# THE PENGUIN TOURS

## *The Diary of a Touring Cyclist*

## By Paul Bland

# Table of Contents

*Dedicated to the brave cyclists who have joined me on these tours. A special mention to Jimmy Forest, and Kevin Moorwood. I know, if it was possible, they would be signing up for the next adventure.*

# Acknowledgements

I have to acknowledge the support of my wife, Jane who allowed me to go off on my annual tour each year without understanding the reason why I needed to do it.

A special thanks to Nicky Rafferty, who painstakingly proofread this book and transformed my ramblings into a readable form.

# About the Author

The Author is a Sheffield born retired Design Engineer, married with two children and five grandchildren.

He discovered cycling as a means of gaining fitness and losing weight. He used cycling as a means of transport and lost five stone in weight. He competed with success at long distance time trials, winning several events.

During his forties, fifties and sixties, he embarked upon long-distance cycling tours across Europe each year and persuaded friends to come with him. He kept a diary of these tours. *The Penguin Tours – the Diary of a Touring Cyclist* is the outcome.

# Prologue

Holidays, for most middle-aged people, usually entail a fortnight putting their feet-up in some hot foreign land, eating and drinking to excess and getting a suntan. The success of the holiday is usually judged on how much weight they've clapped on and the shade of brown their skin goes before it sheds and returns to its natural pasty tone. I could imagine to some this would have appeal, to me it would be hell. By contrast not everybody would want to spend their holiday clad in Lycra, astride a laden pedal cycle, hauling their weary ageing body over some of the hardest climbs in Europe. The severity of some of the climbs would make the legs of tour de France heroes scream out with pain. If that didn't make the adventure hard enough, it is undertaken without any backup vehicle and without making any plans or reservations.

This is the story of a group of ageing cyclists who look forward to testing themselves each year on some of the hardest terrain in Europe. To enhance the experience the cyclists live out of their laden panniers and endure a level of relative discomfort and uncertainty. When I am asked why and at the same questioned about my sanity, I have to search deep for the answer if I ever feel a need to defend myself. I have never been in love with typical 'do nothing' holidays. Vacations should be fun, unpredictable, adventurous, everything the daily routine of work isn't. Foremost in my reasoning is my longstanding love affair with cycling, which sadly has been spoilt in our country to an extent by others obsession with the motor car. Secondly, I still need a challenge despite my advancing years. Twenty years of being a racing cyclist takes a lot of erasing from your make up; something that sadly may never die. And lastly, a basic need for adventure and freedom that is hard to explain and even more difficult to understand. My adventures stem from a romantic notion and a desire for a simplistic way of life in a complex cosy world.

It was born from a very simple idea cultivated during the half-time interval of a football match at Bramall Lane of what has become known as the Penguin Tours. This story documents the journeys of the cyclists who have been conned or coerced into embarking on one of these cycling escapades – some returning for more punishment, and others whinging every pedal stroke of the way and vowing never to return.

On every tour I made a point of taking with me a camera and diary to record the places visited and people I'd met along the way. I did this in the knowledge that I would compile this book one day given the time and inclination. Now that day has come and I look back, remembering some places in great detail whilst some are just a place on the map and mean very little. On trying to recall events, sometimes, my memory has deserted me. Detail is sparse in places, but I would rather leave it that way than enter into the realms of fantasy and make something up. This is not a novel – just a diary of a touring cyclist.

# Introduction – A Lifetimes Obsession

I was born in the fifties and was brought up in a virtually car-free environment. This was a very different world from one where people increasingly depend on the car as the primary means of transport. My old man never had a desire to own a motor vehicle. Only the wealthy could afford cars. Except for the obsessed, who would deny themselves other pleasures in order to own one. He scoffed at and ridiculed those who spent their hard-earned cash on what was then an expensive and unreliable mode of transport. He relied on his bike and public transport. He was probably the first green campaigner and the original grumpy old man, long before green campaigners and grumpy old men were invented. He used a bike for work before a combination of old age and the increase in traffic made the roads, in his mind, unsafe for cyclists.

My father wasn't alone in his thinking as there was far less traffic on the road and parents allowed their children to make their own transport arrangements. The school lanes were free of Range Rovers and Mitsubishi Warriors, and the bike sheds were full. The humble pushbike for me wasn't just a toy or a hobby it was a necessity, an integral part of everyday life.

I can actually remember my old man bringing home my first two-wheeler. It was a cast-off someone had grown out of, but it didn't matter; a bike was the one thing I wanted more than anything. I learned to ride, firstly with the aid of stabilisers, and within days, I had mastered riding without them and never looked back. From that moment on, I had at least one bike to ride and another in the process of being built as a project, a work in progress. I had trackers with cow horn handlebars, three-speed with Sturmey-archer gears, and later racing bikes with sprint rims. I even owned an early molten small-wheeled bike, much to my embarrassment at the time. That was my parent's idea; they thought that somehow it would be safer because of the smaller wheels. Closer to the ground, they perhaps thought and not as far to fall. I never understood how they had actually figured that one out.

It is one of my big regrets that I never got into cycling at club level at an early age. I didn't know anybody at that time in a club and I had no idea how to go about joining one. Cycling must have been still very low profile, back in the sixties. I think it may also have been a class divide; good racing bikes have never been cheap. Playing football was the sport the lads played where I came from. I could well have been severely embarrassed turning up on a club run on one of my mongrels that I had cobbled together from bits and pieces. By the time I started working and was in a position to buy a decent bike, that wouldn't have been out of place in the peloton, I had moved on to other things.

At the age of nineteen, I entered my bicycle-free era. I shunned my lovingly built Holdsworth racer, (pretty much the state-of-the-art at the time) in favour of the more fashionable motor car. Cars are sociably acceptable, even my Morris Minor, with its top speed of nearly seventy miles per hour achieved downhill with a following wind.

Cars, I discovered, make people lazy and in my case very unfit and overweight. The car wasn't the only culprit for my laziness, an excessive alcohol intake and an unhealthy diet of fast food meant I had a big problem – mostly gathering around my waist – a problem that wouldn't go away.

In my mid-twenties I went through a bit of a self-evaluation process – growing up you could call it – I began questioning what I was doing with my life and started to ask why. I blindly followed my peers into manual engineering work that in the short-term, paid well but wasn't what I really wanted to do. Career decisions made after leaving school were a result of apathy rather than choice. I was overweight, through binge drinking, and I was heading for health problems if I didn't make radical changes to my lifestyle.

At the age of twenty-six, I was on a mission to lose a vast amount of body fat in the shortest time possible. My chosen weapon was the humble bike. My fitness regime was intense and aggressive. My long road back to a fit and healthy lifestyle started with the purchase of a second-hand Bob Jackson and a daily ride to work of about ten miles each way, come rain or shine. I went through the initial embarrassment of struggling up hills and arriving at my destination drained and knackered. I received the usual jibes and bets on how long this fad would last. After an initial period of acclimatisation to pain and suffering, my weight dropped dramatically. I confounded all the sceptics and became a proper bona-fide paid-up member of the

Lycra brigade. I joined a cycling club and gradually kicked the football into touch. My football was deeply entrenched in a binge drinking culture – and it had to go. After following my regime rigidly, I started to get something approaching a reasonable fitness level. The exercise became infectious; every fitness fanatic will tell you the same. You just don't know when to stop. The boundaries are there to be broken. All the old clichés are true. You just have to see how far this thing will go before it breaks.

I started competing in cycle races. My weekends were now spent either tearing along the tarmac of dual-carriageway, racing my bike against the clock as a time-triallist, or alternatively, I would be trying to stay away from a pursuing bunch of third-category road racers. I was never good enough to make the first-category riders hurt or even keep with them on some occasions, but at a lower level, I made life tough for those who wanted an easy race. I never mastered the bunch sprint, so a sprint finish was of no use to me at all. Success came from staying away from the pack and that determined my tactics and approach to racing, flying out of the blocks from the start.

It wasn't long before I realised I was more suited to riding in time trials. In time trials, riders are set off at minute intervals and basically, it boils down to a war of attrition, where the person with the best time over a measured distance wins. It was particularly long-distance time trials where I came into my own – the longer the race, the better. Races of a hundred miles, 12-hour and 24-hour, would see me up there in the frame, anything less and I joined the also-rans. I put this down to the fact I didn't have much top-end speed required for short distances, I could push myself for longer than others were prepared to do. I was designed to be a tourist. Long distance time trials required, most of all, a mental toughness that allowed you to push your body to the limits of its endurance. They were also a superb way of burning up reserves of energy and fat – which, in my early days as a cyclist, was a blessing.

The obsession with cycle racing lasted twenty years and I have no regrets; but I needed to call a halt to the gruelling regime of constant training and sacrifice. During my racing days, I couldn't envisage the day when I would finally call it a day. I kept a record of my times and results. It was a necessity to record details as all entry forms required details of past performances. Your acceptance into a race was on the merits of previous results. Fields were restricted to a hundred and twenty entrants and when time trialling was popular, races were heavily oversubscribed. I always thought I would fill this book, but as the years rolled on, the number of events each year reduced. It has been twenty years or more since I have raced a full season now. I made odd appearances after that date, but the number of events is never destined to reach a landmark five hundred. I fell a dozen short.

The question on my mind, after racing for so long, was what will I do with my life now? The end of cycling racing didn't mean a return to an unhealthy lifestyle. I still intended to ride the bike on a regular basis, to and from work and at weekends, to keep relatively fit. Cycle racing did occupy a great deal of my time, through training, racing and travelling to events with friends. I needed to fill this void, otherwise a part of life disappears only to be replaced by a vacuum. I planned to take a holiday each year with my bike. In my racing days, I never took a cycling holiday abroad. I figured that the time-consuming sport I had thrown myself into occupied enough of my life without going on a holiday with a bike. My late summer holiday in September with the family heralded the end of the busy racing season that had usually kicked off in early March.

A lot of my cycling peers did holiday abroad on their bikes. The most popular destination was Mallorca, usually in March and April. It was thought that a week or so at that time of year would hone their fitness and pay dividends in early-season events. There was little point in a holiday like that; I no longer had a season of racing to plan and a high level of fitness to maintain. I decided I needed an annual holiday on the bike to unwind rather than a training camp. I needed to enjoy cycling again, free from the constraints of competition, and free from others that still had a point to prove. But what sort of stress-free cycling holiday am I looking for? I definitely did not fancy a Mallorca-training-type camp with the racing boys. However, I still wanted to exert myself a bit and keep myself fit. I searched for inspiration in my pursuit of a cycling holiday that would best suit my needs. The thought of touring on a bike appealed to me more than being tied to one place for a holiday. Not for me, the cycle camping type touring where the kitchen sink is towed behind on a trailer, but the lightweight variety where the least amount of equipment is taken with you. I fancied the idea of packing all my kit in two small bags and setting off into the unknown and the sense of freedom this gives. I could well imagine a cavalier spirit causing pain and uncertainty at times, but for me, this would add to the adventure. The rest of life is routine. We go to the same place of work and return to the same house every night. Should holidays also be like that?

I dreamed of a holiday cottage in the Alps or Pyrenees to use as a sort of base. If I had to cycle out from this base every day, would I get bored after a week? I go on a base holiday every time I get on my bike at home. Shouldn't a holiday be different? At home, I have to ride through the same bit of estate to get on the quiet Derbyshire lanes where I want to cycle. Why would I want that on holiday? I also appreciate people are different and some like routine. Some would dislike the uncertainty of not knowing where they are sleeping after a hard day in the saddle. For me, I don't see a problem, where a little bit of risk is involved. Everything in life is a compromise, I would be willing to sacrifice a bit of uncertainty to discover new places and sleep in a different town every night. I didn't think it would bother me having to ride with panniers, but I can imagine that for some, it would be a nightmare.

It was the turn of the century before my touring started. For two years, up until the year 2000, I spent holidays with seven other cyclists in a friend's two-bedroom cottage in Plumieux, rural France. Plumieux lies in the centre of Brittany. The south coast from John's cottage was about sixty-five miles to Lorient. Towards Saint Brieuc on the north coast was a little less. Jimmy, John (JC), Kevin, Steve, Sherby, Adrian and I caught the ferry and journeyed by car to our French retreat. For ten days we rode our bikes every day in the sun and partied at night with the locals. We took turns to sleep in sleeping bags on the floor and had a great time. We formed a strong bond and camaraderie in those two holidays and still remain close friends. My short twelve months working with and socialising with these people made me realise that if anybody was up for a bit of an adventure, this group of people certainly were. I didn't realise at that time that my friends from those two trips to Brittany would join me on my cycling adventure tours over the coming years.

# Touring Tips for Beginners

This chapter offers a few tips for would be cycling tourists that I have learned the hard way. It is not intended in any way to be definitive, but it may save a bit of heartache learning from my experiences.

## Where to go?

In my opinion, as far as touring is concerned, England has both negative and positive aspects. If you need reminding, I'll begin with a few negative points. First, there are just too many people on a small island. France and the United Kingdom have a similar population. The UK is a third of the size of France. In this country, we are fighting for space with the motorist. It is a battle the cyclist can never win. The roads are geared to transport the motorist as fast as possible. The policy to use roads as the major source for transporting our goods and services has caused gridlock. Public transport in my experience, in the Sheffield area, has become a joke. Private bus services take long, convoluted routes, making journeys through Sheffield lengthy and inconvenient. The tram system in some cities is good but only if it is going where you want to go. The commuter in the UK, and England in particular, are heavily reliant on using their own motor vehicle through the lack of a viable alternative.

If you tour this country, the national parks are the obvious choice. The further north you go, the more isolation you will find. Scotland and Northumberland are equally as remote as parts of Europe, and you couldn't wish for better scenery but it is not usually accompanied by good weather.

I have toured in this country a few times and I have been fortunate enough to have remained reasonably warm and dry. For anything over a week, and particularly camping, I would not be prepared to take a gamble on the weather unless I had masochistic tendencies.

The next negative in England is the attitude towards the cyclist. A popular motoring television presenter summed up the attitude of the British motorist towards cyclists when he encouraged them to 'work harder and buy a car'. This comment was met with much laughter. It seemed a childish quip from a bloke who looked as though a bit of exercise would not go amiss on his more-than-ample frame. His tongue-in-cheek attitude typifies today's motorist. Quite rational people have told me that cyclists shouldn't be allowed on the road. They quote horror tales of irresponsible cyclists running pensioners down and causing death and destruction. Cars are a status symbol of our success and standing in society. I do not know exactly when this attitude started, perhaps it is a legacy of the Thatcher area. We now have a generation of motorists that have never ridden a bike. A parent has always taxied children to school in the car. I think the empathy our European neighbours demonstrate towards cyclists is refreshing. They respect cycling as a sport and shout words of encouragement rather than abuse. When tackling a major climb in France we have encountered shouts of 'bon courage'. This is a refreshing change from the abuse we receive in our own country. No doubt, there are problems with being a 'rosbif' in France, but not as much as some people would have you believe.

The next advantage our neighbours have over our little island is the scenery. I love Derbyshire and the Lake District but we have to concede that other parts of Europe have the edge. Holidays are for trying something different, the Alps, Pyrenees and the central Massif are something we don't have back home. On an annual basis, we see our heroes battle up Alp d'Heuz and Mount Ventoux. The opportunity to experience these and other climbs is a tempting proposition that is too hard to resist. Years ago, these places were out of reach, but today it is different. With the proliferation of cheap travel to thousands of faraway places, exotic places are accessible. Once you have reached your destination, accommodation is usually cheaper. I would be very surprised if you could get a room for the night in, say, the Peaks or the Lake District and have much change out of fifty pounds. It is also unlikely would actually find a vacancy in the height of summer travelling, particularly without making a reservation. What you can save in bed and breakfast costs over your holiday can go some way to paying your travelling expenses.

On a positive for England, it is on the doorstep. There are a lot of beautiful places, and if you pick the weather it can be brilliant. I have usually toured in this country as an extra. Not much planning is required with travel arrangements – get on with it. You don't lose any days of your holiday getting there, and you will save money. Also, you can ignore the next few paragraphs.

### How to get there?

Once you have decided where to go abroad, you then have to decide how to get there; there are several options and I have tried most of them. Usually travel is down to personal preference. For a Channel hop, the ferry is probably going to be the cheapest. If you want to start your tour from a foreign ferry port, it is going to cost around thirty pounds to cross as a foot passenger with a bike. To be added to that is the cost of getting to the ferry port by train, if it is too far or inconvenient to pedal there. Sheffield to Plymouth is a long way and not a particularly pretty journey. The fifty pounds to get there by train would be well worth the expense in my opinion. I have used Roscoff, Cherbourg, Zeebrugge, Rotterdam and Saint-Malo on my travels without any problems. You don't have to travel back from the same port. A mile or so of traffic from the port and you are on the quiet roads of Brittany. You can share a car to get into Europe but you do have the problem of leaving the car somewhere. Cycling to an airport or ferry port is an option. I have cycled to and from the ferry port at Hull, which is about eighty miles from Sheffield.

In 2018, Jimmy and I parked a car at a travel lodge in Portsmouth and went across on the ferry as a foot passenger. This was the cheapest option as the cost of parking was only £25. This option had the convenience of not having to plan train journeys and follow timetables. The big disadvantage is that you are obliged to travel back to the same port.

**EBE**

Another option is to use a company that specialises in transporting cyclists and their bikes abroad. The European Bike Express is good; it allows access to most of the sought-after places in Europe. There are three routes and you can choose various drop-offs and pick-off points en route. The Atlantic bus goes down the west side of France, the Mediterranean route goes down the middle of France into Spain, and the Adriatic route goes down the eastern side of France, touching parts of Switzerland and into Italy. The bus starts in Stokley near Middlesbrough with several stops and pickup points in England. The advantage of the bus is that you can usually cycle to a bus stop and it will take you all the way to your destination. The criticism levelled at this system is that there are cheaper ways of getting there if you are prepared to find them. Twenty hours or more on a bus is a long time to endure. On the way down, it's not that bad; you can plan your route and grab a few beers. The return journey I find, can be tedious. After a hard tour, you just want to get home as quickly as possible. The big disadvantage is that you lose two days out of your holiday travelling. If you have two weeks holiday or more, this may not be a problem.

## Flights and Ferries

The increase in cheap airfares provides another option for the Europe bound cycling tourist. The main concern with this method is getting to a particular destination. More airports are available today than in the past. Geneva, Bordeaux, Carcassonne, Limoges and Nice would make an ideal starting point for a tour. Preventing your bike from getting damaged is the main concern. I have had a bike damaged by baggage handlers and know of others who have suffered a similar fate. A bike bag or box is a definite requirement for plane travel, but what do you do with it once you have landed? I have used a cardboard box from my local cycle shop as a cheap alternative to a bike bag. The box can be disposed of at the airport and away you go, it's no longer required.

For many years, I have flown to a southern destination and ridden north to a ferry port. This is my preferred option. If you use the ferry to get back home, then there isn't a problem with packing up your bike. You have the option of riding home from the ferry port or perhaps using a train.

## Fly Out, Fly Back

More recently I have used airlines for the outbound and home journey. I have used this method a few times now without any problems. I use a cardboard box for the outward journey and a thick polythene bag and packing tape for the return. The cardboard box is free from the local bike shop and the polythene bag cost ten pounds. The polythene folds down to the size of a cycling cape and doesn't cause a major problem bulk-wise. I would not recommend using the bag for both journeys. There is a good chance that the bag could get damaged on the outbound flight. In my experience, you are more likely to have problems on the outbound journey with airport staff. Steve my touring companion, had trouble at Leeds Bradford airport when they refused his bike in a polythene bag because it may endanger the baggage handlers! Luckily, he managed to find a discarded box at the airport and rescue his holiday. For this reason, I am always very nervous on the return journey about my bike being rejected. I always make sure I have plenty of time at the airport in case of problems with the baggage handlers.

**Eurostar**

The only method I have not used is the Eurostar train. At present, the price is restrictive at over two hundred pounds for a return journey from London to Avignon. In addition to this, a train ticket to London has to be budgeted for. I usually look on the internet for cheap deals by train without success.

An idea I am looking to pursue is to have a lightweight bag made as small and as light as possible that would allow access on trains as normal baggage. The bag would need to compress down, possibly to the size of a cycling cape; this would allow a lot of flexibility and freedom. In France problems arise when cyclists and their bikes are separated, even ending up on different trains. I know of someone who lost his bike this way. He and his bike went separate ways in France and were never reunited. A bike accepted as normal luggage would remove a lot of potential problems. Another option would be to tour with a fold-up bike. There are several on the market but it's something I don't have experience of and therefore cannot comment on this.

### Where to Stay?

Where you plan to stay depends on how much money you want to spend. A half-decent hotel will cost fifty euros per night or more, and a municipal campsite can be as little as three euros per night – a massive price difference. Youth hostels and cheap chamber d'hôte or pensions come somewhere in the middle of this range. The price of accommodation usually depends on the location and the facilities provided. In the past, the middle option is the one I have chosen which is reasonably cheap and avoids the need to carry camping equipment.

It is a good idea to plan a tour with knowledge of where youth hostels are located. A European YHA book is available by post from the YHA. The areas where you are likely to visit the Alps and Pyrenees are well served with places to stay. In Europe, there is an ample supply of cheap accommodation. On my earlier tours, I would not entertain taking a tent due to the excess weight and bulk. However, a tent gives you the flexibility of staying in very remote areas. The difference in cost between staying in a hostel and a campsite can be minimal. Even when I have followed the Tour de France, cheap accommodation has not been a problem. The difference in quality of youth hostels is startling, but the prices are not. On one tour, I stayed at a youth hostel in Albi, best described as a dump – a dirty dingy hole that felt a bit intimidating. I was travelling with three others, so it was not such a big deal. Our next youth hostel was at Carcassonne and there could not have been a bigger contrast. This hostel was in the middle of La City and the hostel had a first-class restaurant and a bar. Youth hostels are usually at the bottom end of the market. The first time I stayed abroad in 2000, I paid fifty French Francs, about five pounds. Nowadays, a youth hostel will cost more than double that, even so it is still fairly cheap. The Chamber d'hôte in France or Pension in Spain are the next level of accommodation and are equivalent to our bed and breakfast. A double room would typically cost about twenty-five pounds, between two people it isn't too expensive. In towns and cities, you will find cheap basic hotel accommodation. Some of these hotels, such as the Formula One, are found on industrial estates and usually provide rooms with three beds. The cost usually works out at about fifteen pounds per person. The Loges de France group are a chain of usually family-run restaurants and hotel accommodations that are an excellent standard, but they are a little more expensive. A good idea is usually to ride to the tourist information office and let the usually charming English-speaking receptionist find you accommodation at the price you want to pay. This is provided you can arrive in town before they close at 6.00 pm. In 2009 I toured Germany and was very pleasantly surprised with the youth hostels – they were well above the standard I had experienced elsewhere. There was also a level of consistency with the quality – all the hostels were excellent and well-run.

Over the last few years, camping has been my preferred option. This has been mainly to do with finance. The price of accommodation has gone up considerably since the strength of the euro has increased. The average cost to pitch a tent is about seven euros compared to, say, thirty-five euros for a Chamber d'hote. Even if you need to buy a breakfast, you will still be at least twenty euros better off per night. That could be a couple of hundred euros on a ten-day tour. Campsites are readily available in popular tourist areas. A lot of French towns and villages have a campsite on their outskirts. I have paid as little as three euros for a municipal campsite with just showers and toilet facilities available. The other extreme is a top-notch site with bars, restaurants and leisure facilities, which will cost about twelve euros. The obvious downside with camping is the lack of comfort, and the amount of gear that you need to take. I have would-be touring companions who will not even consider camping for those two reasons. Their argument is that it is supposed to be a holiday and camping would take away the pleasure. You have to face the fact that daily mileage will be reduced. Camping cannot compare with the versatility of credit card touring. By the same token, if you are on a budget, you will get further camping. If you're able to source lightweight gear, you may only be carrying an extra three or four kilos.

## Bike Equipment

Since I started writing this book equipment has changed – I will not say improved necessarily. With bikes, you now have probably two main options: a traditional touring bike based on a road frame with 700c wheels and secondly, a mountain bike type tourer with flat bars and smaller wheels. Recently mountain bikes have increased wheel size and some 29-ers have the same size wheel as road bikes. These two types could be subdivided into disc brakes and rim brakes. Disc brakes are now a fixture on all but the very cheap mountain bikes and are very good. I have used disc brakes on my commute to work bike and I love them. Doing high mileage used to destroy rims through the winter months as grit and salt used to erode the aluminium until the inevitable failure occurred. This could lead to the cyclist coming to grief as the rim wall falls apart.

Disc brakes are now finding their way onto road bikes. Top-end cyclocross bikes and tourers are now offering a disc version. The Dawes Galaxy – long considered the benchmark for a touring bike – now produce a disc brake version. I should imagine that the rest will follow and disc brakes will be standard on touring bikes.

The good news is that it is not necessary to splash out on a state-of-the-art tourer most bikes can be adapted. The bike needs to be robust and will require lower gears than normal club riding. Mudguards are a good idea; even in warmer climates, you can encounter wet weather. I started touring on an Orange P7 mountain bike with narrower section tyres. A mountain bike already has the benefit of a triple chain set and a wide range of gearing. The smaller wheels are stronger than on conventional touring bikes. Some people find the hand position on a mountain bike a bit restrictive. To help with this, bar ends can be used to add another hand position. After three years of touring, I invested in a conventional touring bike. I opted for a frame with steel tubing, cantilever brakes and plenty of clearance for mudguards and wide-section tyres. There are lighter frames but they usually come at a price. As for wheels, I went for standard Shimano thirty-six spoke hubs with large section rims and thirty-two-millimetre tyres. I prefer wide-section tyres on descents when loaded with panniers. The whole characteristic of a bike changes when weight is added. I would feel very nervous on a fast descent with a few hairpin bends thrown in, on anything narrower than twenty-eight-millimetre tyres.

The bike frame material can be steel, titanium, aluminium, or carbon, depending on your budget. I find it difficult to understand saving a few grams on a carbon frame and then carrying everything but the kitchen sink. I think carbon and titanium are risky options, and I would live in fear of having my expensive frame damaged on a ferry or on a flight. Also, the stresses put on a frame descending with weight can lead to breakages. I have broken two titanium road frames in using them in normal road use. I have had only one carbon bike, a mountain bike and that is still intact. My present tourer is an Aravis with Reynolds 631 tubing, but I have used my Kevin Winter, which is Reynolds 531 and a Genesis mountain bike, which was Reynolds 853. My first tourer was my Orange P7, which was a steel chrome molybdenum tubing. Aluminium is also an excellent tubing and is capable of matching steel options in terms of strength and durability.

I use a triple chain set with a range of sprockets from thirteen to twenty-seven. This gives a bottom gear of around thirty inches. Some people don't like triples in which case you would need a thirty-two-tooth rear sprocket to obtain a similar gear ratio with a thirty-nine-tooth inner chain-ring. The unfortunate aspect of this setup is that a long arm triple rear mechanism will still be required on any sprocket larger than twenty-eight. Recently, compact chain sets have arrived on the scene. They comprise of typically a thirty-four and a fifty chain-ring. If minimal equipment is being carried and the terrain isn't too severe, a compact chain-set may be the solution.

### Bike packing versus Panniers

Once upon a time, panniers were king and bike packing wasn't invented. Bike packing is a newish cycle touring format. With the popularity of mountain bikes and the desire to travel on trails a need for a different type of luggage carrying method was needed. Bike packing gear can be easily attached to any bike without the need for pannier bosses. This comprises, a seat pack behind the saddle, a roll pack in front of the handlebars, and a frame pack situated within the main frame triangle. Also, there can be small bags on the top tube. The drinking bottles are then relocated to the fork blades. The advantage of this rig, is that it allows any racer or mountain bike to be used for a tour. It also makes you critically evaluate how much gear you need to take. It is a minimalist approach and is more suited to low weight, shorter tours, and an all-road capability.

I admit a preference for panniers and that is what I have used for my tours. Unless you are going for a long period or you are camping, then rear panniers will be sufficient to carry all you need. After years of reducing weight, I settled on a pair of twenty-five-litre Karrimor panniers that can expand after unzipping to thirty-five litres if required. They were lying covered in dust on a reduce-to-clear shelf at a bike-cum-car spares shop. I made the purchase still thinking it wasn't possible to fit all my necessities in these small panniers even though there was evidence that suggested I could. Kevin had managed with similar panniers from day one. I had made the initial mistake of buying a pair of massive Altura fifty-litre panniers. If you buy a big pair of panniers, like I did, you will certainly fill them. I started to question the necessity of every item I took with me. Sound advice would be to borrow a pair first and see how they suit your needs. Last year, I added a small handlebar bag, much to the amusement of my cycling buddies, who thought it was a bit old-fashioned. It was a leaving present from my mates at Peugeot when I left in February 2006. I find it useful for items such as maps, a camera and food that I need to keep on hand. Small panniers and, especially the waterproof type, don't have small side pockets. It makes sense to pack items in some sort of logical order. Keep maps, a camera and spare cycling equipment in the right-hand pannier and other equipment not required until you arrive at your destination on the left, for example. When camping, you need more space for the tent. My first two camping trips had equipment strapped to the bike rack, leaving them to get a soaking when the rain came down. I relegated the Karrimor panniers to my commuting bike and bought a pair of Ortlieb panniers to accommodate the extra gear. I fit camping gear such as the tent, mat, and sleeping bag in one pannier; the rest, including clothing and toiletries in the other.

### Camping Gear

A tent, sleeping bag, and roll mat are probably the basics you require. If you intend to take cooking equipment, etc., that is a different ball game and becomes fully laden touring. I have no experience of this latter style of touring. Personally, I think, the logistics make cooking difficult. You need to carry pots and pans, a stove and fuel. This additional equipment requires space in your panniers. I always try to have food onboard in case the campsite is remote and there are no restaurants or supermarkets nearby. Unless it is cold, there is little need for hot food and drink anyway.

With camping gear, I adopt a minimalist attitude. I have a Vango Helium Force Ten tent, which is about 1.2 kilograms. There are several on the market that would do the job. You can pay between a hundred and five hundred pounds for a lightweight tent. I opted for a two-man tent. If you have even the minimum of gear you will need a two-man tent. Two men in it would just be too much of a squeeze and you save little in weight, opting for a one-man tent. I did have a single-skin one-kilo tent, which I used once and sold – a step too far. It was not big enough, and I got wet when I touched the sides - which was very unavoidable given the restricted space. Since I have been using a tent, I have looked critically elsewhere to lose weight and bulk.

As for sleeping bags; a two-season sleeping bag is ok for Europe. The more expensive ones are lighter and compress more. I paid about sixty pounds for a reasonable one. Finally, you will need a roll mat to sleep on. I prefer a blow-up type. I have a full-length one, but I think a three-quarters would have been better and take up less space. Prices for matts range from twenty to sixty pounds.

**Tools and Spares**

I usually take three spare inner tubes and a fold-up tyre with me. I have rarely had a puncture abroad while on tour. I put my low puncture rate down to my preference for robust equipment. Narrow-section tyres are more likely to suffer impact punctures. If you check your tyres for pressure, wear, and flints before you go on tour, you are unlikely to have trouble. A good pump is a necessity – not one of those mini get-me-home ones – also, tyre levers. I take a few spare spokes fastened to the frame with tie wraps and a spoke key. You will also need link extractors, Allen keys and any special tools specific to your bike. If you are travelling with others, a lot of these tools can be split between you and your companions to spread the load.

Take some lightweight cutlery, a plastic plate and a cup. For meals from supermarkets, you need something to cut bread and vegetables and something to drink out of and eat off. For the small amount of weight, or room they take up, they are well worth it.

### Clothing

With cycle clothing, I go with mostly two of everything shorts, tops, undervests and socks. The theory is you wear one kit while the other is drying. Normal clothing made of lightweight material that folds up to hardly anything is the best. This type of clothing can be purchased from outdoor shops. I take a pair of shorts, two tee shirts, a pair of lightweight trousers, one jumper and a pair of sandals. Old-fashioned swimming trunks, (budgie smugglers, as my wife calls them) are a good idea as you will need them for a dip in the pool, and they double up as underpants. Don't take the football shorts-type swimmers, as they are not allowed in France; they've got to be budgie smugglers unfortunately. I take a reasonable looking cagoule that I can use on the bike and use in the evening if it is cold. The advantage of going to a warm climate is that you don't need a lot of warm, bulky clothing. Avoid denim like the plague it is too heavy, it takes up too much room, and it will never dry once wet.

## Toiletries

A bag containing toiletries and a small travel towel is a necessity. Consider weight and bulk when choosing what items to take with you. I have a small travel towel, the type you get from outdoor shops, that dries very quickly. Cheap plastic disposable razors and roll-on deodorants are best for camping. Avoid jumbo tubes of toothpaste – or anything else. I take a tube of soap that I can use to wash everything – including my clothing. Try to manage without the electric razor and electric toothbrush; sacrifices to save weight can be tough. Vaseline, sun cream, and mosquito repellent are necessities. Keep a supply of these items near the top of your panniers, especially in hot weather. A scaled-down first-aid kit is also a good idea.

## Maps, a compass, and a plan

If your new school you have a Garmin or similar GPS system. The price varies hugely from a hundred to five hundred pounds and beyond. If you're a gadget person, they are for you. There are several apps you can download from your phone that you pay a subscription for, such as Map My Ride GPS or Commute. Or there's just Google Maps which is free. For the Lejog trip, Phil started off with Map My Ride GPS and ditched mid-tour for Google Maps.

The uses of computer packages such as Auto route have made planning tours easier, so plan in advance at home on the PC. I take Michelin maps that give sufficient detail of minor roads. Eighty miles a day with panniers is usually far enough for most people. Know your limits and plan your daily mileage accordingly. You need to have an achievable planned destination each day. Allow at least a day's float on your trip in case of problems. A daily route on a postcard is a good idea containing route, compass direction, road numbers, towns and landmarks. It's better to have essential information at hand than having to open a map every few miles. It is important that you arrive at a town before 5 p.m. if you haven't any accommodation booked. I used to take a lightweight sleeping bag and ignore this rule, but this is a dangerous gamble to take unless you fancy sleeping under the stars. Now, if I am not camping, I just take a silk sleeping bag liner for use at youth hostels; it folds to nothing and costs about twenty pounds.

## Kevin Winter Tourer Fully Laden

## The Bianchi – Fully Laden

# Tour 1 – Northern France

After three good years of cycling around Brittany, the cottage we used as a base for our holidays was no longer an option open to us. John was retiring early from the Fire Service due to his poor eyesight. He was selling his house in England and moving to France for good. His holiday cottage was to become his permanent home. John was investing money in this transformation and it would have been hardly fair to expect him to allow us to keep on using and abusing his place on an annual basis.

I would have to seriously rethink my annual cycling holiday arrangements. I quite fancied touring but I didn't really associate with any tourists who I could approach for ideas. Touring had the same appeal to some of my racing buddies as Morris dancing. A few admitted to being involved with touring at an early age, but had no interest anymore. To most cyclists, touring was a phase that was forsaken for racing and was never to be revisited. A lot of cyclists – and I was one – bypassed the touring stage altogether and entered straight into a competition. What a shame. And some, when their racing days are over, abandon the bike altogether, never to be seen astride one again.

My search for a cycling companion to join me on my first touring expedition was proving difficult. My fireman chums, with whom I had enjoyed two good years in France, showed no inclination to don the panniers and join me on tour. Only Kevin showed any interest at all. If I were to be honest, I thought of him as an unlikely cycling companion. I had always got on well with Kevin, there weren't many people that didn't. He wasn't ambitious, so he never tried to be something he wasn't, a rare breed in his chosen profession. In the fire brigade, there was a tendency among the ranks to strive for promotions, in order to secure that final salary pension on retirement. Retirement in your mid-fifties meant that quite a lot was at stake in being able to attain as high rank as possible. In such circumstances, people were competitive and some had exhibited some undesirable traits in order to achieve their goals. Kevin, however, tended not to involve himself and didn't like talking about work and tended to avoid those who did. He was always good company and as a boozy companion on our cycling holiday, he had no equal, even though his cycling ability was a bit of an unknown measure. His lack of competitiveness stretched on to the bike. He had never shown his hand, like some of the others, so nobody knew his true ability. He certainly had a cycling physique, not an ounce of fat on him; at five foot eight, he would hardly make ten stone, just what is required for climbing the steep cols. He was also unique in being the only cyclist I knew who smoked. This fitted in with his laid-back attitude, he knew and accepted the risks to his health but puffed on his fag just the same. He did have a good cycling background, having raced as a schoolboy and at junior level before going to Australia in his twenties, which effectively put paid to his cycling aspirations. Now he just rode his bike to the fire station and back on a daily basis, with the occasional detour into Derbyshire on the way home. His was very laid-back, and his refusal to be fazed attitude gave him mental toughness in adversity. I knew he wouldn't be the sort of bloke to whinge if things got a little tough. It was just as well because, over the following years, events on our tours didn't always go to plan.

In fact, the word 'plan' was a word that wasn't really applicable to any of these coming tours. I can't remember whether it was Kevin or I who *planned* the first cycling tour, but I was increasingly excited with the idea the closer it came to fruition. It slowly came together at Bramall

Lane, home of Sheffield United, during the half time break in a corner where Kevin went for a smoke. I knew Kevin casually even before I joined the fire service. I had shared a bit of banter with this craggy-faced bloke at the match. He took his two children to watch the Blades, just like I did, and he seemed to know what he was talking about, football-wise. Little did I know at that time that in the near future, I would be sharing a couple of cycling holidays with him, and potentially, he would be my first touring partner. What I did pickup from our early exchange of ideas, was how refreshingly simple and laid back the arrangements were, to the point of being non-existent. I have been accused of being laid back and not one to get too bothered with detail, but compared to Kevin, I suffered from paranoia. On this occasion, it was me who was concerning myself with details, while Kevin had this 'don't worry, we will find somewhere' attitude. I wanted to take a small tent just in case we couldn't find anywhere to stay. We reached a compromise and decided to just take sleeping bags, presumably so we could sleep on some park bench or in a doorway if necessary. That's how it came together, a couple of half-time chats and we were ready to go. It seemed so simple; it was almost frightening. In retrospect, I should have known what the guy was all about. A bloke who just jumps on a boat to Australia without fear, although his mates have let him down, and stays there for several years on his own, isn't going to plan to death a couple of weeks on a cycle-touring holiday.

I also think there was an element of fate about that first tour. I had left the fire Service a couple of years earlier – for reasons I can't quite understand – and Kevin was the one I still saw on a regular basis through our visits to Bramall. I say, for reasons I cannot understand, because if ever there was a job that was made for me, that was the one. It was very sport-orientated; it had a gym, shower facilities and a culture that suited my racing aspirations at the time. The job was stress-free and the people were a breed apart. I had not encountered this level of banter and piss-taking ever before. It was, for all purposes, a fantastic place to work. For some reason, when I settle or become comfortable in a place, I feel choked, and claustrophobic. As soon as the ink has dried on some pension scheme that I can look forward to, I start having panic attacks and start fumbling for the exit door. In the past, I have deliberately jeopardised or sabotaged any chances of any long-term employment through stunts I have done, leaving my only course of action to bow out disgracefully. I feel like the person who doesn't want to commit to a relationship because he will miss out on something else, something better. I then find attractive the things that I don't have. At the Fire Service, I pined for a more challenging job with more responsibility and money. As soon as the opportunity arose, I was away like a shot, only to regret my decision, but by then, it was too late.

I discovered this unfortunate trait very early in my career. As a young apprentice engineer, I saw the workmen – men of thirty-five who looked fifty – who had spent most of their waking hours, seven days a week, within the confines of the factory walls. Their complexion was grey, clay-like, through breathing in too many cigarettes and machine oil. They gleefully accepted the trap of excessive overtime to pay for their poor lifestyle. They ticked off the days until their pension arrived and they wouldn't have to 'clock-in' again. I decided that lifestyle wasn't for me. As soon as my apprenticeship was finished, I was out of there like the proverbial shot out of a gun. Since that compulsory five-year sentence, I have spent the remainder of my working life on average, less than one and a half years at various establishments. Some jobs lasted a few years, some only a few weeks. I found the variety of work I wanted in contracting, sometimes accepting what was available – which wasn't what I would have chosen – working long periods away from home.

I devised a scoring system to judge how well the jobs suited me and whether the new position was worth taking the plunge. I considered three factors and one was money. I wasn't a greedy person – who worshipped material possessions – but I needed to pay the bills. The second factor was the work itself, how interesting and how much of a challenge it was. I also accounted for the people I worked with in this score. The third factor was the location. Quality of life is something I value dearly. I have worked as far north as Glasgow and as far south as Hastings. It was hard to be happy in these places, no matter how much I was getting paid. If I had been out of work for a period, money would take precedent. During my racing days, I consciously favoured work that allowed me to train more. I would award half marks where appropriate; it was rare for a job to achieve the full mark in any category. So, my ideal job that would score a perfect three would have me earning in excess of a thousand pound a week, the work would be possibly test riding Colnago bikes while engaging in banter with like-minded cycling fanatics. My ride to work would be a ten-mile ride through traffic-free Derbyshire lanes. If I achieved my perfect score, I probably wouldn't want a cycling holiday anyway.

The reality was in the year 2000 I was enjoying or enduring a job which scored no better than a one and a half at best. I was commuting in my car to Brighouse on a daily basis. I had plenty of time to day dream and contemplate my cycling tour while negotiating the slow-moving traffic on the M1 and M62 each day. I was working through an agency named Trust Consulting and I had become friendly with Patrick, a director at the agency. He used to visit me at a company where I worked, offering to provide consultative services. When I was made redundant in 1994, I turned to him for work. It pays to be nice to people in business; you never know when you may need a favour. I started working at a factory in Sheffield – through Trust Consulting – the previous year. When I was asked if I was available to do some work at their other factory in Brighouse, I felt duty-bound (through gritted teeth) to accept. I just hoped it wouldn't be long before I could get back to my daily cycling commute instead of this traffic-choked hell. The other disadvantage of commuting by car is that your fitness deteriorates. I arrived home too late and knackered to be bothered to ride the bike. There usually wasn't enough daylight left, even if I had felt the inclination to take the train. I was going to rely on muscle memory and whatever riding I could do at weekends to get me through a tour.

First, I needed to get some cycle-touring equipment together. I never owned a pair of panniers. As a schoolboy, I rode to the coast and back with a haversack on my back; that was the extent of my touring experience. There were a lot of questions I didn't really have answers for at this point. What equipment did I need, and what should I take with me for a start? I decided against major investment at this stage. This could turn out to be my first and last tour. The 'For Sale' ads are full of articles purchased by would-be explorers that have been used just once. Where I could, I would utilise what I already had in my cycling armoury. I opted to use my old Orange mountain bike fitted with road tyres. I bought a pair of Altura fifty-litre panniers, a rack and a lightweight sleeping bag, and that was it. Kevin invested even less; he intended to use his road bike and he borrowed a pair of small panniers. His only investment was a lightweight one-season sleeping bag.

Our first tour was naturally to France, where else? We planned to watch a couple of the stages of the Tour de France, particularly the team time trial down in Saint Nazaire. The town is a commune down in the Loire-Atlantique department of France. It is a major harbour with a shipbuilding history and it is situated on the Loire River estuary near the Atlantic Ocean. The town and its shipyard had a strategic importance during the Second World War and took a bit of a pounding. Its successful conversion to a cruise ship building, notably Cunard's Queen Mary II had given the place a new lease of life, hence the honour of having an important tour stage there. On arrival in Saint Nazaire, we would have travelled about a hundred and fifty miles. After, we would head North East and get to Vitre for the finish of the next stage, another sixty miles away. Following our stay, we needed to head north through Normandy to spend a night with John and Linda. John, our host in Brittany for the last three years, had secured a job on a French holiday campsite after taking early retirement from the fire service. After a night under canvas, our only guaranteed bed for the tour, it was a simple matter of riding down the coast to Cherbourg and catching a ferry back home.

I met Kevin at Sheffield train station early on a Saturday morning. I was there in bags of time, as giddy as a school kid on a first date. I hadn't time to ponder what could go wrong before Kevin arrived, looking unfazed as usual. We opted to catch the train down to Plymouth and then the ferry as foot passengers to Saint-Malo. The bikes were pre-booked onto the train to ensure there wasn't a problem with space. I have risked not booking in the past, but I wasn't prepared to entertain the possibility of some overzealous train conductor jeopardising my holiday. I had never been a foot passenger on a ferry. This was all a new experience. It hadn't escaped my mind that a couple of beers would be a very appealing prospect. Unlike the majority of our travelling companions in cars, we could drink without the fear of the French gendarmes breathalysing us. Once we had climbed the ramp of the ferry, we were directed to a boiler room at the rear of the boat. The bikes were secured to the wall with ropes. Our bikes had company in there; a few other bikes were tied up. It was very noticeable that the other bikes had considerably more baggage than we were carrying. I was relaxed in the fact we were doing it the right way.

We struck up a conversation with a fellow tourist who was obviously going on his travels for a good while, at least a year, judging by the vast amount of luggage he was taking. His mountain bike, barely visible, was so laden that it was only just possible to lift the bike an inch off the ground. I couldn't help it, I had to attempt to lift this monster of a bike out of curiosity. Just what hadn't this guy got with him? The bike had large front and rear panniers, plus a large circus tent and sleeping bag on top of his rack. I smiled as I noticed a large mallet tied on top of this luggage mountain, presumably to knock in his tent pegs. I think I would have taken a chance on finding a brick, but not this chap. The owner was a diminutive, slightly built man in his mid-twenties. I was curious and proceeded to quiz him about what was in store for himself and his heavily laden bike. He told us of grief with his employer, which had led him to escape life for a while. He anticipated travelling for about six weeks, and like us, he was planning on seeing some of the tour. We wished him luck, something he certainly would need if he intended to take himself and his heavy load up anything resembling a gradient. How had he ascended up that ferry ramp?

## St. Malo to La Cheze (90 km)

We rode off the ferry and headed south towards central Brittany and our overnight stay in La Cheze. As we rode through the rural villages of Brittany, we were met by torrential rain. We took refuge in a bus shelter for a while. We didn't have any accommodation booked, and for a moment, a bit of anxious anticipation, if not panic, set in. A lot of 'what if' questions started to come into my mind. Thankfully, the rain stopped and we pushed on the sixty miles to our destination. We turned up at our usual watering hole in Brittany, the Auberge du Lie, the place where we had spent our evenings while at John's place at Plumieux over the last three years. Matilde, the landlady directed us to the Moulin de le Fosse (a chamber d'hôte) just down the road. Just like she had described, we came across a gathering of large buildings in various stages of disrepair. A Dutch couple had bought the place with the intention of restoring the buildings to their former glory. A project that I suspect had lost its way. Most of the buildings still lay derelict after a good few years. We were relieved to find somewhere, quite easily as it transpired, to stay for our first night. Initial fears, while sheltering from the rain, of spending the night under the stars didn't materialise. We showered and took a short cut across some fields back to La Cheze for a well-deserved night on the beer with the locals. We ate at Matilde's place. Her husband Bernard was an excellent cook and we had experienced his cooking many times before. Afterwards, we drank beer with another Bernard, a journalist who spoke reasonably good English. We were a little bit surprised when he offered us a lift back to our digs; he had sunk a large quantity of beer that evening. He was a large, craggy, rotund bloke with thick, black curly hair. He appeared as part of the fixtures – a regular drinker. We accepted his lift back, mainly because we would have never found our way back in the dark in our state of intoxication.

## La Cheze to Redon (76 km)

We set off in a south-easterly direction in the morning for a place called Redon on the Brittany border. There was a youth hostel and cheap digs for the night. We booked into the modern building that even had a secure place to park the bikes. We headed down town in the evening. We shared a bar with a few dozen Frenchmen gazing at a television set, which for them, was showing a very important game. The European Football championship was coming to its climax as the French took on the Italians. We shared the drama as the game went one way and then the other. The French won the game and the whole town went berserk. Car horns were sounding all through the night. Kevin and I were in Plumieux two years ago when the French beat Brazil in the 1998 World Cup Final. On that occasion, the village got excited, but this was more-rowdy, we were now in something approaching a big town, and they were really up for a party. It is a long time since the English had something like this to shout about. We felt a little bit like intruders at a private party.

## Redon to Saint Brevin (62 km)

The next day, we set off towards St Nazaire on the west coast to watch the team time trial stage of the Tour de France. Our destination was the youth hostel at a place called Saint Bevin les Pins, a few miles up the west coast. As we came into the outskirts of St Nazaire, the rain came down and we looked for shelter. Whilst sheltering in a doorway, a middle-aged Frenchman beckoned to us. My first thought was of mistrust, but that was unfounded. He invited us inside his house to shelter. He then showed us round his home, proudly pointing out his old racing bike and photographs of the ships he had helped to build in the shipyard at St Nazaire. While on this house tour, his wife was preparing a meal for us. It was a simple meal with wine, but nevertheless, it was a gesture that I found incredible and something I had never experienced before. When I expressed my gratitude for his hospitality and told him of my surprise at his generosity, he just said that this was normal behaviour in France to offer hospitality to cyclists.

We pushed on to St Nazaire and crossed the suspension bridge to Saint Brevin. I was amazed at how steep the bridge was. Halfway across the bridge, the bike became unstable as the wind gusted, making riding difficult, if not dangerous. This was the sort of conditions that the tour riders would be encountering the next day.

The youth hostel at Saint Brevin was very basic. It was a two-storied wooden structure situated on a sandy beach. The place was quiet. The beach was empty, apart from a few fisherman and locals walking their dogs. We learned we had to be away and over the bridge early in the morning as it would be closed once the tour was mobile. We needed to be on the right side of the bridge to make an early exit to our next destination. We couldn't afford to be caught up in the tour aftermath if we were to get away quickly. Our plan was to cycle about sixty miles after the team time trial to enable us to get to Vitre for the finish of the next stage.

## Saint Brevin to Chateaubriant (89 km)

We cycled over the bridge in the morning and took our place alongside the locals who had gathered there three and four-deep at the roadside to watch their cycling heroes. The

French take their cycling very seriously. Campervans, cars, mopeds, cyclists, and pedestrians lined the route. Picnic tables were erected as the French made a day of it. This is not just a casual interest – more of a national institution. Children and adults alike fought over the novelties thrown to the crowd by the cavalcade that preceded the riders. Grownups wrestled kids to the ground for a bidon or a small piece of cheese in a net. They treasured their tack like trophies, god help anybody that got in their way. We caught a glimpse of the riders at the top of the Saint Nazaire Bridge. The gradient and the wind were destroying the rhythm of the usual clockwork precision of this discipline. Some teams were losing riders. Not so the yellow Once team as they came past us as a tightly knit unit at forty-plus miles per hour aided by the strong tailwind.

After the last team had whizzed past, we headed towards Vitre. We cycled past a place called Nozay and found digs somewhere near Chateaubriant. Our chamber d'hôte was a small chateau itself. It was a magnificent old building with outbuildings at the back in which to park our bikes. Horses ran wild in the fields behind. At breakfast time, we sat in a massive dining room with a large oak dining table. The room was like something out of a period drama so old and magnificently maintained. We felt a little bit unworthy, so out of place in this aristocratic residence.

# Chateaubriant to Domront (126 km)

We arrived at Vitre at mid-day in time for lunch and the finish of The Tour stage. The town was decorated for the occasion. It is an honour for a town to be involved in The Tour, and a stage finish was taken particularly seriously. There was a street party atmosphere with food stalls, bunting and hordes of spectators. We watched the anticipated sprint finish, which is the norm for a flattish stage of the tour. We had spent our time hanging around eating, waiting for and watching the Tour. We now had some serious catching up to do. From Vitre, we set off northeast in the direction of Caen. Normandy was not as flat as I had anticipated. The terrain climbed for two miles or so and then descended for another two. These were not sharp descents, but rolling hills, the kind that saps your energy. Towns like fortresses sat on top of hillsides. Up and down we rode until we started running out of daylight. We looked for somewhere to stay on this long road that led to the ferry ports, without any joy. We passed town after town without any sign of life. Up to now everything had gone to plan. This wasn't looking good.

Just as I was preparing myself for a night in some hedge bottom or perhaps a doorway, I saw a glimmering light on in what looked like a truck stop café. A door opened and we both breathed a sigh of relief as we secured a bed for the night. It was 9.30 p.m. and the owner, a middle-aged woman, haggard-looking, had locked up for the night. We knew we were pushing our luck when we asked if there was any chance of her cooking a meal for us. This was the equivalent of the greasy spoon café, definitely at the bottom end of the French cuisine. It was not something you would find in a travel brochure or good food guide. Begrudgingly she cooked a meal, and served us with beer and wine. She hovered over us like a fly, checking our progress and giving off exasperating sounds when we asked for more bread and then wine, encouraging us to eat and drink faster. As we drank wine, we became light-headed with fatigue. Her patience came to an abrupt end. As soon as we had put the last piece of food in our mouth, she ushered us upstairs. We were sent to our room like two naughty school children. We staggered upstairs; I was still clutching a jug of wine with one hand. She curtly informed us that breakfast was at 7.00 a.m. It was obviously some form of punishment for keeping her up that late.

## Domfront to Saint Aubin sur Mer (111 km)

We were enjoying our petite dejeuner amongst truckers using the café as their breakfast stop on their way to the ferry port. Our enforced early start had us on the road by 8.00 a.m. We were heading for Caen and then the seaside resort of Saint Aubin sur Mer and our rendezvous with John and Linda. Caen wasn't that memorable; a large river flowed through the centre. Large bridges spanned the river. Old men lined the river with their fishing poles. We grabbed some dinner at a café in one of the small villages on the way out of town. Thankfully our next night's accommodation was assured. We were on our way to see

John. He was living the dream. Working and living in France had always been his dream, or was it for me I wondered?

It was a handy break in our journey and John would appreciate a visit from familiar faces. We phoned a few miles outside Saint Aubin to tell him we were on our way. He greeted us wearing shorts, a cagoule and hiking boots. The rain had turned the campsite into a sludge heap. This was not the French Riviera; the north coast of Brittany can be bleak at the best of times. The wind and rain can make this dream seem like a nightmare. Living in a tent for six months is not everybody's idea of a blissful retirement. No amount of pictures and artefacts can make a tent feel like home. I gazed around their tent, half in amazement. I kept my thoughts to myself. I tried to picture Jane and myself in this scenario but somehow, I cannot visualise something so bizarre. It would never happen. Jane never stops me going on my tours but on our holidays, she will not tolerate anything short of luxury. On the odd occasion when I have booked accommodation that doesn't come up to standard, she lets me know and doesn't forget about it in a hurry. Separating yourself from the elements by a thin piece of canvas for six months is not for the faint-hearted, even in the warmest of climates. We had a good evening eating, drinking, and talking old times despite the rain hammering on the tent all night. I hoped that by morning, the rain would have exhausted itself and we could enjoy a dry ride to the port.

## Saint Aubin sur Mer to Cherbourg (126 km)

No such luck, the rain was still hammering down. We packed our bags, donned our wet weather gear and said goodbye to our hosts. We had a seventy-five mile-ride to the ferry port at Cherbourg. Fortunately for us, we had a tail wind helping us along. The journey wasn't particularly pleasant. We stopped occasionally and sheltered from the rain in the many villages en route. We would receive directions from the locals. Kevin would puff on a fag while I would feed my face with a pain au raisin or similar delicacy from the bakery.

## Cherbourg to Home

We arrived at the ferry port and finally, the rain stopped and the sun came out. It was too late. We were already soaked. We picked up a box of wine from the discount booze shop to enjoy on the ferry journey back home. We drank our wine and reflected on our first tour. We had exploded the myth about the French being arrogant and having a dislike for the British. We can only speak of our own experiences. We experienced warmth and friendliness from the people we met. Whenever we arrived at a café kitted out in our bright Lycra and opened out a map, we attracted attention, and found the French people only too happy to help. As for the accommodation, we had one occasion when it was touch and go whether we would find somewhere to stay. On the whole, it had been easy to find a bed for the night. We knew that the tour would become an annual event. Where and when were the only issues to be decided. No doubt half-time at Bramall Lane would be the venue for hatching next-years cycling adventure.

The train journey back from Plymouth seemed to take forever. We changed at Kings Cross and continued our journey back to Sheffield. The passengers were treated to a sideshow as more and more twenty-something revellers with rucksacks and sleeping bags joined the train on their way up to Leeds for a pop concert. Like most male primates in the company of the female of the species, they were doing a fair amount of showing off. Their antics kept us amused until we reached our stop. I walked to the exit, and one of them sat with his feet across the aisle. I asked him to move politely. He replied with, "What if I can't be arsed?" I asked him again, but this time not so politely, "Fucking move 'em!" and fixed him with a look that implied I might break them if he didn't. He withdrew, gaining some satisfaction and admiration from his mates, knowing he had pissed me off somewhat. Kevin and I looked at each other and shared the same thought. As we stepped off the train and went our separate ways, I said, "That's what I miss about this place."

# Tour 2 – Poitier to Narbonne – The Black Mountains

Once back home, we told our adventures of our first tour. It sparked some positive reactions from those who had made the annual journey to Brittany for the base holiday. At one time there were as many as six possible recruits enlisted on our next two-wheel adventure. A year is a long time to keep interest alive. Kevin and I were definitely up for another tour, but probably a bit more adventurous next time. We had almost a year to research our options. Hopefully, we would recruit a few more adventurers to join us, we thought.

Work-wise, things hadn't been great; Patrick the boss of the agency I had been working for, had died. He had had a terminal illness. He was only a couple of years older than me and his death was a shock and a tragic loss. He had been ill for several months and his goal was to reach the millennium, which he did easily; beyond that he viewed as a bonus. It was sad that he was robbed of any period of life where he could put his feet up and relax. He was always building his business up to make life easier later on. Unfortunately, there was to be no later on. He did try to cram a lot in the last year but it was too little too late. His death was a wake-up call, you have to live for today, tomorrow may never come.

His death had more than one effect on me. His company would not be pursuing work in the field I was working. There was nobody of his calibre to maintain the business. I would need to find an alternative agency, and that would probably mean working away from home. Most of my speculative inquiries had turned up agencies focusing on the West Midlands area.

Since the beginning of the year, I had been working at a company on the industrial east side of the city. This was probably to be my last contract in the Sheffield area and for Pat's company. It was a daily commute on the bike, but not one that was particularly safe or enjoyable. It was a case of dodging in and out of traffic on a slow-moving dual-carriageway. The ring road feeds the busy M1 and carries heavy traffic throughout the day. The benefits gained from cycling to work are probably negated by the damage being done by breathing in the emissions from the heavy traffic. I always felt better mentally travelling to work on the bike as opposed to driving and adding to the congestion problem of crawling into work stressed to hell. I couldn't help making comparisons with what we had experienced cycling across the channel.

For the second tour our numbers had doubled. When the European Bike Express left Meadowhall, our party of four was en route to France. The other two recruits, besides Kevin and me were not what you would call hardened cyclists but nevertheless very fit individuals. Both had been to John's for the last two years but more for the beer and the banter than for any quality time on the bike. I hoped they knew what they were letting themselves in for.

Sherby was a larger-than-life character, and 'Sherby' was a convenient abbreviation for his name pronounced sherbi-et-ker but was spelt very differently. If a person had a hundred attempts to spell his name, I doubt they would get anywhere near correct. He was of Polish origin and as strong as an ox. He was six foot plus and a natural athlete excelling at most sports. For the last two years, he dragged his old wreck of a bike he called the Falcon, out of the cellar and performed like a seasoned cyclist, without any training whatsoever. One of the longer runs – while in Brittany – was one hundred and twenty miles, and he matched us all pedal for pedal stroke. All this was done in football shorts and trainers, what a star. If ever anybody deserved the tag of Alf Tupper, the legendary comic book character, it was Sherby. Steve, our other recruit, had done a bit of triathlon; his strongest discipline was swimming, not cycling. I discovered this when we did a bit of swimming in local lakes. He had done some cycling but would rely on his general fitness to get over the hills. Both Sherby and Steve would be riding bikes that most cyclists wouldn't go to the shops on; they definitely would not be deemed adequate for a tour across France. Sherby's bike was that old; it was produced in the era before quick-release wheels were invented. On our cycle rides in Brittany, Sherby carried with him a large adjustable spanner in his haversack in case he had to remove a wheel to repair a puncture. Neither of them had proper cycling gear. They would be wearing clothing more suitable for playing football than for serious bike riding.

We decided on a different route to France this year. The ferry limits how far you can get from the north coast before you head back. The European Bike Express Bus offered a chance to start farther afield. We could get picked up along any of their three routes, so we didn't have to make it back to a ferry port. The down side is that it is a bus towing a big bike trailer, and it takes nearly a full day to reach its destination. No matter how many times you stop or how comfortable the seats are it is still not pleasant sitting for that length of time.

## Poitier to Saint Junien (98 km)

Our tour was starting in Poitier, a town two hundred miles north west of Paris. Our destination was Serignan on the south coast of France some four hundred miles away. John was working on a campsite there; we would meet up with him for a day or so and then cycle to Narbonne and catch the bus back home. Our journey would take us over the Montagne Noire (Black Mountains) and into some picturesque parts of France. The mountain range is situated within the Parc Natural Regional du Haut-Languedoc. This is located at the south-western end of the Central Massif in south west France, a popular holiday destination by the French.

We got dropped off at Poitier on an industrial estate. We checked into a hotel to sleep for the night and prepared to make an early start. The next day, we made good time and arrived at our first destination much earlier than expected. Our first night was in a youth hostel in Saint Junien, some sixty miles away. It took some finding. The hostel was an old run-down building. Its appearance was not helped by murky weather. The rain was hammering down. We headed for a few beers in Saint Junien but it looked as if the town had shut for the night. It was a dark grey, unexciting place. We managed to get a foot in the door of a bar that was ready for shutting. We drank along with a few locals. I noticed they were drinking a purple-coloured liquid. We decided to try the Bios de Madison. The concoction was lethal. After a few of these, I don't remember much else about the evening except being carried back to the hostel. I vaguely recollect eating a meal with some locals at a restaurant; the purple mixture began to take its toll and I was very ill.

## Saint Junien to Brive (114 km)

The next morning, we climbed out of Saint Junien and headed towards the youth hostel in Brive, some seventy miles away. We stopped at a café for breakfast after a few miles; the area was agricultural with lush forests. The sun was hot and the road was drying out. The locals were drinking their red wine early in the morning as we drank coffee. We enjoyed the warm weather and undulating roads to Brive. The youth hostel was on the outskirts of town and was dominated by families. We sat outside in the hostel grounds on wooden benches for an evening meal. The French use their youth hostels a lot more than the English do. We took advantage of the warm weather and did our washing, hanging our clothes out to dry on washing lines at the back of the hostel. We headed into town for a drink. There was no shortage of bars and restaurants in this lively, vibrant town. I took it steady with the drink, no more Bios de Maison for a while.

## Brive to Villefranche de Rouergue (120 km)

The next morning, we were on our way to Villefranche de Rouergue. The terrain was starting to get a bit lumpy. The two Steve's were starting to suffer, especially around the backside area. Sherby wrapped his jumper around his old leather saddle, looking for a bit more padding to ease his pain. I took pity on the other Steve and gave him a spare pair of cycling shorts to use. His football shorts, not surprisingly, were cutting into his groin. The youth hostel in Villefranche was a smart, modern place, well decorated with beautifully tiled showers. I was unconvinced that this was not a youth hostel. It didn't have the customary Auberge de Jeunesse feel to it. I shared a room with Kevin and suffered from his loud snoring. Sherby was adamant he wasn't sharing a room with Kevin. He had once unwittingly shared a cabin with him on the ferry back from Brittany. He announced at the time that it was an experience he wouldn't be repeating.

## Villefranche de Rouergue to Albi (64 km)

The locals told us we would be experiencing some hilly terrain when we described our route to them. We soon discovered this to be the case, as we engaged very low gears to climb out of Villefranche de Rouergue and head towards Albi. We were in the Tarn region of France, an area much-loved by the French themselves. Albi is steeped in history; the impressive Saint Cecile Cathedral is described as a jewel of gothic architecture. The bridge over the River Tarn, the Point Vieux, was built back in 1035 AD. We crossed the river into the main part of the town. The place where people live and usually not seen by tourists. When we eventually found the hostel, it was a big disappointment. It was located down a back street in a very scruffy part of town. We arrived feeling very weary. We had spent our last reserves of energy finding this dump of a place. We didn't feel inclined to try somewhere else. We entered this dirty, dingy building with its broken windows and had the feeling we were in the wrong place. We were greeted by a hippy type who assured us we weren't, and he showed us to our dormitory. It felt and looked like I would imagine a Salvation Army dormitory was like. We didn't need to exchange words. We knew what we were each thinking. We showered and headed for a meal and a few beers. We headed back to the tourist district where there was no shortage of restaurants and bars in more pleasant surroundings.

# Albi to Carcassonne (103 km)

We left Albi and headed towards Carcassonne, some seventy miles away. On every tour, I have a stage that stands out from the rest. This was definitely the best day of the tour for me. We booked the youth hostel at Carcassone and cycled through some wonderful scenery. The roads meandered high into the mountains. The area attracted tourism at the lakes near Saint Ferreol le Lac and les Cammazes. We reached the highest point at Saissac. This was a beautiful town that felt like the top of the world, with views stretching out for miles around. We cycled the fifteen miles into Carcassonne and made the mistake of having a few beers in the town, waiting for the youth hostel to open at 6.00 p.m. What we didn't realise at the time was that the hostel was in La Cite', the old medieval part of the town, that was a few miles away on the hillside. La Cite' has a double wall around the town. The outer wall dates back to Louis IX and the inner dates back to the Roman times. You could walk in-between the walls, gaining access to the town at a few places. It has been restored, old bits have been renewed, and the new bits do stick out a bit. It looks like something out of a Disney film. Not surprisingly, it was where Walt Disney got his inspiration for the setting of Sleeping Beauty.

On arrival at La Cite' we booked in at the hostel. We were surprised that a youth hostel could demand such a prestigious plot inside a medieval town. In keeping with its surroundings, the hostel was of a very high standard, having a bar and a good restaurant. We toured the narrow-cobbled streets, restricted to all but essential motor vehicles. It felt as if we were inside a massive fort. The shops, restaurants, and museums capitalised on the location, selling their wares to the tourists. Only in the inner area, Chateau Comtal, a 12$^{th}$-century castle with its museum exhibits, were you required to pay. The majority of the town and its ramparts you were allowed to explore free of charge.

## Carcassonne to Serignan (84 km)

Our final stage of the tour to Serignan was a fifty-mile ride through flat wine-growing regions that stretched to the south coast. The temperature increased, and so did the traffic as busy roads were filled with holidaymakers heading for the coast. Serignan was a little town a couple of miles from the coast. The campsite was sandwiched between Serignan and the seaside resort of Valras Plague. Valras Plague was a typical, quiet, unspoilt French seaside town with a beach, a few hotels and restaurants. The French differ from their Spanish neighbours; they don't tend to saturate their seaside towns with typical seaside fare, nor do they pander to English tastes. Not a chance of seeing Only Fools and Horses, or catching up with EastEnders here. I doubt whether I will get a Kebab or fish and chips on the seafront. Moules et Frites are more likely my only option.

We met John and Linda on-site. They provided us all
with a tent for the night, a day's rest and time to reflect on
the tour.

## Serignan to Narbonne Plague (37 km)

The next day was a half-day ride along the coast to
Narbonne Plage to catch the European Bike Express bus
for the long journey back home.

# Tour 3 – Brittany

The contract in Sheffield took me up to Christmas of that year. The dark winter nights commuting on busy roads left me craving a change of scenery. The new-year, as anticipated, saw me working for a midlands-based agency with nights away from home and the unhealthy lifestyle that entails. Hotel breakfasts and pub meals soon increase the waistline if endured for any length of time. I packed my running shoes and swore I would use them. For a little while, I would and then the attraction of a warm pub seemed more inviting than plodding around strange streets late at night.

Fortunately, these contracts were short-lived. By March, I had accepted a contract south of Derby, at a food factory. It was just over thirty miles away and quite a pleasant route to cycle. I saw this as an opportunity to regain some of my lost fitness. Cycling in through traffic in Chesterfield was nowhere near as bad as in Sheffield. Once in Derby, a series of cycle paths made a trouble-free passage by bike to the other side of the city.

I eased myself into cycling the full distance. I used the train occasionally to reduce the distance by half. Soon, the fitness returned and the waist line reduced. I cycled the sixty miles a day for four days a week. On Friday, I would use the car and stock up my freezer with Chinese and Indian food from the employees' shop on the factory site.

By summertime, I was fitter than I had been for a good few years. I was looking forward to taking my fitness abroad and tackling some serious touring.

This year I had acquired an addition to my cycling armoury, a touring bike. My mountain bike had served me well but I felt justified in the investment of a more suitable vehicle to take me to the next level. I opted for a Kevin Winter frame with its characteristic penguin on the head tube. This was my second Kevin Winter frame, and a few of the local riders had these frames and the Penguin Club was born – hence the Penguin Tours. I kitted the bike out with a triple chainring and some heavy-duty wheels shod with 32mm tyres. I gave myself a budget of a thousand pounds. With a touring bike, reliability is the main concern. Saving a few grams in weight on a bike fitted with panniers is futile.

The previous year's long bus ride home from the south of France had left a deep scar on my memory. I hadn't at this stage ruled out using the bus ever again, but not this year. This year I wanted a tour that wouldn't involve a full day of my holiday sitting on a bus. The Brittany crossing from Portsmouth or Plymouth into Roscoff, Cherbourg or Saint-Malo opened up a lot of possibilities for a tour. It was more preferable to taking the short ferry journey to Calais and encountering flat, featureless terrain for several miles. Although the crossing is six or seven hours, it is well worth the extra travel to arrive in Brittany.

Four of us, Jimmy, Denis, and Doug, and I, caught the train down to Plymouth and then the ferry to Roscoff. Kevin decided he was going it alone to Spain on the Bike Express meet up with JC on a campsite he was working on, and just chill out for a week. It was something I didn't feel keen on and I couldn't persuade him to join us on our Brittany tour. I had been on cycling trips with Jimmy many times before. Doug, however, was of unknown measure, especially as he was nearly seventy. He was a cycling legend, a character and good company, never short of a few tales. He was a builder in his working life and very powerfully built. Some of his exploits were folklore. I remember a weekend cycling trip to Skegness, where Jimmy and I tried to match Doug pint for pint in the evening. The pair of us ended up very drunk and ill, whilst Doug was still going strong, and as sober as a judge. Doug had been a good cyclist in his time and I remember from my early cycling experiences how good he was. In those days Doug was in his forties while I struggled to stay with him as a young man some twenty years younger. He was now starting to look his age, a bit tired and old, even his twenty odd years old Colnago looked as though it had seen better days.

## Roscoff to Quimper (102 km)

We planned for about sixty or seventy miles a day on fairly flat roads and we didn't expect any problems. What we hadn't anticipated was the weather. The first leg from Roscoff to Quimper, a ride of nearly seventy miles, was blighted by torrential rain. Doug had the last laugh as he was the only one to have mudguards. It was something I had not considered, but it was a mistake that I never made again. The ride to Quimper was through beautiful countryside, mostly thick forests shrouded in mist but spoilt by the rain. On arrival at Quimper youth hostel, Jimmy learnt another lesson that should have been obvious: always wrap your clothes in plastic bags in case your panniers are not waterproof. I had to lend Jimmy some clothes for our first night out.

## Quimper to Quiberon (125 km)

Our next destination was the youth hostel at the end of the Quiberon peninsula, a thin piece of land that stretches out to sea from the south coast of Brittany. The southern coast of Brittany around Carnac and Quiberon is a place I had visited before but still enjoy adventuring to time and time again. The peninsula was always longer than you imagined from your last visit. It is about ten miles long, with a view of the sea on both sides. Because it is flat, it feels like it goes on forever, especially for four knackered cyclists at the end of a long ride.

At the youth hostel, we teamed up with two very strange characters. The first individual was a very extrovert American motorcyclist from Sacramento. He looked like and behaved like one of the village people, the one with the handlebar moustache. He was a librarian, a strange occupation for a Hell's Angel. He told us that he had learnt German, and then gone to Germany to study for his degree, free Gratis. He had split up with his girlfriend and had taken off on his bike for an adventure. The second character was a German student the American had befriended.

It seemed that the German had few people he could talk to, only knowing a bit of English and very little French. We headed for a restaurant for a meal and a few beers and exchanged adventures. The German was a very quiet bloke, but the American more than compensated. After a few beers, the German let his guard down and told us that he felt the need to sleep with a loaded handgun under his pillow. This information made us more than a little nervous. We all imagined a scenario where something or someone pissed him off, and he blew away a dozen people before anybody could stop him with a bullet through the head. Perhaps it was a good thing Kevin hadn't come with us after all. His snoring just might have been the catalyst that tipped this student over the edge. It could have triggered the Quiberon Youth Hostel Massacre.

## Quiberon to La Cheze (123 km)

The next morning, we headed north towards La Cheze. We intended to stay at the Moulin de la Fosse. This was the place Kevin and I had used on our first tour and the Dutch family always made us welcome. We needed a favour when Doug's pedal broke within a couple of miles of reaching their chambre d'hôte. We managed to reach their place by pushing Doug on the flat and freewheeling downhill. Their son had an old bike that we managed to salvage a pedal off. The pedal lasted until we reached a bike shop in Loudeac, where Doug parted with thirty euros for a new pair of Shimano pedals.

## La Cheze to Trebeurdan (116 km)

Our next destination was the youth hostel at Trebeurdan. This part of Brittany was made popular by the rose granite that adorns the coast. The youth hostel was on the coastal road and was popular with the locals. It was littered with canoes and mountain bikes. We sat down in the communal restaurant and ate a good meal at the hostel before finding somewhere to get a drink later. We sat and ate our meal with a French girl who was on her own. She seemed a very troubled soul. She told us she had left her children and boyfriend at home while she had escaped for some solitude. To us, this seemed an unusual thing to do, but perhaps in France, it was not.

# Trebeurdan to Roscoff (84 km)

In the morning we headed west back towards the ferry port of Roscoff. The rain had set in again. The road towards Morlaix ran alongside an estuary; it was very picturesque, and it was a pity that it was raining. We found a bed and breakfast in Roscoff and caught the ferry back to England. Brittany is a pretty place but the weather can be just as bad as back home. It is a risk you take with this area. Overall, it had been an enjoyable tour. There were a few times when things did get a little tetchy. Doug and Denis did have a few frank exchanges of views, mostly to do with the direction we should be taking. Denis was the map and compass man who prided himself on his navigational ability. Doug tended to go with less scientific means, mostly gut feelings. This difference in approach infuriated the hell out of each other. This came to a head on the last day when Doug went his own way for a while. We found him later in Roscoff quite oblivious about our concern for his welfare. We teamed back up eventually to have a last night away before boarding the ferry back home in the morning.

Sadly, the outstanding memory I have of the Brittany tour is the rain. The beautiful, lush green forests that cover much of the department require a substantial amount of water to flourish. It felt like we had had the yearly allocation on our tour. Thinking ahead, next year, I would want to tour a lot further south, where the sun burns and the ground is scorched from prolonged periods without rain.

I finished the year doing something I swore I wouldn't do again. I entered a bike race. I was told, misinformed as it turned out, that it was to be the last 12-hour time trial on our local course in the North Midlands. I set myself a very modest target of two hundred and forty miles. In my full-on racing days, I would have aimed to cover another twenty miles. On that day, I managed to just surpass my target. It was enough to give me a top-ten finish and was every bit as hard as I thought it would be. It was good to see some of the old faces, still competing, and still enjoying the pain and agony that competition brings. They asked if a return was on the cards. I replied with, "Who knows what tomorrow will bring?"

# Tour 4 – Valence to Como

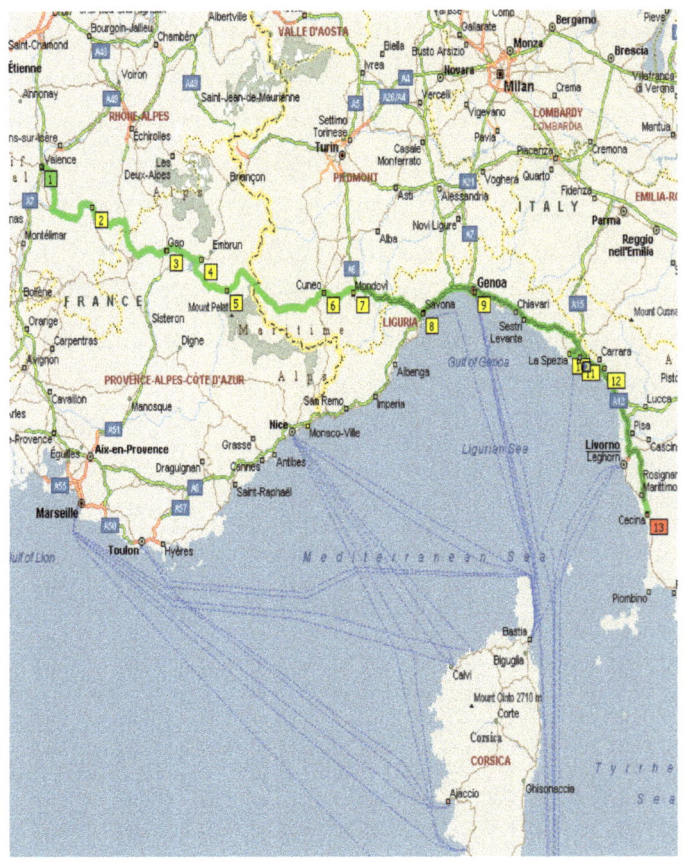

Any racing aspirations I might have had for next year soon evaporated. The contract in Derby ended and I was back commuting in the car. It was one of those jobs I particularly hated, too far to commute easily and too poorly paid to contemplate staying away from home. By the time I arrived home I was too tired to motivate myself to do any exercise at all. I was locked into the all-work and no-play loop, and felt very frustrated with the situation. I didn't have the same frank relationship with my new employer that I had enjoyed with Pat. He had often told me what a job was worth and how much he could afford to pay me and I fully believed him. When I asked the new agency for a rate increase to allow me to stay in digs the odd night, I was told that they couldn't afford to pay more.

A bit of probing revealed how much my services were costing the client. Sure enough, my suspicions were confirmed. I was even stunned at the greediness of my new employer; he was paying himself twice as much as he was paying me for doing very little. The consultancy, as they like to call themselves, had probably forty people, such as myself, to feed off. They would argue that if it wasn't for them, people like me and others wouldn't have work to go to. They would also argue that they have expenses, but surely this is beyond being acceptable? I now had a very big bee in my bonnet that made my daily commute to work feel even worse. I couldn't confront my greedy boss without dropping into trouble the person who had supplied me with information.

I went for a few interviews with other consultancies. I needed to get away. It was hard trying to maintain a professional attitude with Mr Greedy when I wanted to spit in his eye. I was pondering an offer from Peugeot Parts in Coventry. It was March time and I went to France for a fiftieth birthday treat, which would give me time to think logically about what I wanted to do. On my return, I had no decision to make. Mr Greedy had contacts within Peugeot and he had knowledge of my Peugeot interview. He took exception to my disloyalty and terminated my contract by letter. I was down at Peugeot the following day with a suitcase in hand, ready to start.

I was one of six contractors based in the engineering department. I was sold the job on the basis that there were a few sports-minded people like myself and I would fit in superbly well. I wasn't disappointed. Although running was the main after-work activity, I did find a keen cyclist amongst them. I had not done a great deal of running since my Fire Service days, almost seven years ago now. After a month of getting dropped off the back by the after-work running club I could feel my running legs return. Most nights were spent running; sometimes as many as ten miles were covered in an evening session. By June, I had negotiated a four-day week by working a ten-hour day. I ran for three days and cycled my three-day weekend. What seemed a bit of a gamble at the time had turned out to be a better package than I could have imagined. I was ready now (I thought) fitness-wise for anything a tour could offer.

Each year a conscious effort was made to be a little more adventurous than the previous year, pushing how far and how difficult we dare go, to now we had got away with it. The disadvantage of this type of touring, which I find exciting, strangely enough, is that things can and will go wrong. A cautious, worrying type would give this type of cycling holiday a wide berth. A base type cycling can only take you fifty miles maximum from your starting point. This type of touring holiday starts with being several hundred miles from where you want to be and there is no turning back. When Kevin planned this tour, I just had the feeling that this time, we had bitten off a bit more than we could chew. I kept my reservations to myself at the time. He had meticulously planned each day's stopping points and mileage using his piece of string. I hadn't the heart to pour cold water on his enthusiasm and sound like an old woman. Also, last year's tour had certainly not been the same without his unique, carefree attitude, everything had been a bit intense and serious.

Our plan was to get dropped off by the Bike Express Bus in Valance in France, cycle over the Alps into Italy, cycle down to Cecina in Tuscany, spend a day with JC and then head north to Como in northern Italy to pick up the bus home. Simple on paper. A seven hundred-mile trip in eight days did seem a little much but not impossible for hardened cyclists (or nutcases) like ourselves. Plans made in the comfort of your home with perhaps a bottle of wine without being able to appreciate the severity of the gradients or the intense heat of the sun in mid-July can be a bit optimistic, if not foolhardy.

There were three of us making the journey, Kevin, Steve and myself. Steve had been with us to JC's in 1998 and 1999. He also did the Poitiers to Perpignan tour without much of a problem. This tour would be a lot harder and would probably test Steve to his limit. I did feel that it would be a big task for him. That says quite a lot as I tend to be the one with the maverick or it'll be all right attitude, in this partnership. Kevin had planned the route without any serious reservations. So, who was I to argue and fill others with self-doubt?

The tour got off to a bad start when we couldn't gain access to our hotel room, for reasons I will never know. The first night we always pre-book, as there is no chance of finding anywhere to lay our head in the early hours of the morning. These cheap hotels on industrial estates are unmanned; they rely on pre-booking and then recognition of your credit card on arrival. At three in the morning, I must admit to not being fully awake and responsive to any instructions in French. After a few unsuccessful attempts to gain access, we gave up in frustration. Looking on the bright side, an early start might not be such a bad idea.

## Valence to Savine Le Lac (195 km)

At sunrise, we headed west out of Valence; once out of Valance, we hit the traffic-free and rolling countryside that we had travelled hundreds of miles to this part of the world for. After about twenty miles, we experienced a rare event – a puncture. I don't exactly know why, but I have never experienced a puncture in France. It could be the lack of broken glass and the sharp flints found in rock salt we put on our roads in England that's not used in France, who knows? Perhaps the fact that I use a heavy-duty and fatter section tyre to alleviate impact puncture on bad road surface, or increased loading may contribute. Or perhaps I prepare my bike meticulously for a tour and ensure that the equipment is in good condition. Steve, for some reason had decided to tackle this tour on a bike that can only be described as not fit for purpose. As I helped him change the innertube, I couldn't help but notice the bald tyre and loose bearings in his back wheel and felt a little annoyed and frustrated. The tour was in jeopardy; I had serious concerns about this badly maintained heap of scrap holding together all the way to Como.

After our enforced stop, we headed for an appropriately named place, 'Die', for a break. We had covered forty miles and up to now, the terrain had not caused us any problems. Despite its name, Die was quite a pleasant place with a few cafés and restaurants, which allowed us to rest and refuel. After Die, the terrain started becoming more testing. The sun was beating down and we were stopping more frequently to take on water. It became evident that Steve was not in much better condition than his bike. We were now in a mountain range. As we climbed hairpin bends through a steep wooded area, Steve was falling further and further behind.

We reached Gap very much the worst for wear, particularly Steve. Our plan to get good mileage under our belt after our enforced early start was starting to take its toll. We had covered a hundred miles to Gap and the next twenty miles to Savines Le Lac. Our destination for the day was flattish, but we were crawling along at a snail's pace. We stopped at shops, petrol stations, you name it, to refuel with liquids. We rode alongside the large lake, crossed a bridge and went in search of the youth hostel. There cannot be many more picturesque settings than this for an overnight stop. We were all a bit too exhausted to overindulge in food and drink. Instead, a silence hung over us like a cloud. Steve was so tired he was barely able to open his eyes. He had completely lost any patience and his sense of humour for any banter and piss-taking, which is the norm on such occasions. I reminded Steve, tongue in cheek that he was the highest serving officer in the Fire Service present, and I expected more in the way of leadership from him. His reply wasn't very polite, he was in no mood, and I didn't tease him further.

## Savine Le Lac to Mondovi (169 km)

The next day, we headed down the other side of the lake amongst the holidaymakers on our way to Barcelonette for our first break. Steve was struggling to hold the most pedestrian pace and he decided not to stop. Kevin and I enjoyed a bite to eat and a coffee at Barcelonette, a charming market town with views of the Alps before us. I wasn't happy with Steve continuing alone, even at a slow pace, but I accepted that if he felt more comfortable doing that it was perhaps not a bad idea.

We set off towards Italy, expecting to meet up with Steve before the border. We stopped for another drink in Larche before starting on the Col de Larche climb proper. A few kilometres from the summit, we noticed walkers descending with waterproofs on and cars with their lights on. Kevin and I were frying in the mid-day heat and couldn't understand what was happening. Just before the summit, a mist engulfed us and the temperature plummeted. It left us scrambling through our panniers in search of warm clothing to don to combat the cold. We rode through thick mist, barely making out the abandoned border control as we descended the other side of the col, the Col de Maddalena.

We plugged away at a good pace for over a hundred miles that day and still no sign of Steve. At Mondovi, we were looking for a place to stay before darkness prevented us from going any further. We got our foot in the door of a hotel as the owner was preparing to close for the night. Our most optimistic planning had us a further thirty miles closer to our destination. The reality of the heat and the terrain had got the better of us. After feeding our faces, we refocused our attention on trying to locate Steve. My initial thought was that he had come to grief somewhere on route. I then thought that he may have drifted off course and we had passed him and he was behind us. Having witnessed his performance on the first day, I would have thought he was incapable of another hundred-plus mile ride, so the possibility that he was in front of us seemed remote.

## Mondovi to Lerici (239 km or 150 miles!)

When I managed to contact Steve by mobile, I was surprised when he told me he had reached the planned destination. I also felt a little embarrassed that we hadn't. He had ridden virtually non-stop until dark, but he had managed to surpass all our expectations of him. It appears it had been a typical hare and the tortoise race. While Kevin and I had been having stops for drinks and food, he had plugged away and had finished more than twenty miles further up the road. I calculated in my mind how much time we had lost by stopping and even then, it seemed unfeasible that he could have made up that amount of time considering his fitness.

Kevin and I resisted the temptation to overindulge in drink and decided on an early start to claw back the deficit on Steve and get back on schedule. It was a daunting task. We needed to cycle more than a hundred and forty miles to reach Massa before dark. We descended into Savona and

80

followed the coast road to Genoa. The terrain was hilly as we climbed and descended time and time again into small towns while cars drove on flat roads on concrete pillars where bikes were not allowed.

Genoa was a nightmare in itself to traverse. Traffic congestion and only a vague idea of direction added to our frustration. We found that our touring bikes didn't have the acceleration of the other vehicles we were competing with for space on the roads. When traffic lights changed to go, we were left standing by lorries, cars and young females in high heels sitting astride their Lambrettas. Eventually, a young scooter rider came to our aid. He asked where we were heading and then proceeded to guide us though the city and out the other side. Just before he sped off in the distance, he told us about his own cycling exploits in which he cycled down to Rome a few years ago. We thanked him for his help; he had saved us going in circles for hours on end.

We headed along the coast road towards La Spezia. The original plan was to be at Massa for the overnight stay, another ninety miles away. We had already covered seventy-five miles that day and we were feeling the worst for wear. After another hour or so, we encountered some very hilly terrain. After following the coast, we came inland to experience some serious climbing, culminating in the Col de Bracco. It was a relentless climb, hairpin after hairpin, dropping down only to climb again. By the top I was weak with exhaustion. We had stopped several times, each time, the climb became harder. We were grateful for the descent into La Spezia. We realised that we were on our last legs and we had no chance of reaching Massa. We had reached a crucial point in our tour. We realised our schedule was an impossible task. There was no chance of pulling it back. We had definitely bitten off more than we could chew by a long way.

We had covered over one hundred and forty miles and still no sight of Steve. We kept going for another ten miles until we reached the resort of Lerici. The severity of the tour was starting to take its toll. For the first time, there was doubt that we would reach our destination. We were both suffering from dehydration and exhaustion. Kevin also had a problem with his backside. The combination of heat, sweat and friction in that area had developed into infection and swelling that threatened to stop him from riding his bike altogether. We booked into the only hotel that had a vacancy, and then we had to share a double bed. The proprietor enquired if we were happy with that arrangement. He seemed a little uncomfortable when we said it was. He may have thought that we were lovers, who knows? At nine o'clock in the evening, we didn't have the energy or inclination to try anywhere else on the off chance we could get single beds, or be bothered how this arrangement may have appeared.

We headed for the restaurant recommended by the hotel owner. It was on the sea front. The owner was a big, larger-than-life character, heavily built like an opera singer, greasy hair, dirty apron and a bellowing voice. We asked for spaghetti to start, followed by pizza. When we inquired about the dishes, he told us and the entire restaurant that his wife made the best pizza in all of Italy. He was probably right. After devouring the spaghetti, we were faced with this mountain of pizza that was large in diameter but also about three inches thick. It was thickly garnished with bacon, mushrooms, peppers, olives and several types of vegetables. We had no chance of finishing this dish. We hardly made a dent in the main meal and were left wishing we had given the spaghetti starter a miss.

Halfway through the meal we tried to contact our ex-companion Steve. After trying for some time, I managed to make contact. I asked him his whereabouts, and I was gobsmacked when he told me he had made it to Massa. I was filled with numbness and utter disbelief. I didn't believe it was possible. It would have taken somebody way above our ability, a Lance Armstrong perhaps, to ride that well. When he insisted, he was in Massa, I told him that he must have caught the train. When he didn't deny it, I realised he had been having a bit of fun with us. All the pieces fit. He had been playing us along for a couple of days, typical fire brigade humour. We had been worried about the shit while he was putting his feet up. I was too exhausted to be angry. We laughed about it and agreed to meet up in Cecina.

## Lerici to Cecina (137 km)

The next day, we rode the eighty miles to Cecina on relatively flat roads. Kevin was still suffering and we were thankful we didn't have another day of mountains. We passed Pisa and spotted the famous leaning tower from a distance. We reached Cecina a pleasant town where we ate and phoned JC for instructions from there. We were only a few miles away. Next, we passed through a place called La California towards Bibbona. We arrived at the campsite where we located our tanned hosts, John and Linda, and of course, Steve, who was looking a lot fresher than us. John had kindly put me and Steve together in a tent, leaving Kevin in a smaller tent on his own, isolated enough to escape the noise of his snoring.

## Cecina to Como (By Train)

After rehydrating and relaxing around the pool I sensed a reluctance from the other two to get back on the bikes and cycle the two hundred and fifty miles to Como. Steve had already abandoned his cycling aspirations to become a train traveller and Kevin was still suffering with his backside. I was outvoted by a majority vote to catch the train up to Como. It wasn't a straightforward journey. It involved catching a total of five trains and depended on all the trains being on time. Starting with: Cecina to Pisa, Pisa to Genoa, Genoa to Milan, Milan to Monza, and finally Monza to Como. Funnily enough, everything went like clockwork. The trains arrived and departed on time. Milan was the nearest we came to disaster while negotiating the vast number of crowded platforms with our bikes. I think such a logistic challenge in Britain would have ended in failure.

We booked into a youth hostel in Como. The sleeping quarters consisted of two very large dormitories, one male and one female. After a night on the town and a good few beers and cigarettes, in Kevin's case, we retired to bed. As expected, Kevin slid into his famous snoring routine. The acoustics were perfect; the noise amplified and resonated around the building. Steve picked up his bedding and retired to the female dormitory muttering "for fuck sake" under his breath. I lay in bed laughing uncontrollably as everybody started waking up and coming out with what I can only guess were expletives in many different languages. The rest of our tour was spent cycling around Lake Como and Lake Lugano. The former was beautiful but quite busy. We had two days cycling at a leisurely pace instead of grinding away and not knowing whether we would have made it to Como in time for the bus. The tour was a typical example of trying to bite off more than you can chew.

The question on my mind this year was: how much damage had the previous year done? The three of us last year had well and truly taken a bit of a battering. We did a lot more miles than Kevin had planned, however, each day, we fell further and further behind schedule. The main reason was that some of the roads and tunnels planned in the route were not for cyclists. A spare day should be built in just in case someone has a bad day or someone is ill. Things to consider for next year. Surely, we won't make the same mistake again?

# Tour 5 – Bayonne to Empuriabrava – A Pyrenean Coast to Coast

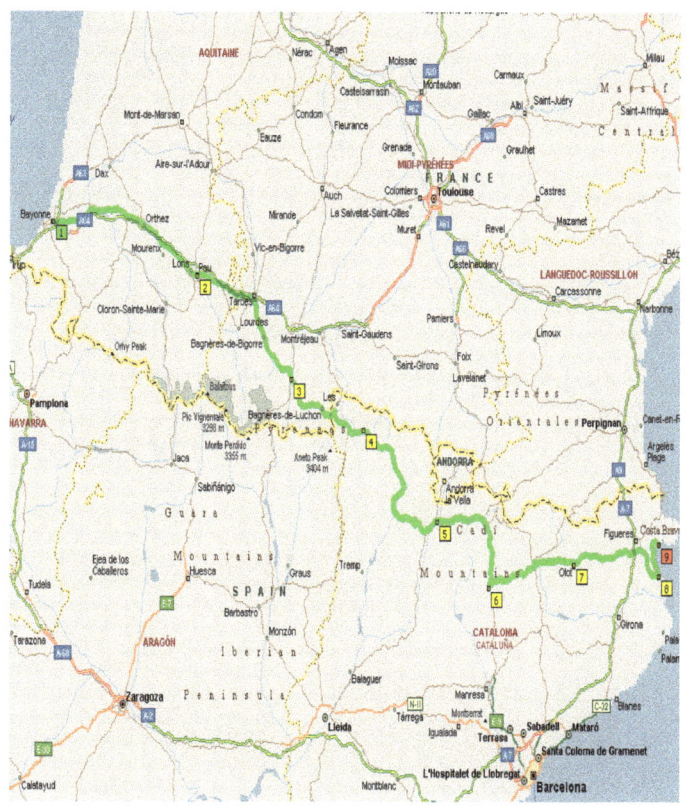

The year 2004 got off to a memorable start. In January I was off to Australia for my daughter's wedding. She met her husband-to-be, Damien, in America on a working holiday. I was going over there for the best part of a month. I hoped that Peugeot would keep my job open, but I couldn't really blame them if they told me not to come back. In the end, they were quite good about the matter.

The trip went well, and as much as I enjoyed my time over there, it wouldn't suit a cyclist. The cities were very busy, with several miles of nothing in between. The roads were long and straight, with little to break up the scenery. Every place we travelled too took forever to get to, and then there wasn't much when you arrived. It seems unfair to judge a country on a month-long visit, but the small bit of the vast continent I did see, didn't do anything to make me want to stay.

I returned to work to find my friend and training partner Ian had decided to leave. He had been in Coventry for three years now and had had enough of the travelling. He had accepted a permanent job back in Barnsley, for less money. I was now the only contractor staying away from home. The nights seemed lonely when you had no one to share a pint with after an evening's run. It did put a bit of a damper on the job, when I had been enjoying a bit of stability in my working life. I was still running with the after-work group as much as I had been doing the previous year. I was even competing in a few mid-week running races that were held in the Midlands area.

I enrolled on a Computer Aided Design course at Coventry College. The benefit of the course was two-fold. It would keep me out of the pub, and it was a way of keeping my mind active and a useful addition to my CV. Contractors have to continually update their skills. The more tools a contractor has in his toolbox, the more useful he is to an organisation. When work is hard to come by, those that offer a wider range of skills are those that are likely to be kept on longer.

I devised a way of increasing my weekly mileage on the bike. Each Monday, I travelled down on the train with my bike. I then used it to commute to and from my digs on a daily basis. I finished work Friday and rode the eighty miles home for the weekend. The ride home at dinnertime was done with panniers containing my weekly washing. Sometimes I would pick a more scenic route, and push the mileage up to a hundred miles. The route home was quite picturesque. I chose roads that ran parallel with the busy M42, keeping my route traffic-free. The nearest thing I would get to a big town was Ashby-de-la-Zouch. I would then follow the cycle paths through Derby to avoid rush-hour traffic. After that I then had the option of a Derbyshire detour up the A6 to Matlock and then Bakewell. Alternatively, if I was tired or the weather was bad, I had the option of a shorter ride up the busier A61 through Alfreton and Chesterfield. Either way, I had good fitness for whatever my cycling aspirations happened to be that year.

Like most keen cyclists, I loved to follow the Tour de France on television each year. The big mountains are where all the damage is usually done. How hard can these climbs be? This year, and the following years, I intended to find out first-hand how hard they were, before I got too old to manage them, starting this year with the Pyrenees. The Pyrenees is a range of mountains in southwest Europe that form a natural border between Spain and France, with

Andorra sandwiched in the middle. They span from the Atlantic Ocean (Bay of Biscay) to the Mediterranean (Cap de Creus). A coast-to-coast ride that would involve tackling some of the Tour de France cols seemed an ideal holiday adventure. The highest cols we would be tackling were only a little over two thousand metres, seven hundred metres below the snow line, but still high enough to make legs ache, especially carrying a heavy bike fitted with panniers. The EBE bus determined the starting and pickup point for our Pyrenees trip. Bayonne was our drop-off point in France on the Atlantic side, and the pick-up point was Empuriabrava in Spain on the Mediterranean.

Three of us were to make the trip this year, Kevin and myself, as usual, and Denis. Denis had been on the tour to Brittany, two years ago. That trip would seem like a stroll in the park compared to what this year had in store. Denis was a fireman and hopefully, he would emerge with his sense of humour intact. Kevin plotted a route that took advantage of any youth hostels on the route, which we knew would only serve as a rough guide, a very rough guide.

## Bayonne to Pau (105 km)

The first day we cycled from our drop off point to Pau, a popular tourist town in the Pyrenees. The rural roads from Bayonne to Pau were quiet but unspectacular. We stopped at a pretty market town called Navarrenx. The town was confined within solid ramparts and was built as a Bastide in 1316. After a while, you get quite blasé about these beautiful places as France has so many. We ate lunch and then continued our journey to Pau clocking about seventy miles for the first day.

Pau is the capital of the Pyrenees-Atlantique department. The focal point was the Chateau de Pau, a magnificent castle by all accounts, but we didn't have the time or the inclination to visit. We were proving unsuccessful in finding vacant accommodation in the town centre. The tourist information office directed us to a Gite de France, another chateau a couple of kilometres outside the town in a suburb called Idron. Once at Chateau d'Idron, a stocky, longhaired Frenchman speaking good English greeted us. We wondered if this man was part of the French aristocracy who had fallen on hard times and was having to resort to entertaining English cyclists to make ends meet. When we asked about eating arrangements, he gave us a few options, one of them being eating in the chateau with his family. We took up the offer and dined in the chateau with the owner's family. The meal cost thirty euros each, which included several bottles of wine. The evening further dispelled the myth of the French being arrogant and loathing the English.

## Pau to Arreau (95 km)

Day two we headed for the cols of the Pyrenees. Our first stop was at the commercial centre of religion, Lourdes. We wandered around the stalls in the town, unimpressed by the tack and memorabilia on display. From Lourdes, we headed for Bagneres de-Bigorre and then on to Campan.

The road up to Saint-Marie-de-Campan was congested with cyclists heading towards the Col-du-Tourmalet to watch the stage of the Tour de France that was finishing at La Mongie. At Marie-de-Campan, we were prevented from going any further. We were climbing Col d'Aspin from one end while the Tour de France cavalcade approached from the other. We watched the Tour at the foot of the Tourmalet in torrential rain. Our enforced rest wasn't a problem. Riding in these conditions would have been difficult, although it didn't seem to bother the professionals.

When all the riders and backup vehicles had passed, the police reopened the roads to mere mortals like ourselves, and we carried on up the Col d'Aspin, picking our way through camper vans and other cyclists. A lot of the cyclists were American. They had come to see their hero, Lance Armstrong. Their bikes were expensive lightweight machines, the best that money could buy, complete with matching trade team jerseys.

They were following the tour. They parked their cars at the bottom of a col, rode up it, and moved onto the next stage. They were astonished at these three crazy English cyclists who were climbing the big cols, complete with heavy bikes and cycle panniers. We joked light-heartedly with them, suggesting that what they were doing was not proper cycling, just cheating. We meandered up the hairpins to the top of the Col d'Aspin and stopped at the top to take photographs and admire the scenery. There was evidence that the Tour de France had visited. Scattered about was all the rubbish that careless humans leave behind in their wake. It looked scruffy even though a half-hearted clean-up operation had taken place. There were still a few campers preparing to spend the night there. We descended down the col, negotiating the tight hairpins into the town of Arreau. We booked into the two-star Hotel de France and spent an evening, exchanging stories with a couple of English motorcyclists who were following the Tour. We drank a substantial amount that evening. If we had had an insight into what lay ahead, we might have prepared a little better for what was to be a stage to test any amateur cyclist.

# Arreau to Salardu (75 km)

Day three was the hardest of our tour. A few miles from Arreau, we arrived at the foot of the formidable Col de Peyresourde at 1569m. At the top, we stopped briefly and then descended very rapidly into Bagneres de Luchon. We then climbed the Col de Portillon at 1293m, not that high by the Pyrenees standard but a very hard climb. By the time we had hit the foot of this climb we were hot and tired. We had to make a couple of stops partway up to rest in the shade. The heat pounded down while the gradient was hard going with panniers. For the first time on this tour, we were under-geared. Denis and I had triple chain-wheels and we were managing to keep moving forward. On a hairpin bend near the top, Kevin couldn't keep his thirty-eight chain-ring turning even with a twenty-eight-rear sprocket. He lost momentum and came to a stop; he got off and walked for a while. We reached the top and noticed an unmanned border crossing that told us we were in Spain. By the time we arrived at a place called Salardu, there was very little left in the tank. The town sat at the bottom of a mountain called the Bonaigua (2072m), although we didn't realise that at the time. Salardu was a nice place with a modern, well-equipped youth hostel in beautiful surroundings, that served good food. Later, we enjoyed a few beers and explored the medieval town.

## Salardu to La Seu d'Urgell (116 km)

Day four and we set off from the foot of the Bonaigua.
The gradient wasn't as severe as the Portillon, but it went
on forever. It was lunchtime by the time we reached the
top. At the summit, we stopped at the Sky Station Café.
The temperature was a lot cooler at the top we then
descended the other side of the mountain. Cows wandering
onto the road on the fast descent presented a hazard to
traffic. The next climb was the Col del Canto (1725m),
again a tough climb but more by its length than gradient.
After the descent, we headed for La Seu d'Urgell or Seo de
Urgel, depending on which road sign you read. The traffic
started to get heavier as we headed into town. The road ran
parallel to the river, dominated by water sports pursuits.
The town, which was crowded and dirty, had little appeal.

The youth hostel was oversubscribed so we booked into a pension (posada), a Spain version of a bed and breakfast.

## La Seu d'Urgell to Berga (70.5 km)

Day Five was my favourite ride of the tour. After a few miles on the busy road out of Seo de Urgel, we turned onto a minor road. We wound our way upwards on a deserted road that periodically disappeared into the mountain. The scenery was stunning. We stopped at a place called Cambrils for lunch. This was a pretty village in the middle of nowhere – not to be confused with another Spanish town on the coast. It was still a very hard day. We arrived at Berga and booked into a youth hostel overrun with schoolchildren. The hostel had the advantage of being cheap and serving beer at only one euro a bottle.

## Berga to Olot (73 km)

Day Six was the last day in the mountains. As we got nearer the coast, the weather got hotter and the cols got smaller. The terrain was still hard as we wound around the mountainous landscape. Our attempt to cut short our journey landed us in trouble with the local police. We ignored a road sign, banning cyclists from this tunnel, to avoid a torturous accent. A police car stopped us no more than half a mile into the tunnel and made us turn around. After a lecture in which we claimed ignorance and a lack of understanding of Spanish, the police parked at the entrance of the tunnel, acting as a deterrent. We set off up the mountain as swiftly as we could to avoid any further trouble. We arrived at Olot and celebrated that we had seen the back of the Cols. We booked into a Pension overlooking a pretty square with brightly painted houses. We stumbled upon a brothel by accident. The bar was empty apart from a few over-friendly, attractive women. We were too tired and drunk to realise what was happening. It wasn't until I was offered this rather attractive female body for fifty euros, did I suspect, that perhaps we were in the wrong place for a quiet evening. Needless to say, we all declined what was on offer.

## Olot to L'Escala (66 km)

Day seven was a steady fifty-mile ride to the coast. L'Escala is a charming coastal resort, not too commercialised or crowded. It was the ideal place to spend an evening drinking and experiencing fresh seafood after a hard tour. We booked into a hotel near the sea for the night.

## L'Escala to Empuriabrava (25 km)

The next morning, we cycled sixteen miles up the coast to the much busier Empuriabrava to meet the bus for the tedious journey home.

# Tour 6 – Beaume to Montpellier - The Massif Central

I sensed the contract at Peugeot was coming to an end. Several of my colleagues had been given their notice, and I was one of only three contractors left. When I had started at Peugot, there were ten of us. I was hoping to finish my two-year course at Coventry College before my contract ended. Three years in a contract is unusual and something I had not experienced personally before. Contracting, by its nature, is there to serve a short-term gap. It was turning out to be a lot longer employment than some of my permanent jobs. If I was honest, I was ready to move on. The impending closure of the Righton car plant, a few miles away, was likely to see the remaining contractors leave. A clear-out of contractors and voluntary redundancies would allow some of the car workers to relocate to the Tile Hill warehouse. A lot of the warehouse operatives, including my Landlady Norma, took advantage of the very generous redundancy carrot that was on offer. For the likes of contractors like myself, we would leave with nothing, other than a handshake and a farewell. But that is the trade-off for being free spirits or mercenaries, depending on how you view it. We were paid well by comparison with our PAYE peers but the downside was we had little or no employee rights or pensions. Luckily, I hung on past June to ensure I had enough money for another touring adventure. My newly acquired AutoCAD skills were already paying dividends. I was using these skills in their new warehouse extension, prolonging my usefulness, but this was just buying time. I put my cares behind as I plotted the 2005 adventure. I knew that on my return I would be busy scouring the job market, hopefully finding something nearer home.


After the Alps and Pyrenees, the next most famous mountain ranges featured in the Tour de France are the climbs of the Central Massif. In terms of tackling climbs on a bike, there isn't that much difference in terms of altitude or difficulty between the three; climbs marginally over 2000m are about as high as they get. With this in mind, it was time we acquainted ourselves with this mountain range.

The Massif Central is an elevated region in south-central France, consisting of mountains and plateaus. The area experienced volcanic activity which has subsided in the last 10,000 years. These central mountains are separated from the Alps by a deep north-south cleft created by the Rhone River, known in French as the Sillon Rhodanien, the furrow of the Rhône. The Allier, Ardeche, Aveyron, Cantal, Correze, Creuse, Haute-Loire, Haute-Vienne, Loire, Lot, Lozere, and Puy-de-Dome are Departments of the Central Massif. The largest cities are Clermont-Ferrand and Saint-Etienne. The mountains are not of the Alps standard but are nevertheless challenging and include Puy de Saucy (1886 m), Plomb du Cantal (1855 m) Puy Mary (1787 m) Mont Lozere (1702 m), the highest non-volcanic summit and Mont Aigoual (1567 m), near Le Vigan and Puy de Dome (1464 m).

To experience the Massif Central, I planned a tour that would take us from Beaune, (20 km south of Dijon) to Montpellier on the south coast. I calculated it to be about four hundred miles. This would be manageable in a week, allowing for any problems. We used the Bike Express coach to drop us off at our starting point. Beaune was a pleasant surprise and was a contrast to the large industrial towns, which are usually the stopping points.

This year's tour had four onboard, Kevin, Jimmy, Maurice and myself. Maurice was the newcomer; I had shared several tours with the other two. Maurice was an exile from Newcastle, this was very obvious when he spoke. We had shared many a ride together in Derbyshire since he moved down from the North East some ten years ago. He was a strong rider and ex-racing man and he would add some much-needed banter when the going got tough, and no doubt it would. He had resisted the attraction of a Penguin Tour long enough and I hoped this would be the first of many.

We arrived down at Meadowhall in good time to climb aboard the Bike Express at 8.00 a.m. for another nearly 24-hour journey by bus. In the company's attempt to maximise profits, it wove its way towards Calais, picking people up on route. There was a lot of stop-starting and detouring. If you then consider the coach was limited to 60mph, when it was up to speed, and factor in the motorway stops, it made for a very frustrating journey.

## Beaume to Roanne (166 km)

The first day we rode on mostly flat roads from Baume to Roanne. In retrospect, doing a hundred miles in blistering heat wasn't such a good idea. There is a tendency to stack up a large mileage on the first day. It could be the long, frustrating period of being confined on the bus combined with an early start or maybe a subconscious longing for a rest day when things get tough, as we knew from experience that they inevitably would.

The one overriding memory I have of that first day was a café stop after about eighty miles in the saddle. As we sat in the shade, an elderly woman served us with the worst coffee I had tasted in a very long time. Her face was painted like the mime Marcel Marceau. She glided about with a permanent smile cemented on her face. We could hear the sound of her husband inside the café playing on the piano. There was nobody else inside. These two really pleasant people amused themselves, not really worried about distracting customers, with their eccentric behaviour and crap coffee.

We arrived at Roanne tired, hot, and dehydrated. We had not tackled a hill and yet we were exhausted. The Youth Hostel at Roanne was like most hostels in large towns, modern, functional, and lacked character. After a shower, we all perked up and headed downtown with enthusiasm for large amounts of drink and food. We replaced lost fluid with alcohol in the evening, probably too much. The four of us shared the same dormitory in the local Youth Hostel. Tempers were a little frayed when Kevin's snoring kicked off. I had told Jimmy and Maurice what to expect, regarding Kevin's snoring, but they obviously hadn't listened. In the morning, Maurice vowed never again to sleep in the same room as Kevin, even if he had to pay a thousand pounds a night.

## Roanne to Ambert (94 km)

The second day everybody felt a little rough, too much beer and sleep deprivation. The weather didn't help to raise spirits; the hot weather had been replaced by thunderstorms and torrential rain. We sheltered in a bar, still in Roanne, and watched the locals drinking wine before 10 am in the morning. When the rain had slowed, we set off. We rode from Roanne to Ambert; the terrain was now hilly, with very little flat road. The conditions made the seventy-mile ride feel like a lot more. The Col de Beal was probably the highest peak of the day, climbing steadily to 1350 metres. The temperature dropped dramatically once on top of the cols. There was a long and difficult descent into Ambert. The bends were tight, and the road surface was poor, making the bike hard to control, the panniers made the conditions seem a lot worse. We booked into a Logis de France in Ambert, to ensure that Maurice and Jimmy got their beauty sleep. I shared a room with Kevin, and suffered the usual fate of being awoken several times in the night by some high-decibel snoring.

## Ambert to Le Puy en Velay (69 km)

On day three we planned to ride to Issoire and stay with Brian, a fellow cyclist who moved to France about ten years ago. After a discussion at breakfast, it was decided on a majority vote to miss this leg out. It would have meant a fifty-mile detour over some substantial cols. There was a feeling that if we did go to Brian's we would arrive in

Montpellier absolutely knackered or even miss the bus back.

We rode to Le Puy en Velay instead. The place was buzzing with life and there was plenty to see. The centrepiece is a church perched on top of a large piece of volcanic rock. The Saint Michel d'Agduile Chapel was visible when descending sharply into the town. I took a picture of the church, and everybody I showed it to, found it an amazing sight, defying belief. The place is just full of history. A bishop of Le Puy, (Gothescalk) led the first French pilgrimage to Saint Jacques in Santiago de Compostella in the ninth century. The 1600 km walk is still undertaken today by enthusiasts.

The Youth hostel was a contrast to that in Roanne. It was a large old building down a back street with plenty of character. The rooms were varied in quality; Jimmy and Maurice got the penthouse suite at the back of the building. Kevin and I got a room on the ground floor that looked onto the street. The room didn't have curtains or blinds and passers-by peered into our room. It was like being on display in a human zoo. After a few beers, this didn't bother us, and we played to our audience, administering cream to our sore backsides.

## Mende to Camprieu (75 km)

Day four's original plan was to take some minor roads and end up at Florac. At dinner, we had a discussion with a French waiter, was advised us to revise our route and head for Mende. Our plotted route would have been horrendously hard which would have included Mount Lozere. There seemed little point in subjecting ourselves to unnecessary torture; the route was already hard enough. The long and fast descent into Mende bore witness to how far we had climbed. It was a wide, well-surfaced dual carriageway that weaved for several miles downhill; we must have hit fifty miles per hour in places. Mende was a pleasant town. It had a medieval old town and a modern part that had an excellent bike shop to explore. We had no trouble finding enough bars, restaurants and a cheap hotel.

On day five, we headed in the direction of Le Vigan but we didn't expect to get there. By now, we were not adhering strictly to plan. Our new schedule involved stopping when we were ready, and wherever we could. After some climbing, we rode on a plateau for miles. After a couple of hours of riding on this bleak, uninteresting landscape, we came across the Tarn Gorge. The scenery was spectacular. We descended the Gorge into Ste. Enimie - a pretty touristy place. It was lunchtime, and we entered a café looking for a meal. We left without eating there. Flies plagued the place; the locals dined and drank their coffee unperturbed by them. The flies were on the tables, the counter, the food and the customers. We found a fly-free sandwich shop, fed our faces and then climbed the winding road out of the massive gorge.

We descended the Gorge again into Meyrueis, which was a nice little town. We sat and had a coffee at the side of the river (la Jonte) that runs through the town. After climbing out of the gorge once more, we were getting tired, and were looking for somewhere to stay. After riding for a few miles on a plateau, we came across a place called Camprieu in the middle of the Parc National des Cevennes. The place was so small it wasn't listed on our maps, there was one hotel restaurant, two shops, one church, one playing field, and a few houses. It was what we labelled Deliverance Country - after the famous film. The place had a bit of a spooky feel to it. We weren't actually spoilt for choice in that area, as the landscape had returned to the bleakness, we had encountered on the other side of the

Gorge du Tarn. From having very low expectations of the place, we decided after a short while that we had certainly dropped lucky. It was, without doubt, the best night of the holiday with regard to food and hospitality. We ate and drank like lords, for very little. The staff couldn't do enough for us. The one negative point was the beds; they certainly left a lot to be desired. They were at least a hundred years old and sagged in the middle; it was like sleeping in a hammock. I suppose you can't have everything! By the time we hit the sack, we had had enough red wine to ensure we had a decent night's sleep.

## Campieu to Monpellier (82 km)

On day six, we rode off the mountains and headed towards flatter terrain. After a few miles of riding on the flat, we started a descent that was a bit scary in places, it twisted and turned for ten miles and ended at a town called

Valleraugue in the valley below. Once at Vallerauge, the road followed the river slightly downhill into Ganges, where we stopped for lunch. After lunch, we rode on flat roads into Montpellier, arriving on Friday afternoon; we had two days in hand and we didn't catch the bus until Sunday afternoon.

Montpellier is only six miles inland from the coast, and a nice place to be stranded for a couple of days. It is the capital of the Laguedoc-Roussillon region and the administrative capital of the Herault department. Walking down the wide expanse of its Place de Comedie, you are surrounded by large, impressive, grandiose buildings. We booked into a good hotel allowing ourselves a little bit of luxury in contrast to the very basic accommodation we had encountered on our trip. In the evening, we explored the many bars in the quieter part of the city.

Saturday, we rode down the coastal road and found a beach and just chilled out for a day. We vacated our nice hotel in favour of a basic Formula One hotel on an industrial estate at a place called Saint Jean de Vedas, which was the pickup point for the bus. Luckily, we spent Saturday evening in the one excellent restaurant that the place had to offer, saving us from the Macdonald's and Burger King fast food establishments. That was the disadvantage and the beauty of our tours; no two nights were the same. Sunday, we rode inland in the morning, exploring the surrounding countryside. In the afternoon, we relaxed with a few beers and watched the Tour de France in a bar in the afternoon, while waiting to be picked up by the bus.

# Tour 7 – Mulhouse to Orange - The Jura Mountains

By 2006 I was settled in new employment. Towards the end of 2005, I found myself a new job or should I say, it found me. Ironically, it was at Bramall Lane, that I met an old friend and former workmate, Andrew. He was someone

I'd kept in touch with for a short time but lost contact with while I was working away from home. I knew he was a Blade but he didn't go to many matches at the Lane and it was the first time I'd seen him there. We had worked together in the nineties at Sisson's before I was made redundant. We chatted and the conversation led to what we were doing work-wise. By chance, a vacancy had arisen at Pinxton, where Andrew was working. After a couple of interviews, I was offered a full-time permanent job.

As jobs go, it was OK. The money was rubbish but where it scored highly was the fact that I was sleeping in my own bed and the ride to work was good. The work was interesting and the little mining village of Pinxton had some colourful characters. The real bonus was the twenty-mile ride to work, and to put the icing on the cake the firm had a shower. In the summer I had the advantage of adding another twenty miles or so to my journey on the way home. In bad weather I could reduce my journey by catching the train for half of the way back. By the time our tour came around in June I was relatively steaming. I started pushing myself on my way to work. Despite the several roundabouts, dozens of traffic lights and less than flat terrain I had reduced my journey time to fifty-eight minutes.

In 2006 I was to tackle The Jura Mountains. The Jura is a range of mountains extending for 225 miles (360 km) in an arc on both sides of the Franco-Swiss border from the Rhône River to the Rhine. It lies mostly in Switzerland, but a good part of the western sector lies in France. The highest peaks of the Jura are in the south, in the Geneva area, and include Cret de la Neige 1,718 m and Le Reculet 1,717 m, both in France, and Mount Tendre and La Dôle at a similar altitude, both in Switzerland.

It was in my previous employment at Peugeot that I first heard about the beauty of the Jura Mountains. Peugeot had a very large car factory at Mulhouse and one of the French bosses there decided to send his offspring to Coventry to improve his English. Initially, we thought the lad was a French spy, observing our working behaviours and reporting back to father how lacklustre and lazy the engineering department were at Coventry. I certainly warmed to the lad when he asked if he could borrow a bike for his journey to work instead of using a company vehicle. He salvaged a Peugeot mountain bike that had been dormant at the factory since the time when Peugeot cycles had a respectable name. After a little maintenance, Lauren was mobile and became one of the boys, commuting to work on his bike. Lauren was soon sharing with us cycling tales like all cyclists do. He lived in a small village outside Mulhouse. Apparently, it is a very quiet place and nothing happens, except the previous year when Lance Armstrong was there familiarising himself with the terrain for a time trial stage of the Tour de France. Lauren was impressed by the man's dedication. No other tour rider was there, or maybe they were but just not recognised. While Lance has fallen from hero to zero since he disgraced himself with his drug taking, it doesn't take away the fact that he was a very gifted and dedicated athlete. I personally think they pursued and hounded him with more enthusiasm than any other athlete I have known – no stone was left unturned. I don't think for one minute that the powers that be were wrong in doing so. I do believe that other, more charismatic legends, have got away with it because they were not investigated with the same intensity that Lance was. They remain gods with their status still intact and Lance has nothing. Would Lance have won those tours if drugs had not been used? Personally, I think he may have won some, but not all of them. I do think that cycling is now a cleaner sport and they have the systems in place to detect drug use. Hopefully, and this will deter cheats in the future.

Soon Lauren was telling us about his cycling exploits in the Jura Mountains. I had the impression, from his description, that it was like being like Derbyshire with longer gradients, but nothing as severe as the Alps or Pyrenees. He did enough to persuade me it was worth a visit.

While looking for a tour in 2006, I noticed Mulhouse was a drop-off point with Bike Express. After several debates, that prelude every Penguin Tour, a route from Mulhouse to Orange was agreed upon. I had received mixed opinions about the weather conditions in that region during July, nevertheless we decided this was to be our destination. A detour over Mount Ventoux was included just in case the tour lacked a little bite. I hoped the 2006 tour would include the same personnel as the previous year. Everything seemed to be on course until two weeks before when Kevin phoned me to pull out. Kevin finished work at the fire station that year and instead of riding his bike more during retirement, the reverse had happened. A change of routine had thrown his training plans into disarray. No amount of cajoling could change his mind. Kevin had even planned the route and sent me the maps and directions, perhaps an insight into what lay ahead had put him off. Kevin's planning consisted of two maps with a pencil line drawn from Mulhouse to Orange, the logic being that it was the best policy to adhere as near as possible to the pencil line, knowing that would be the shortest, but not necessarily the best route to take. That just left Maurice, Jimmy and myself to tackle the tour and find out for ourselves.

We caught the bus and endured the usual mind-numbing journey on the bus to arrive at a basic hotel on an industrial estate in Mulhouse. No amount of warm lagers and red wine in plastic cups can anesthetise you from the boredom of this bus ride. It is amazing that we still come back each year for more. After the usual French breakfast of croissants and coffee, we set off on stage one.

## Mulhouse to Le Russey (100 km)

Mulhouse is pronounced Mylose and is an industrial town and commune in eastern France near the Swiss and German border. It is the largest town in Haut-Rhine and the second largest in Alsace after Strasbourg. The town was founded around textile and tanning, latterly chemical and engineering. The quicker we could move on from the drop-off point, the better.

Once out of Mulhouse, the scenery improved dramatically. The small villages and the construction of them on the road to Altkirch gave them a Swiss feel. Every town ended in heim (Rixheim, Riedisheim, Zimmersheim, Zillisheim, Walheim and many more heims). The Swiss theme continued when we stopped for lunch and paid the bill in Swiss Francs. After dinner, we noticed a difference in the weather as well as the architecture; the buildings became more French and the rain came down. Maurice did warn me that rain was a feature of this area – and took pleasure in reminding me of this fact. As for Jimmy, he looked totally knackered. Usually he has been the strongest, but his lack of training was showing. I just hoped it was a bad day, as there was some serious climbing ahead.

At about sixty miles, we started looking for digs. Usually on tours, we had a tendency to do too much on the first day, just in case we encountered problems further down the line. This time, the weather was a strong deterrent. After finding several places closed, we found digs in Le Russet at a small bar-cum-hotel in a small town. There was also a tendency to get absolutely pissed the first night. This first night was unusually quiet, it could have been the weather or fatigue, but the evening passed without anybody getting too drunk.

## Le Russey to Morez (103 km)

We departed from Le Russey with blue skies above, this lifted spirits as we expected rain. The terrain was undulating with lakes and rolling countryside but nothing too heavy. As we climbed up to Morez we had cycling enough for the day. I had hoped to get to the youth hostel at Les Rousses, but in reality, fatigue had ground us to a stop. We pulled off the main road and we descended into the town below. A thriving, pleasant little town, dominated at one end by a factory that produced glasses. It would have been good to get to Les Rousses because we would have woken the following day to a descent instead of the two hours of climbing we now faced.

## Morez to Seyssel (87 km)

We climbed out of Morez onto the main road. Two hours later, we were still climbing. We passed the youth hostel sign at Les Rousses and realised there wasn't much chance we could have reached that yesterday, even in our wildest dreams. Again, I had been guilty of underestimating the terrain or overestimating our fitness. Once past Les Rousses, we were in a winter sports country with ski jumps and ski runs. The air was clean, crisp and fresh. We were a little preoccupied by our surroundings, so much so that we missed a turning at La Dole onto a minor road and instead ended up on the Col de la Faucille and a descent into Gex. Once off the mountain, the journey from Gex to Seyssel wasn't very memorable.

Seysell was a pleasant surprise. We rode through the old town and over a bridge that spanned the Rhone in search of a hotel alongside the river. We were directed to a small hotel just outside the town. From what was a very unpromising start to the evening, we had probably the best night of the tour. The small hotel was primarily a lodge frequented by fishermen. The owner welcomed us but then told us it was his night off, so we would need to find a restaurant. He enquired on our behalf about a restaurant but unfortunately, no luck. He then took pity on us and cooked us the best meal we had experienced for a very long time. With an ample supply of beer and red wine, the evening was perfect as we sat outside taking in the views in the warm air.

## Seyssel to Tullin (90 km)

We followed the road that ran parallel to the Rhone. For fifty miles, we enjoyed almost perfect cycling condition, quiet roads, pretty villages and warm weather. It was an area enjoyed by holidaymakers without being overcrowded. We followed the quiet roads through Yenne, heading in the general direction of Voiron, a medium-sized town on our route. Well before Voiron fatigue had set in (especially Jimmy). Admiring the views had been replaced by the preoccupation of being able to get off the bike and rest. Traffic was building up near Voiron and our plan was to skirt around the town and find a place on the other side on route. We ground to a halt at Tullin. It wasn't a case of wanting to stay in this town because of its charm, because it didn't have any. It was a contrast from the previous night. It was a dirty, depressing place. The digs were well in keeping with the place itself, dirty and uninviting. It was basically just a doss-house. The owner of the hotel seemed a shady character, and he obviously didn't trust us as he asked for his money upfront. We dined out at a poor Italian restaurant, and then watched a music festival that was taking place at the other side of town.

## Tullin to Crest (85 km)

We rode out of Tullin and saw a delightful looking Logis de France no more than two miles away, if only we had known. At this point, I thought it would be wise to ignore Kevin's pencil line and follow the white patches on the map depicting the valleys. By now I was taking some flack, for making the tour too hard. I responded by reminding Jimmy that he had brought too much with him and had brought a lot of problems on himself. Jimmy had brought far too many clothes, like heavy denims, He should also have done a bit more preparation in the way of riding his bike on a regular basis to make sure he was fit. It was all becoming a bit tetchy. Fingers were being pointed and blame was coming in my direction as though I was some sort of tour representative who had misled his customers in a fancy brochure. Even Kevin's name was mentioned, they blamed him for concocting some devious evil plan to entice unsuspecting cyclists into a torturous tour, and was then sitting at home laughing about it. I was well and truly pissed off with the pair of them. I have never had this problem before and I vowed not to have it again, even if it meant going it alone every year. It's an adventure holiday that was planned without any prior knowledge of the area or conditions. What did they expect? Should I have researched it beforehand to make sure it was easy enough for everybody? I tried to show a calm exterior even though I found it hard. I knew on the bus home, and in the years to come, the three of us would be having a good laugh about this.

I hoped my revised route, despite adding on a few miles, would hopefully be not as hilly. Every time we hit a hill Jimmy was suffering badly, slowing our progress. The original route took us through a place called Die. I knew from a previous tour this was a hard cycling country. Our new route was taking us more westerly in the direction of Valence. After about thirty miles we hit Romans and then headed south towards Chabeuil, where we stopped to eat. Chabeuil was a pretty place with a canal running through the centre of the town. We decided to push on to Crest, about another twenty miles away. The terrain had been mostly flat; it needed to be because we were knackered. We booked into a Logis de France in Crest and experienced a bit of luxury in contrast to the previous night.

## Crest to Carpentras (95 km)

Our original plan was to ride over Mount Ventoux, approaching it from a northerly direction and descend into Carpentras. Our revised plan took us a lot further west, missing out the mountains altogether. We now intended to ride to Carpentras and then ride Mount Ventoux without the panniers. This would involve returning back to Carpentras, picking up the panniers, and riding a further twenty-five miles to Orange.

In theory, the plan looked feasible, but it nearly didn't come off. Although the roads from Crest to Carpentras were relatively flat, it proved too much for Jimmy. The accumulation of fatigue and heat exhaustion finally took its toll. We stopped at a village called Cairanne for a coffee about fifteen miles from our destination. It was then that Jimmy announced he didn't want to push on to Carpentras. He also didn't want to attempt the Ventoux because he was too knackered. This split the group, I was the villain, Maurice sided with Jimmy and both decided to look for a hotel in the village. I intended to ride to Carpentras on my own. Unfortunately for them, the only hotel in the village was shut and we limped into our destination together as a group.

Carpentras as a town was a big disappointment; it was busy, noisy and unspectacular. The hotel we had was overpriced for the facilities it had. We had no choice but to pay the price, the other hotels were full. We dined out to avoid being further stung by the heavy price of their cuisine and drinks. That evening, we got drunk. We planned to rise early the next morning and do a runner from the hotel without paying as a protest to the exorbitant prices. The plan grew more legs as more beer flowed. Maurice and I managed to talk Jimmy around to the plan. He wasn't convinced. The next morning, we didn't awake until eight o'clock, so the plan was dead.

The cigarette-shaped observatory at the top of Mount Ventoux was visible from our bedroom window. Despite Jimmy's protestations and reluctance to tackle the climb we set off for Bedoin, about twenty miles away, the foot of the climb. Bedoin was trying hard to cash in on the notoriety of the famous Tour de France leg-breaker. Bike shops, hotels, and bars thrived on the cyclists who thronged to the area to tackle the climb. We filled our bottles with water at the bottom and surprisingly, all three of us set off. The mountain climb was certainly popular. It was heaving with cyclists from the novices to full professional cycling teams with backup vehicles. There were parties of cyclists with backup vehicles and cameras to capture the experience. You had to stay alert as there were as many cyclists descending the mountain at speed as there were going up. Luckily, the first part of the climb is sheltered from the sun by trees. At Le Chalet Reynard, the landscape changes, it is open and resembles a lunar landscape. We stopped at the shop cum restaurant to get water, others there were tucking into their well-earned meal. Some had medals around their neck, proudly showing them off, I assume, after conquering the Ventoux. We pushed on the last couple of miles to the summit. We passed a few cyclists walking with their bikes, and were passed by a professional cyclist being timed up the ascent by a guy in a following car. We passed the Tom Simpson memorial on the right and decided to stop on the way down rather than on the way up. The top provided superb panoramic views, as well as camper vans and traders trying to cash in on the thirsty, hungry punters wanting a bit of tat to celebrate their famous ascent. We took the obligatory photographs and descended the short distance to the Simpson memorial and took a few more photos along with dozens of others. We descended back down to Bedoin with great speed, avoiding those coming up.

## Carpentras to Orange (30 km)

We rode back to Carpentras and picked up our panniers. The twenty-five miles to Orange felt more like a hundred miles. At this stage of the tour, twenty-five miles can take nearly two hours, even if the terrain is flat. We arrived in Orange with a full day to spare. We used our day to explore the surrounding countryside by bike. The area is famous for wine. Among the small towns we came across a town called Chateauneuf du Pape, home of the famous wine of that name. Orange was quite a nice place to chill out and reflect on the tour, and consider what we would and what we would not do next year. As departure time approached, we prepared ourselves for the long coach ride back home.

# Tour 8 – Geneva to Calais

The year 2007 got off to a very bad start. It seemed like somebody had been saving up a lot of bad news and decided to unleash it in the first part of this year. I knew Kevin hadn't been himself for a while - with him missing last year's tour. I wasn't ready for what was to come. I received a phone call in January from JC in France. He told me Kevin had been diagnosed with terminal cancer. This probably explains his lack of appetite for the bike. The guy I had started touring with had probably seen his last tour ever. I took a couple of bottles of wine over to his house and he told me of the grim prognosis. The cancer was in his lungs and liver and he had no chance of recovery. The doctors had given him three months to live without chemo or six months if he underwent treatment. I can't remember Kevin touching a bike again. I continued to see him at Bramall Lane for the football matches. We went on a couple of walks in Derbyshire, which he found easier than cycling. He underwent chemotherapy to prolong his life, but his strength suffered and he accepted a more sedate lifestyle. He had a week of relative comfort sandwiched between his cycles of chemotherapy that left him unwell.

Other things were conspiring to make 2007 a pretty depressing year. My mother died at the beginning of April. Her health had worsened since Christmas. She had suffered from Alzheimer's for several years and was becoming more and more confused. She went into a nursing home where she could get the constant attention she required. She was taken into hospital at the end of March and she stayed there until she died at the beginning of April. I held her hand until she took her last breath. I knew this day would come, but it is still a very traumatic period in a person's life. Eighty-seven was a good age, but her last seven or eight years were lived without much enjoyment as her memory and her frailty had robbed her of any quality of life.

By June, I suffered another setback. I lost my job. Not that this was anything new in my life. Having been a contractor for long periods I also had an idea when a job would end. The first sign that things were going pear-shaped was when the company's share price started to plummet. The MICE group was a massive organisation, our company was a very small part. News of its difficulties was featured in the press. When share prices drop from forty-five pence down to eight pence, you know things are not going well. Soon after, the company ceased trading and the men with dark suits, posh accents and big cars rolled in. The company was stuffed. After two weeks of stocktaking for the administrators, half of the workforce, which included me had been made redundant, the remainder had another couple of weeks and then they were shown the door. I was sad about losing my job. It wasn't particularly well paid, but the work was interesting and the people were pleasant enough. Some had been there a long time and quite naturally, they felt their world had come to an end. I had also enjoyed the twenty-mile ride to work and the thirty-mile ride home on the light nights over Beeley Moor.

Kevin went on a family holiday for two weeks in Spain. He came back in a bad way. He found the plane journey difficult, and his last holiday was blighted with pain and illness. I saw him in hospital twice after he came back. The last time, he was waiting for a specialist bed to be installed at his home. He wanted to spend his remaining time there and was counting the minutes down until he could be released. On one of my visits, he told me I should tour by myself. I relived with him about his lone trip to Australia. His mates had backed out one by one, leaving him to board the boat alone for what was then a six-month journey to the other side of the globe. I had heard the tales a few times during our tours together, but I never stopped him. It was lifting his spirits, recounting his adventures.

I was planning on going on tour as soon as possible. I had the ideal opportunity; I was out of work and I needed time alone to clear my head of the many demons that seemed to be plaguing me. I had never been on a tour on my own. I had never wanted to. I remember the bus picking up a lone cyclist and it really made me wonder what was wrong with the guy, he couldn't be normal? Obviously, I wished Kevin had been strong enough to go, even if it was only ten miles a day. We went for a walk in Derbyshire together and he said he would never ride his bike again. Walking at a sedate pace was all he could or would be able to manage. This made me feel quite sad as I recalled all the tours we plotted and discussed at Bramall Lane during the half-time interval of the football match. Cycling tours were never going to be the same again for me. I thought of other options, but nothing worked somehow.

Denis was going on a family holiday and Maurice was going later in the year on a base holiday. The time wasn't good. I needed to get away now. I decided unless anybody was willing to fall in with my plans, I was going it alone.

I was conscious of my employment situation, or should I say unemployment. I knew I was likely to pay two hundred pounds on the bus, which I could hardly justify in the circumstances. I set myself a challenge of making the transport arrangements as cheap as possible. I didn't intend to skimp on the food and the odd night of luxury in a reasonable hotel, but I could save on my transport budget. It was an opportunity to explore this option. I wasn't going so spoil a holiday for anybody else if things didn't work out.

I scoured the internet for a cheap flight. A one-way ticket to Geneva for less than sixteen pounds looked good value, it was booked over the internet and I ended up paying thirty pounds when taxes were added. It felt quite good just doing it. I didn't have to get on the phone to anybody else and discuss dates and the choice of destination. I was happy so I just hit enter, done. I decided I wasn't going to book my bike on the plane for an extra ten pounds. It turned out to be a mistake I later discovered. I thought I could just use a cardboard box and pack everything in that and declare it as my main piece of luggage, a cardboard suitcase in effect. As long as I kept the weight down to twenty kilograms, what could be the problem? A trip to the bike shop for a strong cardboard box was necessary. They use these large boxes for shipping bikes – which they break down and dispose of - which they were only too glad to give me. The bike was dismantled and packed. My panniers were used to hold the frame rigid in the box. Loads of "Fragile Handle with Care" tape sealed up the box and I was ready to roll.

Simply hitting the enter key on a computer is quite easy in the comfort of your home after a few beers, now I needed to make it happen. I had only a week to plan the trip. My map reading isn't brilliant, as my wife will testify. I struggle to navigate around Derbyshire on a Sunday walk. On previous tours, I had quite gladly let others hold the maps, even though it is hardly rocket science. Last year, Kevin had already part planned the route and handed me the maps when he pulled out. His planning that year only consisted of drawing a pencil line in the direction we needed to follow. In previous years, he had meticulously prepared daily route cards on postcard-size paper with names of the places we passed through and the distance to the next town.

I picked up the three Michelin maps I needed from a bookshop in Sheffield on Wednesday, after what was to be my last hospital visit to see Kevin. My plane flew from Luton at six o'clock the following Tuesday morning. A very early start suited me. Geneva was described by a friend who had travelled there as being like Rawmash with a big lake, not at all spectacular. It was too late to worry about the merits of my destination. The deed was done. I would arrive early morning giving me ample time to put a few miles between it and myself. Luton Airport was a short train ride away from Flitwick, where Jane's sister lived. I could save money on airport parking, which is worth at least twenty pounds. I drew my pencil line on my maps, avoiding any big cities and that was about as much planning as I intended doing for the trip.

I did my usual Saturday morning run. I was upstairs in the café at Bakewell overlooking the cobbled courtyard, enjoying banter with a couple of the Penguins. My mobile rang unexpectedly. It was Steve Worthy. Kevin had died in the early hours of Saturday morning. I rode the fifteen miles home feeling sad and choked. I can't remember many occasions when I have felt this depressed. I thought he had at least a few weeks left, apparently it wasn't to be. Life isn't very fair. I desperately wanted to go to his funeral, but it was more than likely to be in the week that I was to go on tour. I asked Steve to let me know the funeral arrangements in the vain hope I could make it back in time.

I put my bike box in the car and set off for Flitwick, some hundred and twenty miles down the M1. I was embarking on my trip during some of the worst floods in living memory. I found my route to the motorway blocked by a flooded road, as the emergency services stopped traffic using parts of Sheffield. If I had believed in fate or had I been in any way superstitious I would have thought somebody was trying to persuade me not to go. Perseverance paid off. After several attempts, I successfully joined the motorway and arrived at Flitwick an hour later than expected.

I left the car and boarded a train for the airport. I had not travelled this route before to Luton airport. If I had, I would have been prepared for the steep escalators at the station down to the bus station and the minibus ride up the hill to the airport. With a normal amount of luggage, there isn't a problem. An oversized cardboard box with a mind of its own weighing twenty kilograms feels like more than a handful. I bumbled my way to the airport, finding myself apologising several times as I got in everybody's way. I made a mental note, next time I need a carrying strap of some description, not much help on this occasion as I struggled to keep control of my outsize luggage.

It shouldn't have come as much of a surprise to me when I arrived at the checking-in desk that I had an oversized object. I would need to re-route my bike via the oversized luggage check-in at an extra cost of twenty pounds. The bike box went through the screening process without a hitch. I was relieved. I didn't fancy repacking the bike again. The only item that failed to make the trip was my bike lock. It was confiscated from my hand luggage. It was considered an item that could be used in terrorist activity. There isn't any point arguing, the bike combination lock was left in the hands of a vigilant operative. I didn't declare the number, let them figure it out for themselves.

A couple of hours later and our plane was circling a big lake and preparing to land. The weather was cloudy and dull. The awful weather I feared hadn't been left behind. The contrast between this journey and my tedious bus journey was staggering. After two hours, we would only be eighty miles down the M1. We would have had a couple of stops at motorway services and a few stops to pick-up cyclists with their tandems, various bike contraptions and luggage. We would still have twenty hours of useless, time-wasting activity in front of us. My mind was racing ahead to what I needed to do on arrival. What spanners did I need, had I forgotten anything?

I picked up my box at the airport, changed into my cycling gear and headed for the airport exit. I found an open space outside where I could assemble the bike. I cut open the cardboard box, found the tools and set about putting the bits together. I took the Stanley knife and shredded the cardboard into strips and filled up a couple of bins conveniently situated left there for my use. So far, so good, everything was happening at a pace. I mounted the bike and I was away. The road looked busy, with fast dual carriageways – not cycling-friendly. I followed a cycle lane to get out of the airport and continued for a few miles until I was lost. I found myself in a shopping area with a café. The first café of the tour, an ideal place to get my bearings I thought. The situation was a little unreal. It took me a bit of time to comprehend what was happening. With the bus, your mind has time to acclimatise to the reality that you are travelling miles away from where you know. You are reinforcing with the long journey on the bus and ferry that it is real. I felt fear and excitement at the same time. This morning, I was in Flitwick, Bedfordshire. It was not yet dinnertime and I was lost on a bike somewhere on the outskirts of Geneva. There are not enough days like these unfortunately.

# Geneva to Morez (53 km)

I cycled on busy roads that took me across the border into France. I didn't have an option. I was warned that Geneva wasn't particularly pretty. They were right. The traffic thinned as I headed for the Jura Mountains. I passed through several small suburbs heading for Gee and the foot of the Col de la Faucille (apparently meaning easy in French – who said the French don't have a sense of humour?). I stopped to cape up as the rain started to become heavy. I took my first photo, I aimed my camera at where I thought the mountain should be, but all I could see was clouds and mist. I climbed the col without breaking a sweat. On a summer's day I would be overheating and taking in plenty of fluids, that day, I was freezing cold and being drenched by an endless water supply from the clouds and the traffic. I reached the top of the col and headed for a café to thaw out and refuel. I had covered twenty miles, if that. I was in the middle of nowhere, just a café devoid of tourists, just a madman on a bike. I set off for Le Rousses, where I knew there was a Youth Hostel and a few hotels. On last year's route, I planned to stop at the Youth Hostel there, but we stopped a few miles short at a town called Morez. I can remember the climb out of Morez being a hard one, but this time, I would enjoy its descent.

I arrived at the Information centre at the holiday ski resort of Les Rousses cold and wet. The information I gathered from speaking to the receptionist wasn't what I wanted to hear. The youth hostel was a do-it-yourself arrangement as far as the meals were concerned. The shops were shut and I didn't have the strength or the inclination to hunt around for food, I just wanted to feed and now. I donned my entire wardrobe and braced myself for the long descent into Morez. My teeth were chattering violently as I descended the hairpin bends into the town centre. Luckily, the miles went by quickly in contrast to the two hours of climbing up the mountain last year.

I came to a stop in Morez at the same hotel as last year. Within ten minutes of arriving, I was soaking in a hot bath, where I remained for what seemed like an hour. I headed for a restaurant for refuelling and a couple of beers. I had fallen woefully short of where I thought I would be. I calculated I had done just thirty-six miles. I paddled through the puddles in sandals until I found a suitable French restaurant. A few drinks and my spirits were lifted. I returned to my hotel feeling a new man and thinking,

"What's the problem? It's just a drop of rain, nothing to worry about."

Back at the hotel I notice I have a text message. It's from Steve Worthy, letting me know that Kevin's funeral is a week today. I had already mentally written the funeral off. I anticipated it would be midway through my tour. I argued with myself that we had some great times together and that was more important than attending his funeral, it's just a ceremony. There was a thought in my head, probably alcohol-induced, that maybe I could make it back in time. I turned on the television to have a look at the weather. The weather map suggested that this rain was localised and fifty miles on either side of the Juras would be a lot brighter. I retired to bed a man on a mission.

## Morez to Selongey (159 km)

After a sleep, I decided I wasn't going to spoil my holiday by trying to pull out all the stops to get back for Kevin's funeral. I don't think he would want that. I'll ride within myself on the quiet forest minor roads as I had planned. If I did find myself achieving an early return, then that would be great. I would know in a couple of days how things are going to turn out.

I climbed out of Morez and was met by a steady drizzle. The temperature was definitely up a couple of degrees. After a couple of miles, I went through the town of Mobier and a clock was showing nine o'clock and nine degrees. It was not actually the tropical weather I had hoped for. I had to follow the N5 through Champagnole and onto Dole for lunch. It was not a busy road, but not what I was here for. I dined at Dole and plotted my route for the day. Auxonne was the end of the route nationale for me as it headed for Dijon and the built-up metropolis that I hated so much. I continued my journey from now on, on small, quiet roads. I intended to enjoy the quality cycling I had craved all year. After Beze, fatigue struck and I needed a bed for the night. After the slow start, not helped by the climbing in the Jura's, I found I had pedalled over a hundred miles, this in in contrast to the poor start on the first day. I travelled on for almost an hour before stumbling on an absolute peach of a hotel and restaurant. The Sarl La Tourmaline on the Rue du Moulin is in a sleepy little place called Selongey. It took some finding, hidden away in the woods on its own grounds, at the side of a river. The old cartwheels, lanterns and artefacts outside gave the place a homely feel. The place was class without being pretentious. The en-suite room was massive, with a large double bed. I dined like a king in their restaurant, including indulging in my favourite starter of smoked salmon. It was all washed down with vin rouge. The lady owner mingled with the customers, inquiring if everything was 'bon'. In fact, everything was 'tres-bien'. The staff were friendly. The chef quizzed me about my journey, and seemed genuinely interested. He had worked in Morez and he told me the people of Morez were a strange breed. Apparently, they had a reputation for being hostile to strangers. He may have been right. They hadn't made much of an effort to make conversation, but to be fair, neither did I. I made conversation with an

American woman at the next table. She overheard me sharing my cycling exploits with the chef and her curiosity got the better of her. She was teaching English at the local school, on a temporary basis. She was a similar age to me, and I found it strange that she wanted to be on her own, miles from home. I didn't pry, and she didn't volunteer the reasons for her situation. Perhaps she wanted some time on her own to sort herself out. I wondered if that was what she thought of me. Who knows?

I paid the bill of sixty-four Euros, feeling that they had made a mistake. They seemed happy with the transaction and so did I. Surely, that is how it should be. The next place had a hard act to follow.

## Selongey to Margerie Hancourt (140 km)

I continued with my forest trails. I wanted quality riding rather than quantity. My pencil line passed between Troyes and Chaumont; at least thirty miles from each. The Foret de Chantilon provided enough green on the map to ensure solitude. I headed for Bar Sur Aube and then Chavanges. The latter had a deliverance feel about it; quant but eerie and strange. For about forty miles, I was travelling blind. There was a gap in my regional Michelin maps. I started on 520 Franche-Comte and then continued on 519 Bourgogne. The forty miles I was missing was on Michelin map 14 Ile –de-France. It hadn't been available at the time, and something as trivial as a map wasn't going to stop my tour. My day's cycling ended at Margerie Hancourt, a small village some fifty miles south of Reims. I came out of the forests and tried to find civilisation. The tiny village was bisected by the D396 on its way to Vitry Le Francois. The Auberge de la pomme d'or, as it was called, sat on the main but very quiet main road. I arrived at six o'clock with a healthy mileage under my belt and decided to call it a day.

The feature of touring is that two nights are never the same. When you book a week in Majorca, you either warm to, or you end up despising your host. Many times, I have arrived at my holiday destination and my heart has sunk through disappointment. Later, anger would emerge as you realised how the brochure or advertisement had deceived you. With touring, you have a second chance; you've not booked, so you aren't committed. You can usually tell from the outside if the place is going to be rubbish. You don't have to book straight away; you call for a drink first and make your decision over a beer. If it turns out that after a beer, you've dropped a clanger, it's not a problem; it's only for one night. Also, this isn't a busy holiday resort; it is in the middle of nowhere. They want your custom, no they are desperate for it.

My hosts for the night were an odd pair. Mirelle was dark and perhaps in her late forties. She was painted up like Briget Bardot and had squeezed herself into sixties-type clothes that were too tight for her. I guess she must have been a doll in her time but the cracks were appearing everywhere. My mother had a term for it 'mutton dressed as lamb'. Francis, her husband, I guess was the complete opposite. He didn't give a damn about his appearance and was one of the boys. For all her tarty looks, she was the business head while he drank away the profits with his pals in the bar. They had a single room for thirty Euros or a double with a shower for forty euros. I said I would take the single room. She tried her best to persuade me to have the double. For devilment, I said I would still have the single. She got her revenge by charging me two and a half Euros for using the shower. She was a bit of a weirdo and I didn't take to her much, and she lacked any sense of humour. Their daughter was very pleasant, I assumed she must have been adopted.

## Margerie Hancourt to Laon (146 km)

In the morning, I remembered I was riding blind again, without my map. The first place showing on my final Michelin 511 was Epiernay. I kept on the D396 and headed towards Chalons-en-Champagne. The traffic started to build, sending off alarm bells in my head. I was deep into champagne country only being about thirty miles from Reims.

It was lunchtime before I picked up my pencil line and was back on the quiet roads again. I stopped to eat at a small town called Mareuil sur Ay. I sat in what looked like a popular eating house for the locals. After being ignored for ten minutes I was taken into a back room and was invited to help myself. I followed the lead of the locals as I tucked into what I can only describe as an eat-as-much-as-you-can, French-style buffet. The food was exotic, varied and plentiful. I was encouraged by the locals to return and eat heartily. I duly obliged. I was a little surprised when the waitress appeared with two plates, one with a large piece of meat and the other with a massive piece of shepherd's pie. I had the choice – the buffet was only the starter. I chose the shepherd's pie. She returned with the plate piled high with vegetables. I finished with a coffee and contemplated how I was going to manage to ride a bike with this amount of food inside me. This had been, without a doubt, the best meal I had had for a long time. I sat there smug with myself for dropping – on such a brilliant place. Perhaps I would retire here and eat like this every day and not bother making anything. I asked for the bill and got another shock. I thought thirteen Euros was the bargain of the century. In Derbyshire, you would pay nearly that for a cream tea.

I climbed up through Haut Villiers and the Foret de la Montagne. As the name suggests, the road was quite hilly and undulating all the way to Laon. I stopped at a tiny place called Marfaux to take a picture at the immaculately kept British war graves there. I stopped to read the inscription in English. *'THE LAND ON WHICH THIS CEMETERY STANDS IS THE FREE GIFT OF THE FRENCH PEOPLE FOR THE PERPETUAL RESTING PLACE OF THOSE OF THE ALLIED ARMIES WHO FELL IN THE WAR OF 1914-1918 AND ARE HONOURED HERE.* The lines of the stones were in perfect symmetry and equally spaced as if planted last week by a CNC machine. There wasn't a crooked stone amongst them and no sign of neglect or graffiti. How sobering and how moving that was. I may be cynical, but in England, the stones would have fallen into disrepair years ago. The grass would have been neglected after some cost-cutting exercise by some over-zealous councillor who had diverted some of the funds for some obscure minority organisation, but not before some of these immaculate headstones had found themselves on eBay or some car boot sale. As I cycled on, there were more and more – just as impressive. It wasn't just a gesture by the French but more a commitment for all time.

It was quite a pull up to the fortress of Laon. I started feeling really knackered on my way up to the town centre, running on empty. There were several signs and advertisements for hotels, but in my weary state, I couldn't find one. I rode the small forest roads, and I had wandered forty miles or so east of my pencil line. The missing map had caused me more problems than I could have imagined. My period of guesswork and intuition had wreaked more havoc than I could ever have anticipated. I had learned a lesson that, really, I shouldn't have needed to.

The fact that by now, I should have been showered and downing a few beers prior to an evening meal played on my mind. I booked into the Hotel de la Banniere de France, the first hotel I found in the old town. I guessed I might pay a premium for the medieval location and I was right. The room was twice what I had paid up to now. To make things worse, the owners were far from being the happiest, friendliest hosts I had met. The German owners were perhaps used to more sophisticated guests, instead of a lone knackered cyclist. I showered and hit the town and took advantage of one of its many reasonably priced eating houses. I got the maps out in the restaurant and I calculated I was only a hundred and sixty miles from Calais. A mere two days of quite doable cycling on what would be easy terrain.

## Laon to Arques (182 km)

Instead of getting up and riding to a café and enjoying a reasonably priced petite dejeuner in the atmosphere of some amiable French establishment, I decided to rub salt into my wounds and eat at the hotel. I really must have wanted to boil my blood. How they got away with serving half a crusty old French stick and a single croissant and hold out their hand for eight and a half Euros (yes six pound and forty pence), god only knows. It made airport parking, and ferry snacks look very good value for money by comparison. I'm afraid I couldn't be sure that that nice little café bar was just around the corner.

Saturday's ride turned out to be a bit of an epic, but I never planned it that way. I thought I would get past Arras and that would be a good platform for Sunday's ride into Calais. Sadly, I was starting to think about the journey's end. I didn't want to get into Calais too late and find a problem getting somewhere to stay if I couldn't get a ferry. This was a new adventure; in previous crossings, I had booked a passage. Surely, a foot passenger with a bike isn't going to be too hard to accommodate?

I headed east out of Laon, heading towards a place called Perrone for a lunch stop. I struggled to find a traditional French restaurant. A lot of places were shut and the ones that were open didn't look very inviting. I settled for a pizza type fast food restaurant that wasn't particularly good but provided the fuel for a few miles. Laon seemed to signal the end of the charming country village. Later that day I kept my eyes open for a possible overnight stop. I had a feeling that I might struggle to find something. The area was pleasant enough but not exactly a tourist trap. I had a refuel at a mobile cake shop. This was similar to a sixties mobile shop, and reminded me of one I used to work as a teenager. It was in an era before everybody owned a car and massive supermarkets didn't exist. I worked for one of the local bakeries that sent their goods out into the communities using about twenty vans. In rural France, a lot of old ways still exist, they are trapped in a time warp and, luckily may never escape into the chaos of our shopping nightmare.

I made the decision to bypass Arras, a fair-sized town where I would have been assured a hotel and a bed for the night. I felt a bit like a pontoon player who should be happy with sticking with a healthy seventy miles under my belt. Instead I decided to live a little dangerously and ride into the unknown. From the map, there didn't look much out there. I passed more war memorials at Baupume and beyond. I reasoned with myself that Arras was in fact twenty miles east of my pencil line anyway. It is always good to have at least a few reasons for a decision; there is no turning back on.

I was coming up to the hundred-mile mark and I was passing small towns without hotels. I stopped at a cake shop - a weakness of mine – ordered some buns and asked the shop assistant in my best French where I would find a hotel. She shrugged her shoulders and suggested St-Omer. That was twenty miles away, if not more. I rode easterly in the direction of St-Omer, hoping to find something en route. I was almost there when I came to a place called Arques. There were a few factories and, to my relief, a Logis de France. The Logis chain of hotel/restaurants, although a bit more expensive, the quality is always assured. You can spot a Logis by the yellow fireplace and chimney on a green background. The quality varies from one chimney, signifying simple and value for money, to three chimneys, which are excellent with all the amenities of a top hotel. There are about three thousand Logis de

France and the beauty is the prices are very reasonable and I have not found one that has been poor.

The la Grande Saint Catherine Hotel was a two-chimney one and was excellent. It was a long time coming, but it was worth the wait. It was a good hotel befitting the last night of the tour. The owner proudly told me that the town of Arques was famous for fine glass, the type that I was sinking quite a few of that evening. I looked at the map at dinner, little wonder I was knackered, I had done one hundred and twenty miles at least. I would be at Calais by lunch, even earlier if I went straight there.

## Arques to Calais (50 km)

I tucked into my five-and-half-euro petite dejeuner, well worth the money and a comparative steal compared to my breakfast in Laon. I planned a bit of a detour, heading west through a few forest roads. I met a French cyclist who advised me on the best approach to Calais via Guines. He obviously knew a thing a two about the area. The road he described ran parallel to a canal before approaching the busy ferry port from the west. I arrived in Calais by mid-day. The thirty-eight miles or so had flown by. It felt a bit like a rest day. Ironically, I had started my tour with a similar mileage.

The ride on a bike to the ferry always seemed to go on forever. You would pick up the signs early, giving false hope that the boat was just around the corner. I arrived at the P&O booking office and was told that there was no room on board the one o'clock ferry. When I asked why, the receptionist told me there had been a large contingent of cyclists booked onto the ferry and there wasn't enough room for another cycle. I thought how odd, I had not encountered any cyclists on my route. I noticed quite a few motorcycles outside. I wondered if she thought for some strange reason that she had mistaken this middle-aged bloke clad in Lycra for a twenty-something leather-clad motorcyclist. On the off chance that she had made this mistake, I emphasised that I was on a pedal cycle. The penny dropped. A phone call later, and I was on the one o'clock ferry. I shared banter with the motorcyclists who had been down to the south coast of France and found the sun. For me, no such luck weather-wise.

I fastened my bike to a pipe at the side of the ferry with a rope. The motorcyclists had to bolt their machines to the deck with strong straps to stop them from moving. I could understand why there wouldn't be room for another motorcycle; the deck was swamped with expensive-looking, brightly coloured two-wheeled machines.

Once the ferry had docked in Dover, I made the short bike ride to Priory station. The traffic was heavy for a Sunday and I just wanted to get back home as quickly as possible. I bought a ticket to Flitwick for just over thirty-six pounds. I had just missed the train, so I bought something to eat and a paper and caught up with what had been happening in the world. I phoned Jane to let her know I had landed on home soil before embarking on my journey home by train and car, I focused on what I needed to do when I got home, things that had been driven to the back of my mind during the past week.

Tuesday morning, I was up at the crack of dawn and travelling to a new contract in Newark. Forty miles felt a long way to go for a morning's work. I had to make an appearance, even if it was for just the morning, I couldn't afford to lose the contract. I had my dark blue suit and a black tie on the back seat. Lunchtime I would travel back to Sheffield for Kevin's funeral. I only had time for a health and safety induction and a few other introductions before I was racing back to Sheffield and Hutcliffe Wood Crematorium. I stopped mid-way to put on the suit and tie. The Chapel was full of Fire brigade uniform staff, some I knew and a lot I didn't. I wondered if Kevin would have been impressed – I guessed not. I just managed to squeeze inside the small chapel, but a lot was left outside. It was the busiest I had seen this place. The service took on a military flavour. I felt a bit of an outsider looking in on what was a very formal affair. The centrepiece of the floral tributes was a red bike crafted from flower petals. Every attempt was made to escape the sobriety of a funeral. As the curtains were drawn, 'Be young, be foolish, but be happy' rang out. I made an attempt to see Janice on the way out. See looked radiant in a bright yellow suit. She had a look on her face that said, "What's everybody being miserable about?" I embraced her, holding back my tears. She was putting on a really brave front, I didn't want to make it any more difficult. She was surprised to see me. "I didn't expect you back yet." I think she knew if it was humanly possible, I would make it back. I left her to play the perfect host as I moved off to join some of my ex-touring buddies outside, Sherby and Steve Worthy, we shared a bit of banter and talked of tours past and drove off to the Crosspool Tavern to continue our tales over a few drinks.

At such emotional times, it is quite easy for our mouths to promise things that will be forgotten very quickly. Plans were made in that pub, and I really would have loved for them to come off. We had each other's phone numbers, so there could be no excuses for a venture not getting off the ground.

# Tour 9 – Nimes to Zeebrugge

The contract at Flowserve in Newark was only a short-term solution. I stayed for just four months. The people and the banter in the drawing office were first-class. The atmosphere was very relaxed and, all in all, a very enjoyable place to work. The kettle was constantly on the boil, a sandwich trolley came around in the morning and the afternoon, and the people there always had time for a chat. The place was big, run-down and very old-fashioned in some ways. It felt like a blast from the past but had some big plus points, like a good canteen. The big problem with the place was that I was just too far from home. It was forty-five miles, but it was on cross-country roads that were very slow going, and it was painfully frustrating. It was just too far to commute each day, and the chance of using my bike was out of the question. I was required to put in long hours, so I stayed in bed and breakfast accommodation during the week. I sometimes took my bike on the train on Monday morning and cycled home on Friday after an early finish. After several attempts to secure employment nearer home, I succeeded when I was offered a job at a small company on the east side of Sheffield. My new employer, Lechler, was German-owned and, more importantly, offered a relatively easy commute by bike.

It was around New Year when Steve Worthy rang with a plan for a 2008 tour. I had been tipped off by JC, who had been over from France at Christmas, that he would be in touch with a plan. I wasn't prepared to believe it until it happened. The last time I went with Steve, I seem to remember him putting his bike on a train on only the second day. Now he was telling me his ambitious plan that had me wincing at the severity of the ride, while at the same time exciting me with the prospect of a south-to-north navigation of our beloved France with Belgium thrown in for good measure.

Steve was retiring in March after thirty years in the Fire Service. It was something he thought he must do before the onset of old age. He planned to fly to Nimes on the south coast of France, spend a night with JC in Saint Remy De Provence and then cycle to Zeebrugge; catch the overnight ferry to Hull and then cycle back to Doncaster. This looked quite an ambitious ride, even by our standards. It would be the best part of eight hundred miles; I was unsure as to whether this was an option. I would anticipate at least ten hard days of cycling on my own, with Steve as a companion, maybe another two or three days on top of that. It was surpassing the amount of time that I allowed myself on an annual cycling holiday. I would have no holiday left for anything else that year and that could become a problem. The tour could be shortened to finish in Calais, which would reduce the distance significantly. It was left open-ended; it would all depend on how things were going at the time.

This year two others were to join us, Jimmy and Denis. Jimmy had not made the tour last year but had been two years previous to that. Denis had not been since the Pyrenean tour back in 2005. By March, four seats had been booked on a Ryanair jet from Luton bound for Nimes. In total the one-way ticket was to cost forty-two pounds each. Twenty-five pounds of that was to transport our bikes in a cardboard box. Getting ourselves and our cardboard boxes containing our bike to Luton was a problem that would be considered nearer the day.

With a few weeks to go, I started to focus on the tour. We hadn't booked any transport to Luton. I hadn't budgeted for a £140 taxi ride to Luton. This would be divided into three: Jimmy, Denis and myself. Steve was the only one of us travelling from Doncaster, so he was using the train. The train would work out cheaper initially, but we would have to get to the station, so that would amount to about the same. We were now looking at ninety pounds each to get there. We were now nearly up to the price of the Bike Express but we would be half a day less travelling.

I received a call from Jimmy telling me he had sourced a taxi to take us to Luton for £110. I told him to book it, provided the bike boxes would fit. Keith, the taxi driver, was confident the boxes would fit when the measurements were given over the phone. We were sorted. I received a last-minute phone call from Jimmy. He couldn't get the seat pillar out of his frame, and the bike wouldn't fit in the box with it in position. We finally solved the problem by removing the saddle. The box closed with a bit of bulge showing, it would have to do. The lesson to be learnt from this is not to leave the packing until the last night. If any major problem occurs, there isn't time to fix it. I was no better myself. I was frantically packing at the last minute. I discovered that there isn't a uniform-size bike cardboard carton. The one I was using was definitely smaller than last year. I totally dismantled the bike, fitting parts in any space available. I finally boxed up the bike but not after much packing and repacking.

Keith, our taxi driver, arrived early and after a rare trouble-free ride down the M1 we arrived at Luton to meet with Steve. We booked in and took our bike box to the oversized baggage. Although we arrived in plenty of time, the minutes flew by as we caught up with old times. We ended up abandoning our umpteenth cup of coffee to make a mad scramble for the departure gate.

## Nimes to St. Remy (40 km)

We landed in Nimes to be met by JC at the airport. The heat was intense. We dragged our bike boxes to a shady spot just outside the airport. The race was on to assemble the bike in the quickest time. Steve looked as though he had taken first prize only to puncture on the final hurdle even before his tyre had seen the tarmac. JC led the way on the country lanes from Nimes to St Remy. We parked our bikes in John's garage and proceeded up to his flat. As JC's accommodations go the flat is probably better than the tents he has got used to over the years. The biggest disappointment as I saw it was the shower. It wasn't a shower more of a dribble, barely enough to wet you. As we took it in turns to be dribbled on, John broke open the wine and olives as we revved up for a night on the town. We discovered wandering through St Remy that we were in the birthplace of Nostradamus an astrologer famous for prophetic verses. He has been credited by his enthusiasts to have predicted the French Revolution, the rise of Napoleon and Hitler, and even the September 11<sup>th</sup> attacks on the World Trade Centre – not bad for somebody born in the sixteenth century.

## St Remy to Rochemaure (101 km)

John joined us for twenty miles in the morning on our northbound journey. We planned a detour to see the Pont du Gard near Remoulins – an aqueduct constructed by the Romans to carry water over the river Gardon. We found the beautiful setting to be a busy tourist attraction, especially among young schoolchildren. Jimmy's Discovery team jersey attracted the attention of three American cyclists, two of them women. The seven-time Tour de France winner Lance Armstrong rode for the Discovery team. The Yanks thought Jimmy was wearing the jersey for some loyalty or admiration towards their American idol, when the real reason was, they were reducing them to clear at our local bike shop.

We headed on the minor roads to Bagnolis for lunch. There we sat, in the cobbled square at one of the half dozen café's on offer, and refuelled. We took a full hour and a half for lunch, a trend we adopted early on in the tour, which severely disrupted our momentum. The break from pounding the pedals gave us time to study our route and formulate a plan. Kevin usually took care of route planning, which was meticulously worked out with a map, a piece of string and handwritten in different coloured biros that denoted milestones and overnight stops. I learned over the years to have the utmost faith in this method because it had been tried and tested. What Steve put on the table before us was an A4 printout from some computer software program. The printout showed a total mileage, from St Remy to Zeebrugge, of less than seven hundred miles and I just didn't believe it. On this premise, Steve reckoned that by doing seventy miles a day, we would arrive in Zeebrugge in ten days. The seventy-mile mark would take us to a place called Le Teil. I put my reservations behind me and off we pedalled into the Mistral wind that was blowing in our face like a hot fan oven.

My frustration got the better of me and I came up with a brainwave to take a quieter, more scenic route. I took the team northwest on some small, narrow lanes. The lanes got hillier and the road surface got heavier. The cracks in our fitness level began to show. I could see that my idea was losing popularity by the minute. How could the roads, only a matter of a few kilometres from the Rhone Valley, be so hard? The death of my idea was final when I led our party to a church at a dead end. We backtracked and found St Marcel d'Ardeche, a little town to shelter from the heat with a large water trough to fill our bottles. We didn't need a vote, we were all glad to see the D86 once again.

We arrived at the Le Teil tourist information office to find nothing available. Fortunately, we managed to find a couple of rooms available in a town called Rochemaure a couple of miles up the road. We resisted the temptation to have a drink. A few extra miles and we could relax at the day's end at our hotel. Once there, the hot winds made the chilled beer taste even better. Jimmy and I sat drinking in our sweat and cycling gear, finding the lure of the cold beer more enticing than a hot shower. The beer on empty stomachs soon took effect. We reluctantly washed our weary bodies and changed clothing before making our way across the road to feast on pizza.

## Rochemaure to Ampiu (113 km)

We set off next morning on the D86 down the Rhone valley. By now, I was pretty sick of this road. The heat and headwind made for very hard going even though the roads were reasonably flat. One of our crew was starting to wilt. We stopped at a small place called Vion for lunch. Denis was feeling sick and didn't want anything. A bad sign, the number of calories we were burning meant we should be eating like horses, otherwise we were asking for trouble. We studied Steve's A4 piece of paper; we needed to be at

Condrieu to be on schedule. I wanted to push on considerably more but a puncture and tired legs dictated that we settled for a small town called Ampuis, just a few miles up the road from Steve's planned stop.

We followed the previous format of using the Office de Tourisme to find our digs for the night. Once in the town, we had difficulty finding our hotel. The directions we were given bore no relation to where the place actually was. We wandered up and down the main road to no avail. In desperation, I asked a woman outside a dingy cafe. To my surprise, above this café, was our hotel for the night. The place was a dump. The two rooms had a shower and shared a toilet at the end of a corridor. Odd furniture and random pieces of lino decorated the place.

We showered and wandered the narrow, busy main road in search of somewhere to eat. Dining at the hotel was not an option worth considering. We found a nice restaurant that was a touch on the expensive side. We bit the bullet and dined there. Denis was still off his food, which was a pity as the food was good. Denis apart, we all enjoyed the meal even though the portions were not designed with hungry cyclists in mind.

## Ampiu to Le Echarmeaux (109 km)

We had breakfast at the hotel as it was included in the price. The breakfast was typical French. The service was slow, to say the least. Our host deliberately dragged her feet, giving us a very low priority. We waited for our milk as she chattered and served her regular customers. I think she thought we were German, as this could be the only reason for our poor treatment.

Thankfully, this was the day we came off the main road through the Rhone Valley. We took a route to the west of Lyon on the D30. Our hour-and-a-half lunch break had now been replaced by shorter, more regular stops when we felt it necessary. We couldn't afford the luxury of a long stop as our speed had slowed considerably. The riding changed from the rolling good surface and sometimes busy, by French standard, main roads to quieter rural country roads. This is what I had been waiting for – picturesque French villages, and empty roads. Denis was not enjoying the scenery, he was suffering. When Jimmy punctured, Steve and Denis carried on and we arranged to meet-up where the road met the N7 some fifteen miles ahead, if we didn't catch them up before. This is a strategy I don't subscribe to – it is fraught with pitfalls. We had little choice, as by now, we were losing a lot of time. Every time the road hit a gradient Denis went backwards. Jimmy and I reached the destination and fed our faces on the wares from the local patisserie before Steve and Denis arrived. Somehow, we had overtaken them, and we had no idea how this had come about. Thank goodness for the mobile phone, otherwise we would have charged off down the road after devouring our pasties under a false assumption.

At Lozanne, we turned onto the D385 and started the gradual ascent to the summit of the Col des Echarmeaux. At first, the slope was hardly noticeable. Bit by bit, over the course of twenty miles, the gradient became steeper. We stopped at a cafe for cold drinks, but the cooling effect on the system lasted for only a couple of miles before the body returned to boiling point once again. A couple of miles from the summit, Denis and Steve opted to shade from the sun. Jimmy and I continued to the top, preferring not to break our rhythm. At the summit, we sat in the shade outside a dilapidated hotel, drinking ice-cold beer. It was more than twenty minutes later before our two companions appeared. I was unsure where this place put us in relation to Steve's bible (A4 spreadsheet) but I think it was well short of our daily quota. The chances of Denis turning another pedal stroke once he had reached the summit of this climb were less than nil.

Our digs for the night had been decided upon; it was where we had been sat for the last three beers. Les Echarmeaux was just a beautiful view on the way to somewhere else. Motorbikes and sports cars would race up and down its bends and admire the view for a while, but the opportunity for a large hotel to thrive wasn't possible. The Hotel des Nations provided the basic requirements for weary travellers, just. The people were friendly and the food was pretty good. The owner stored our bikes in his garage. He showed his vintage mid-fifties, green and white, two-tone Peugeot, which he had restored. This was a good indication on the amount of trade his hotel was doing. Perhaps his business premises might be his next project. He then showed us to our rooms. The view was unbelievable, a panoramic view down the Rhone Valley with mountains in the background. Denis still wasn't enjoying his food. I felt tomorrow would be the make-or-break day. At least tomorrow we would be enjoying a few miles of descents.

## Le Echarmeaux to Autun (109 km)

We had the start we had hoped for, twenty miles of mainly downhill. We stopped as the road levelled out at La Clayette to take a photo of the very impressive chateau there. We headed for Charolles and stopped at Toulon sur Arroux for lunch. Three of us ate while Denis was still not eating and was giving us cause for concern. We decided to split Denis's luggage between us in an attempt to motivate him to carry on. We carried on at a steady pace. The extra pannier strapped to my rack and Denis's lightened load had the desired effect at first. As the miles rolled on, the effect wore off, once again, Denis was falling behind. Autun, a medium-sized town, was intended as a café stop. It turned into an overnight stop as Denis announced he couldn't go any further, even with the three of us carrying his luggage.

We booked into the Hotel Commerce et Touring, which was a Logis de France on the main road. The hotel was of a good standard, the people were charming, the food, and accommodation were superb. The one drawback was the sound of thundering Lorries in the early hours of the morning.

Over dinner we planned a chat on how we should tackle the next few days. We were finishing earlier each day. Today we had covered less than planned despite the fact we had the advantage of a downhill start and Denis was travelling without luggage. It was evident that eventually, we would fall too far behind and would be unable to make up the lost time. The debate didn't take place. Denis received a phone call that altered our thinking completely. His mother-in-law had died and he was deeply distressed. He needed to get back to his wife, Sandra as soon as possible. The next day, the various options for returning home would be examined. We planned to do this through the tourist information office.

Next morning an early breakfast was followed by a brisk walk to the Tourist Information Office, which saw us explaining our tale of woe to the young Frenchman behind the counter. Our ideal scenario was to get Denis back to England, complete with the bike. To do this, he would either have to hire a car for the one-way trip to the ferry port and then get a train from Dover or to get a box to put the bike in to allow him to use either the train or a flight. The flight option involved getting Denis and the bike to the airport. The car option was immediately ruled out by our young Frenchman, it wasn't possible in this town and he didn't think it would be an option other than at Dijon, over nineties miles away. The bike shop in the town was closed and the likelihood of the shop having a suitable box was remote. Time was ticking by and a train was leaving for Paris at 10.45 a.m. We made contact with John in St Remy in desperation. He tried one or two of his contacts who he thought might help. In the end our only course of action was to leave Denis's bike with the hotel owner and hope to have somebody pick it up later. She was very obliging and agreed to leave the bike in her garage. She insisted on a written disclaimer from us to relinquish her from blame in the event the bike was stolen. I produced a handwritten letter copied from a text sent by John and the bike was handed over. I left Denis my mobile phone and John's number in case of a language problem. By 11.00 a.m. Denis was on a bus to the railway station and the tour was ready to roll minus one recruit.

## Autun to Les Riceys (133 km)

The stopping and waiting had been frustrating for the remainder of the group. When we set off on the bikes, the speed was definitely a lot higher, we rode as though we had our legs untied and the average speed increased by five miles per hour. We stopped at Semur-en-Auxois, a small fortress town with cobbled streets and medieval gateways.

The most striking piece of architecture was the thirteenth-century church of Notre Dame. The town had been the venue for the French road racing championship only the day before and the roundabout approach in the town was decorated with old bikes sprayed with gold and silver paint. I told Steve he had an opportunity to swap his wreck for a better model. We cycled down the road to the bridge over the river Armacon on the heavily cobbled streets and then climbed up to the main street and then up the hill to find a decent cafe for lunch. Afterwards, we then had to retrace our tracks almost losing our fillings on the large cobbles in the process.

We pushed on through Montbard, aiming for Laignes. Despite the late start, we had over eighty miles on the clock by the time we reached Laignes. We carried on our route and reached les Riceys before we found a hotel. Le Magny was by far the best hotel we had experienced in a few years, but its old-world setting in the middle of nowhere suggested that we were about to pay a premium. It looked like a French version of a country club. It was a Logis so we hoped it was within our budget. Rooms at sixty-six Euros a night are not what we normally pay, but our options were becoming limited. We bit the bullet and enjoyed the drink, food and surroundings in the knowledge that our next digs would be considerably cheaper.

## Les Riceys to Reims (Taissy) (160 km)

We headed off towards Reims. After Bar Sur Seine and Brienne le Chateau, we found ourselves on the road I used last year on my solo trip. We passed the hotel at Margerie Hancourt where I had stayed. We headed towards Vitry Franqois and took a lunch stop at Blacy. It was a truck stop cafe. The minor D2 road went across the N4 which was very busy, an ideal place for a cheap lunch. It was after 2.00 p.m. and the place was empty. It was like an American diner with French waitresses. We were invited to help ourselves to the salad buffet. I knew from a previous experience last year that this was just the starter. I didn't share this with my starving travelling companions. To be fair I didn't know for definite. The salad bar was visited several times as we piled on the pasta, meats, boiled eggs and coleslaws. We wiped out the salad bar. The waitress asked us what we wanted for the main course and gave us a few options. None of us could manage another mouthful, to the obvious displeasure of the proprietor. We bought some drinks and chocolate for later in an attempt to quell the atmosphere.

We followed the small roads to Challon de Champagne, where they disappeared and became motorways. We sought the help of a Frenchman on a sit-up-and-beg bike. He navigated us through onto a minor road to Reims, via a trading estate, when all routes sent us down a busy motorway road. We tried asking a couple of motorists, for directions to no avail, they couldn't quite comprehend the fact that we were sat astride a pedal bike and didn't want to commit suicide.

We skirted the west side of Reims and found a complex at Taissy, which housed several cheap hotels. We began our search for accommodation, the third hotel we tried, a Premier Classe, had a room for three very weary cyclists. A room in this type of hotel is basically a plastic box that they have quite remarkably managed to squeeze three beds and a shower into. They are cheap and are usually found on trading estates just off motorway junctions and provide a cheap overnight stop for weary travellers. This particular one at Taissy was like a maisonette on the Manor estate in Sheffield; it was full of boisterous Frenchmen acting loud, animated by alcohol. Our three neighbours were drinking Becks out of bottles and were well intoxicated to the point of being abusive. They were taking the piss out of us, but fortunately we didn't understand what they were saying, although we had a good idea. We had chained our bikes to the balcony but one of them was making gestures inferring that he would be away with our bikes. He was making scissor actions with his fingers, implying that our locks would be cut and we took his threat seriously. We went for a beer and a brainstorming session on how we could get three blokes, three bikes and six panniers in a plastic box and still manage to navigate our route to the toilet and sink. We stood two bikes upright, suspended from coat hangers by the front wheel, and a third across the bottom of a bed.

## Taissy to Le Quesnay (136 km)

We awoke the next day to another warm but overcast day. We had only got onto the main road when the heavens opened. We took refuge in a bus shelter until the torrent of rain had died to a trickle. We headed for Serny le Reims and then Bethenay. The thunder and lightning made for a scary start to the day. We rode over flat farmland and watched the lightning strike the ground. The storm heralded the end of the intense heat we had endured for this tour. The roads to the north of Reims were quiet with strange-sounding names, Nizy le Conte and Dizy le Gros – where we stopped for lunch. We managed to find some quiet lanes away from the main drag, and this time it was flattish rolling countryside.

We arrived at the fortress town of Le Quesnoy, only 25 km from the Belgian border. During the First World War, the Germans had turned the town into a fortress using the sixty-foot-high ramparts and moats designed by Vaudan the military architect of Louis XIV. The town was eventually taken by a New Zealand regiment on 5th November 1918, but not before two hundred Kiwis had lost their lives. We rode over a cobbled street into the old town and found it was lacking in hotels. The only hotel in town, we were reliably informed by the Frenchman at the tourist office, was above a Moroccan restaurant on the outskirts of town.

We had very little choice, our bed for the night was at Chez Ahmed, not the usual French hostelry. It wasn't our worst digs of the tour, but it was far from being the best. The bright purple wallpaper was peeling from the wall, and the furniture looked like it was from a bottom-end house clearance shop. The only plus point you could say was that it wasn't massively overpriced at fifty Euros between us, about thirteen pounds each, including breakfast. We showered, changed and wandered the town looking for what might be an alternative eating experience to the Moroccan restaurant we were sleeping over. Our walk was fruitless, so we returned to sample our host's cuisine. Not being familiar with Moroccan, we ordered far too much; we gave it our best try but we failed to clear the vast amount of food they laid on our table. For once, we went to bed with our bellies bulging with enough calories to last another tour.

## Le Quesnoy to Zeebrugge (140 km)

We started what might be the last day of our, but we didn't know for certain. We believed we had about a ninety-mile journey in front of us, but we couldn't be sure, the reason being we didn't have a map. Steve had stopped plotting the route after France, and my map didn't cover all of Belgium. On the last leg, we were literally flying blind. The Frenchman at the tourist information office said a hundred and sixty kilometres, Steve thought it was a lot less.

We passed through Jenlan, a town that shared the same name as the beer we were drinking last night. At Peruwelz, we entered Belgium. The names of the towns had a strange ring to them, not very French such as, Waregem, Tielt, Wingene, and Waardamme. We dined outside a supermarket in Ronse. The waitress serving up our meal of a baguette and brie sandwich was using a language not familiar to us. We knew we were not in France. The mostly main roads we used had a cycle lane running alongside. We found some quiet roads approaching Brugge. Cycle signs with Brugge written on them meant small roads suitable for cyclists not wanting to encounter juggernauts in my eyes. We encountered exactly what it said on the tin, deserted narrow roads with accompanying cycle lanes. I asked a young female jogger who confirmed in both English and French that we were on the right track.

We rode into Brugge, the Flemish name for a place of bridges across the Bascule bridge onto the cobbled streets. We posed for photographs, thinking we were at our destination. In fact, what we did find out was that Zeebrugge was fifteen kilometres away down the road. We didn't have a map and our perception was that Brugge was a couple of kilometres at most away from the ferry port. We asked for directions, stopping at a chemist. If in doubt, ask at a chemist, they always speak English. We then set off at pace to the ferry port arriving with an hour to spare before the boat was to set sail.

We didn't have a reservation and we didn't have a clue how much we would pay. The cost for a ticket was about eighty-five Euros, about four times the cost of last year's ferry trip, I recall. For this price, we got a cabin for the night and a trip up the coast to Hull. We wouldn't have the problem and expense of getting from Dover, all-in-all quite a reasonable deal. We took advantage of the lunch and breakfast deal and once again, we tried our hardest to wipe out the generous buffet on offer.

## Hull to Dronfield (120 km)

The ferry docked in Hull on Friday morning. We timed it just right for the rush hour traffic. The cars crawled out of Hull and we dodged in and out of traffic, picking our way out of the centre. The main road out of Hull turned into a nightmare as the traffic thinned and the lorries hurtled past. We had just six or seven miles to go before the Humber Bridge and relative solitude. We feared for our safety and felt quite relieved to replace the busy A63 with quieter Lincolnshire lanes. We rode through Scunthorpe on our way to Gainsborough. I pointed out my old digs at Scotter as we passed through the village, and the old Ericsson factory where I was employed. It had only been a few years since I had spent a year or more there but how they had changed. The old farmhouse had been totally renovated and the factory had been boarded up and abandoned. We stopped at Rosies Cafe on the way to Retford for a traditional tea stop. We dined before we parted company with Steve. Jimmy and I were heading for Sheffield and Steve was heading for Doncaster; another tour completed! By the time Jimmy and I had parted company, we had eight hundred and fifty miles on the clock – our longest tour by a long way.

# Tour 10 – Freidrichshafen to Rotterdam

Another year had rolled by and I was still hanging in at Lechler. It wasn't by choice – the recession was making it difficult to move on. With other companies handing out pay cuts instead of pay rises, I suppose getting nothing made me very lucky. I had the advantage of having a relatively stable, secure income rather than a good one.

The last tour took a bit of getting over, not just the mileage but the damage to the bank balance. We hadn't managed to squeeze in the odd night at a youth hostel or

B&B. By our usual standard we had travelled Club class. Jimmy was already making noises about giving next year a miss. He had a point I needed to look at ways of reducing the cost if the tours were to continue.

I wasn't actually crying poverty but two factors influenced my decision to consider going a bit more low-budget touring. Firstly, I had fallen in love with a piece of sculptured titanium that was the best part of three grand. My old Cannondale was about knackered and was ready for an upgrade. The nought per cent finance the bike shop was offering was too good an opportunity to miss. The deal was done and the Litespeed Sienna was soon sitting proudly in my garage amongst my other steeds. This is something I don't do on a regular basis, mainly because I can't afford it. My belief is that the most important thing about a bike is the engine. It did feel good to actually go out and buy it instead of just drooling over it. This euphoric feeling was all the better because I didn't make a regular habit of such extravagance. My second big expense hadn't happened yet, but it was something I needed to budget for. My daughter and her family were intending to move to Australia in March. I could envisage a trip to Australia, if not every year, at least every other year. Those sorts of holidays don't come cheap, with a flight alone coming to more than a grand each. By the time I had spent a few weeks there, the Litespeed outlay would seem rather meagre and insignificant by comparison.

I remember very early on in my touring days mentioning tents. The "T" word to Kevin wasn't met with much enthusiasm. The second word of his reply I'm sure was "off". I don't think the subject was ever mentioned again. To be honest, the thought of carrying a tent long distances, finding a pitch or field to camp and then enduring Kev's snoring wasn't appealing. But that was then. If I was to continue touring, I might now have to consider this low-budget option. If it was have-tent-will-travel or no tour at all, then I had no choice. I hadn't been camping for a long time; perhaps great leaps had been made in lightweight tents, which wouldn't be a massive burden on a bike. The travel light/travel far ethos still has to remain. The thought of taking all day to do fifty miles towing a trailer is not what touring is about, in my opinion.

I roamed the internet and spent too much time in camping shops looking for inspiration. Bike forums on the internet introduced me to the dark side of touring. Strange men on bikes who were into stealth camping. They used camouflaged hammocks and freeloaded their way across continents, sleeping anywhere they could for nothing. I decided that sort of adventure was a step too far.

This year was the tenth tour since I planned the first one with Kevin at the turn of the millennium. I wanted to do something special to celebrate the fact. The original plan for 2009 was to fly from Doncaster to Gerona, watch a couple of stages in the Pyrenees and then ride home. The highlight would be the finish in the ski village of Alcalis Andora. To do this, a tent would be a prerequisite to savour the atmosphere of a mountaintop tour stage. I had two other people interested in sharing this adventure initially, Steve from last year's tour and Chris who had not been before, both later had a change of heart. As the time approached to book a flight, Chris went missing Lord Lucan style and Steve went cool on the idea, fearing it was too much for him. When the time arrived to book the flights, I was on my own, looking at the best part of a thousand-mile epic. I didn't fancy the trip as much going it alone, but I was prepared to do this, rather than not do a tour at all. I remembered the miles alone on the road on my last solo excursion. When the sun is shining, solitude is not a problem but bad weather always seems worse when braving it alone. In the end, Steve came up with an alternative tour for me to consider. There was no way I was going to talk Steve round to my plan, so I succumbed to his for the sake of companionship. I rationalised my change of heart by putting on hold my planned tour for another year. By next year there might emerge another masochist from the local cycling fraternity who was willing to accompany me. Inside, I knew that this could be the end of the tours as I had known them. The next decade will see me pass the sixty mark and become an OAP before the decade is through, certainly food for thought.

## Sheffield to Friedrichshafen

The first day's journey looked daunting – three train journeys, one plane flight and a bike ride. It all went amazingly well except for a hiccup at Doncaster station. I loaded my bike box in the Golf at 6.30 a.m. and headed for Sheffield Station, where Jane was dropping me off on her way to work. The box seemed bigger and heavier than last year, measuring 1450 x 800 x 300. There is no such thing as a standard bike box. Jane helped me out of the car and over the steps to the platform I needed for Doncaster. The train to Donny was no problem, I just looked for the bike logo on the door and struggled on board. I had attached a couple of nylon straps to the box to use as handles and they seemed to work a treat.

Catching the Doncaster to Peterborough train was a nightmare. It was the express service to London and the train was about a mile long. I stood on the end of the platform designated for bike travellers. I wasn't on my own; a bloke with a mountain bike waited with me. I secured the services of a trolley just in case, by some remote possibility, the guard's van was at the other end. Sure enough, myself and the mountain biker were standing as far away from the guard's van as possible when the train arrived. The biker got astride his machine and pedalled furiously to the other end of the platform while I pushed my massive box along the platform clipping people as they were getting off the train. I must have said excuse me and apologised a hundred times before I was greeted (not the appropriate word in this case) by the man with the key at the other end. I was grateful to the mountain biker, who told the guardsman that a bloke with a massive box would be arriving shortly, otherwise I would have missed the train. The guardsman looked pissed off and gleefully told me I would have to pay extra for the box. I argued, but the guy asked me if I wanted to catch this train or not. I felt like saying, "No, I just wanted to give my box a ride." I decided it wasn't the place for sarcasm and jumped aboard. I didn't pay extra for the box, but I'm sure it made the guard's day telling me I would have to. The cross-country train journey from Peterborough to Stansted Airport passed without any further incident. My box sat alongside another cyclist's bike box, an Aussie, who was off to conquer the Pyrenees with the aid of a support vehicle. He was planning on doing it in five days, which is pretty good going. I loaded my box onto a trolley and waited at Stansted Airport for Steve to arrive.

We arrived at Friedrichshafen on time, as our aircrew proudly boasted. We opened our boxes at the airport and assembled the bikes while being observed by a bemused taxi driver. He spoke English reasonably well, as he told of his fond memories of his visits to England (Cambridge). We asked what we should do with the cardboard, and he suggested we stack it behind a bin and just go before we attracted any attention. We obliged, and in our hasty retreat, we set off in completely the wrong direction. We arrived at the Hostel just in time for dinner, which ended at 7.00 p.m. Our first impression of German Youth Hostels was a good one. The accommodation was good, the building and surroundings were pleasant, and the variety and quality of food were superior to that of other countries we had experienced in Europe. The evening was rounded off with a couple of beers in the town, followed by an ice cream, which I managed to drop on a woman's foot. She laughed about it, and I was given another free of charge.

Nice people, these Germans, apart from the bloke back at the hostel who took pleasure in telling us the English had lost 4-0 to the Germans in the Under 21 football championship.

## Friedrichshafen to Balingen (140 km)

We sampled our first German youth hostel breakfast. Again, the quantity and variety of food on offer was far in excess of the French equivalent. As well as the usual bread roll and a croissant we had cereals, fruit, meat, and cheese as well. The breakfast was just the job for two cyclists on a budget, who were facing a long bike ride.

We set off in the morning through the town, thinking that cycleways were the answer; by evening time, we weren't so sure. In large towns, they are good at keeping motorists and cyclists separated, but still sharing the same road. Also, when the road gets repaired, so do the cycleways. We breezed through towns and cities with other commuters and felt perfectly safe doing so. Out of town, it was another story. The rural cycle-ways take you away from the road and are usually lost down some unmade road. The material used for these segregated cycle paths took on many forms, smooth asphalt, concrete slabs, block paving, loose chippings and green lanes. Some of these cycle routes required a full suspension mountain bike plus a satellite navigation system to get you back on track to your destination. Steve's planned route by road was sixty-five miles, by the time we arrived at our destination, we had done ninety.

We set off from Friedrichshafen keeping the massive Lake Constance to our left shoulder. We headed through Salem, Pfullendorf and then stopped for drinks and ice cream at a nice town called Sigmaringen. Reaching our next stop at Albstadt was becoming a bit of a nightmare. Off-roading on touring bikes is not what we were looking for, but we got sucked into trying to stay off roads occupied by traffic. Roads that looked like minor roads on our Michelin map were quite busy in reality. We took directions from a German mountain biker who we weren't convinced knew his way, but we got to Albstadt eventually. From there we took on some food and drink and rode to Tailfingen and then onto the youth hostel at Balingen.

The youth hostel at Balingen set the bar even higher. It was fairly small, having only forty-four beds. It was a part of the castle of Hohenzollern; the hostel was used originally as the servant's quarters. It was half-timbered and had been completely modernised inside, with the original beams left showing as a feature. We were asked to remove our shoes before entering the building as they might damage the polished wooden floors. The rooms were given names rather than numbers, which added a bit of individualism to our accommodation. Balingen is a good place for a night out, as there are plenty of places to eat and drink. We sat at a bar next to the river at the back of the hostel with a good view of the castle.

## Balingen to Baden Baden (112 km)

This was a good day for taking in the views; with plenty of climbing and descending through picturesque villages. We rode through Gerslingen, Vohringen, Sulz, Hopfau, and Lienstetten before stopping for lunch at Fruedenstadt. After lunch, we climbed for hours over the Black Forest road through Oberal, Ruhestein and then descended into Baden Baden. We had just seventy miles on the clock by the time we hit our destination, a rest day by our comparisons. Several factors affect mileage, terrain, weather and fitness. On this year's tour, we had a couple more to add to that list, how many times we got lost, and how many times we had to stop to consult the map. The latter was becoming a feature of this year's tour as we were changing roads quite often, which broke up any momentum, rather than grinding out the miles. We didn't know where we were going.

The youth hostel there took a bit of finding. We stopped several people before we finally found the place, on the North side of town, hidden away next to an open-air swimming complex. The hostel was an old building, but like the others, was clean, well-equipped and ran with German efficiency. The hostel surprisingly, didn't offer an evening meal, so we wandered the many bars and restaurants within walking distance.

## Baden Baden to Thallichtenberg (163 km)

In the morning we went for breakfast to find the large reception had been changed into a dining room. All the equipment was on wheels and like a stage to a musical, all the props and furniture had been changed while we slept. Space was at a premium. German staff made the most of what space they had. The quantity and quality of the breakfast hadn't been compromised and was still far superior to what the French hostels had to offer.

We set off on what was to be our highest mileage of the tour. We had fallen a little behind schedule. A long day in the saddle was required, and by the time we reached our hostel at Thallichenberg, we had covered a hundred and five miles. We followed a route through Beinheim, Seebach, Wissembourg, Dahn, Landstuhl and Kusel. The towns tended to suck you into their centre, all roads lead you there. That is exactly what we wanted to avoid. Once through Kusel, we looked for the hostel. The hostel was hidden away up a mountain off the main road. The road soon had me scrambling for the small inner ring of my triple in order to keep rolling. At the top sat a castle that housed the hostel. The Castle was built in 1200 and is the largest ruined castle in Germany.

We consumed a few beers and ate at the hostel. We were hungry and anything half reasonable served would have tasted good. We started with Doritos – not very German – with a side order of dips followed by pizzas. The hostel's location limited our choices, and we didn't have the energy or inclination to roam far. Our German female host for the night made us feel as though everything was too much trouble, she wasn't big on hospitality. We were her only customers. I imagined the other guests had cars and could be bothered going into town to escape our charmless host.

# Thallichtenberg to Daun (106 km)

We spent an hour planning our route, only then to set off in the wrong direction. We didn't want to descend into town and lose height only to find we needed to climb back up again. There was always an eagerness to get rolling in the general direction we thought we wanted to go and get our bearings later. On this occasion, this act of improvisation must have added at least an hour to our journey. We headed in a north-easterly direction when we needed to be heading northwest. When we eventually got on track at Idar Oberstein, the rain started. We had no option but to shelter under trees somewhere between Allenbach and Morbach, as riding conditions were made impossible by the volume of water coming down. The skies were black and visibility dropped to a few metres as we waited for nearly an hour for the rain to slow. When the rain eased a little, we rode another ten kilometres into Morbach. By the time we reached Morbach, we were cold, wet and hungry. We ordered food at a restaurant and had a long wait for our spaghetti as the storms returned to cut off the power. From Morbach, we had only a short ride before we were descending into the Mosel Valley, a beautiful part of the world.

The Mosel Valley stretches from Koblenz to Trier, which is about a hundred and eighty kilometres. Steve had visited this area before, but for me it was a new experience. We stopped at Bernkastel for a few photos. Kues is a popular starting point for boat trips along the river Mosel.

We planned out a route to Daun, which was about fifty kilometres away. We had lost a lot of time and getting to Daun would be a good result. We gave each other place names to memorise rather than consulting the map every couple of miles, in an attempt to save time. I tried to remember Urzig and Kinderburn (Spelt Kinderbeuern). We went over the bridge to pick up the cycle path that runs parallel to the river. At Urzig, we climbed the steep gradient out of the valley, receiving gestures of encouragement from some of the local residents. We had a bit of complex navigating to do around Kinderbeuern before finding the single road (421) that led us through Hontheim, Strotzbusch, Mehren and then Daun. We looked for a town plan on entering into the centre. We scoured the map in search of the YH sign or the word Jugendherberge. In keeping with the hostels, apart from the first, we had a bit of climbing to do. In this case, the directions took us up a steep cinder track, there must have been a road, but we never found it.

After housing our bikes and showering, we headed for the bistro to be offered exactly the same menu as the night before. We ate there, but enough was enough; we vowed not to do it again. The only thing that was different was the German sausages on tap, which were very spicy; I dreaded to think what they contained. Our host and cook for the night was a young Turk who was friendly and made us feel welcome by contrast to the miserable woman at the last place.

## Daun to Masstricht (150 km)

From Daun, we set off to Maastricht on the same road that we came in on. We learned our lesson from the previous day and retraced our steps back to the main road. We made good time as we kept on the same road taking us through Stadkyll and stopping just before Eupen at a pub for lunch. We took a route left of Aachen on our way up to Masstriicht. By the time we reached the youth hostel called the 'Stay OK', we had well over ninety miles under our belt.

To our dismay, the receptionist at the hostel told us they were full. We couldn't believe it. It had taken us ages to find this place as people sent us in the general direction without telling us exactly where it was. To make things worse, the hostel looked really good, modern, clean and spacious.

We asked where he suggested we tried next. He pointed us in the direction of the 'botel', a boat converted into a hotel, half a mile down the river. That was also full. We sat and had a drink on the botel, trying not to panic. We crossed the bridge and combed the streets in the town for hotels and bed and breakfasts. We asked the locals drinking in many of the pubs. They picked us out a few doors to knock on that didn't look like B&Bs. Of the three doors we knocked, only one answered. She was full but she made a phone call to a friend of hers who had a room for the night. Unfortunately, the room was in the district of Amby, a few miles out of town. The chances of finding this place seemed pretty remote at the outset. We asked time and time again and eventually homed in on the house we were looking for. All we had been given was a piece of paper that we presented to a passer-by, hoping it made sense to them. It worked. We knocked on the door and an attractive lady in her mid-thirties wearing a short wrap-around mini-skirt answered. She introduced herself as Tanya. Her house was semi-detached, similar to what you would expect on an estate back home. The house was extended on the front and back and was a little elaborate but immaculate. It crossed my mind and Steve's that Tanya was some sort of upmarket call girl. We may have been serving her a massive injustice. It was just her clothes seemed too tarty for the normal run-of-the-mill landlady. We showered and changed and headed for a restaurant recommended by our host. The food was magnificent, a far cry from our usual youth hostel pizza. It was only spaghetti bolognese, but it was the real deal, not something processed and warmed up later.

We probably had the worst night's sleep we had all holiday. Our room in the attic was far too hot. We had a fan going all night that kept me awake without doing anything to cool me down. It was just too hot to sleep.

## Maastricht to Chaam (105 km)

We went down for breakfast and Tanya had changed into a plain Jane. She had shorts and a tee shirt on and didn't look the same woman. She served up a more than adequate breakfast. Tanya wasn't overfriendly without being rude. Perhaps she felt a bit uneasy with two hungry cyclists in her house. We waved her goodbye and headed off back to Maastricht.

We were heading for Genk and then Mol along mostly busy roads which seemed hard work. Our lunch stop was a place called Turnhout. We sat outside a café in the high street eating our Chicken salad with chips.

We picked up the pace in the afternoon as we headed for Baarle Hertog. We made these places memorable by memorising the name Barry Hertog. Just as we thought we were making good time, Steve punctured and then the rain came heavy.

Once through Baarle Hertog, we were on the road to Chaam or Charm, as we called it. In Chaam, we followed the sign for the youth hostel. Up and down this country road, we rode several times. We found several campsites, but alas no hostel. We asked local people the whereabouts of this elusive hostel, without any luck. Did the place exist? The sign in the town said so, so did the map, and so did Steve's printout from the YHA website. Frustrated, I went to the petrol station to ask for directions only to be told that it had closed down two years ago. This was the second time in two days that we had failed to book into a Dutch Youth Hostel. The Stay OK hostel – as they call them here – hadn't been okay at all. Steve was outside chomping at the bit, desperate to find this place and wondered, what I had been pissing about inside a petrol station. When I resurfaced, I told him the bad news, I watched his jaw drop before I told him that I had an address of a B&B only minutes away. The B&B address was something the petrol station guy had retrieved from the Dutch equivalent of Yellow Pages. Within minutes, we were staring at a big detached house that was to be our bed for the night. This time we were greeted by Inga, a silver-haired woman, in her early sixties. She was very friendly and was used to housing cyclists. She made us feel more than welcome. We felt at ease in a house that was tidy but full of old furniture and books. We had a big room to ourselves with en suite facilities. The house was massive, it felt like a tardis, decidedly bigger on the inside than it looked on the outside. Steve said she used to be a school teacher because of the odd detail she would correct us on. She charged us twenty Euros each, which was more than a bargain – what a find.

We roamed the small town looking for a restaurant. There were several bars, but none served food. We ended up eating at a Pizza parlour run by Asians, I was unsure of their nationality. They cooked the pizza on site and served up two massive Quattro Stagioni's. They were the size of two dustbin lids. I had to help Steve with his. It was just too much. We returned to our digs to find Inga had hung up our washing to dry in our room and put towels on the floor to catch the water. What a gem.

## Chaam to Rozenburg / Rotterdam (91 km)

Monday was the last day of the tour. We checked the sailing time on Inga's PC to confirm it was 9.00 pm. We had a sixty-five-mile ride to the ferry port. We headed out of Chaam in the direction of Breda. We were looking for a place called Etten Leur, which is to the west of Breda. It was a focal point to aim for that would hopefully guide away from the city and into the direction of Zevenbergen. Skirting big cities like Breda on major roads in a car isn't a problem; on a bike, it's a different matter. Our route zigzagged on cycle ways, joining in with the hundreds of commuters and schoolchildren following their daily routine, alien anywhere else in Europe.

As we got nearer Rotterdam, we stopped at a place called Willemstad a small town with a harbour and some good pubs and restaurants. We bought some fruit from the market there and sat at the water's edge and rested up awhile. We set off, heading for the large bridge nearby. We needed to cross a very large expanse of water. Once over the bridge, we took a left and headed for Piershil. The heavens opened and once again, we took refuge in a bus shelter. We cycled after the showers had eased and made it to a good old-fashioned Spar shop. In the absence of a restaurant, we bought bread cheese and tomatoes and made our own meals for a little more than two Euros each. We sat by a river and just managed to eat up before the rains returned with a vengeance.

When we set off that morning, I assumed that we were heading for the Europort at Rotterdam. Where we really wanted to be, according to the natives, was the Hook of Holland and a place called Rosenberg. Perhaps it was the same place? We boarded a small ferry to get across a small expanse of water and kept riding towards the coast. Eventually we came across a sign on the cycle path giving the direction for Hull.

We bought tickets at the P&O kiosk while bracing ourselves to be stung and we weren't disappointed. A hundred and fifteen Euros for a one-way boat trip as a foot passenger isn't cheap. Once on board, we paid twenty-two pounds for a joint evening meal and breakfast ticket. It's fair to say we took good advantage of their buffet and eat-as-much-as-you-want policy. In the morning, we had a good eighty-mile ride back home. Steve had sussed a route that kept us away from the busy A63, the main dual carriageway to the M18. It was part of the Trans-Pennine cycle route. We tried to pick the route up near Hull centre but we lost it due to it being poorly marked. Our government's attempt at encouraging people to ride bikes as a carbon reduction strategy is simply pathetic. We persevered and ended up in industrial estates and dead ends. We used a track at the side of the river, which was overgrown with nettles, as we inched our way towards the Humber Bridge and the quieter roads of Lincolnshire towards Scunthorpe, where Steve and I parted company for another year. I called at Rosie's café at Saundby for lunch before a rode the final leg through Retford, and Worksop on my way home.

It looked unlikely that my touring exploits would carry on seamlessly into the next decade, mainly due to a lack of finances. Nicola's much-delayed immigration to Australia took place in August 2009. The housing market crash had resulted in her house not being sold and I was hoping, rather selfishly, that might have put paid to her plans. It was a strange hand of fate that helped her realise her dream.

Prior to Nicola going, we had spent quite a lot of time together, mainly through her newfound interest in running. It started as a way of losing a few pounds but, like her dad, it developed into an obsession. Her general fitness at first wasn't good. I was recruited as her trainer and from humble beginnings of short jogging trips around the estate, she developed into a tough competitor. Within a year we both joined a running club and were competing in half-marathons and cross-country events like seasoned campaigners. It was through the running club that she met Kate. Kate was looking for a house to rent and a deal was done. She booked her flights and Nicola; Damien and Dylan were preparing themselves for a new life on the far side of the planet.

The trip to the airport was a sombre affair, it felt like a funeral. Everybody felt ill at ease. Damien thought that we blamed him for taking Nicola and our grandson Dylan away. His way of dealing with his uneasiness was silence. What a horrible day that was, they don't come much worse.

Dylan was the only one really excited about the trip; the rest of us were preparing ourselves for the tearful farewell. We keep in touch twice a week through the webcam that they bought us. To see a picture on a computer screen while talking to them was better than nothing but only just. The picture quality was sometimes poor, and when the connection was lost at least a dozen times during a conversation, it made this method of communication less than adequate. The eleven-hour time difference also made life difficult. Chewing the fat at two o'clock in the morning when I am up at 6.30 a.m. for work wasn't ideal.

My plans for the coming years would be to use up my whole year's holiday allocation at the beginning of the year. While there was frost on the ground in England, I would be baking in the Australian summer. The down side of this arrangement will be that my holiday entitlement and savings would have been spent before we hit spring. I won't be able to take a bike over there but I would take my running kit and try and keep up with my daughter. I would hate to think that my annual tour was a thing of the past. If there was a way out of this dilemma, I would seek it out. A change of employment was a solution. Contracting allowed me to choose my own hours and provide the funds I needed. I hoped it wouldn't be long before I was packing my bike for more cycling adventures.

# Tour 11 – Bordeaux to Calais

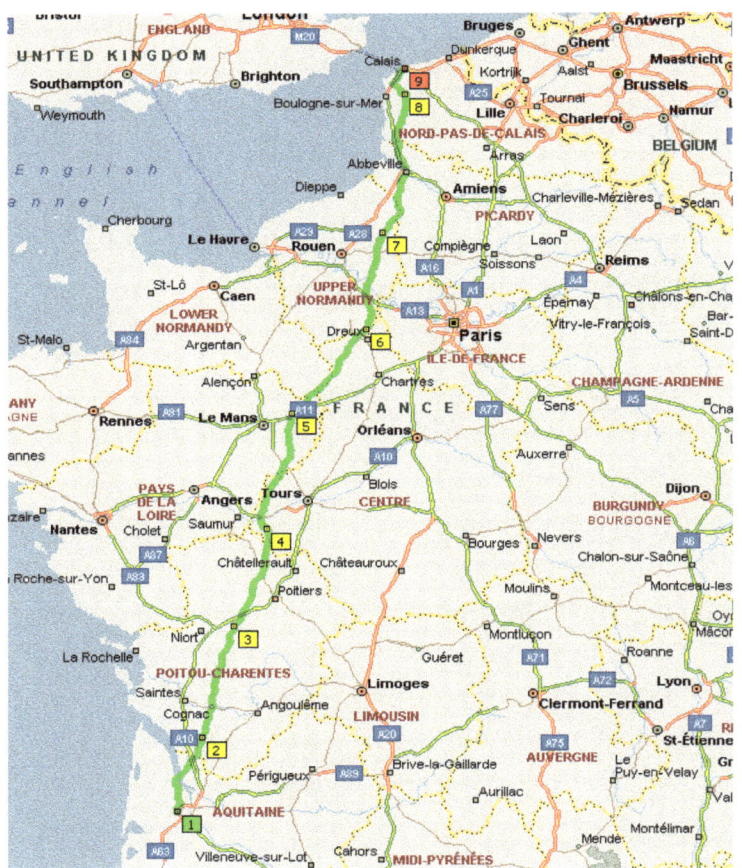

As, expected I took the majority of my annual leave in March. Jane and I were off to see our daughter and family in Australia. I was excited about the prospect. Nicola planned a few trips while we were over to make it a holiday to remember. The holiday was split into three parts, a week in Cairns up in Queensland, a couple of days in Sydney and the remainder going on day trips from Bathurst. By the time we were setting off, Nicola was talking about coming back to England. Even so, we had already decided to make the trip. I knew she was feeling homesick from our discussions on Skype. She felt she had to make a decision before Dylan started school in August.

The plane journey to Sydney was a far from pleasant experience. Sitting on your arse in the same small seat for twenty-four hours is mind-numbingly boring. Between eating, drinking and watching films, there were times when the journey became unbearable. The re-circulated air left an unpleasant taste in my mouth and the smell of sweaty bodies was awful. But it was all going to be worth it.

Once in Australia, we had a great time. So many highlights it was hard to pick out the best moments. Swimming off the Barrier Reef with all the fish was an unforgettable moment. Dubbo Zoo was also great, a cross between a safari park and a zoo where animals had the freedom to roam. Animals were just separated from spectators by a ditch. We travelled round on hired bikes, a welcome change from sitting in a hot car. Even on days when nothing was planned, it was a joy to put the running shoes on and run a few miles in the clean, warm air. March time was Autumn time in Australia and the temperature was just right for me. Moreover, we had three birthday celebrations while we were over there – Dylan, Gordon (my son-in-law's father) and Nicola's.

All too soon, the holiday was over and we were sitting on a plane heading back to England. I mulled over my leave sheet at work. I had enough leave left for a week's tour. Some of the Australia trip was holiday left over from last year. What I was short of was money. I had bought an old house at the beginning of the year to fix up. The idea was to rent out to provide an income in my retirement. In reality it was turning out to be a hungry monster that was devouring my time and money. I honestly thought I could channel all my energy and resources into this project and somehow distract myself from the cycling bug and the yearning of the open road. I was wrong.

With my finances as they were – I decided it was time for a different type of touring holiday, a cheaper one. The main expense to be considered was the accommodation, which could be as much as fifty euros a night. I bought myself a small, lightweight tent off eBay. The tent cost me forty-six pounds, brand new for a supposedly a hundred and twenty-pound tent. It weighed only one kilogram. If this adventure didn't get off the ground, I figured I would get my money back. I now had the unenviable task of persuading some fifty-odd-year-old to go cycle-touring with a tent instead of a credit card. I contacted Steve Worthy – last year's partner – without any luck. His reason was he was doing an iron man triathlon in August. I couldn't think of a better preparation than dragging a heavy bike-complete with camping gear–across France for seven hundred miles. I got the feeling that the iron man was a convenient excuse. Why would anybody in their right mind-who had plenty of money – opt for denying themselves home comforts if they didn't have too? Jimmy, on the other hand, had missed last year's tour on the grounds of finance.

The 2008 tour had been an unusually expensive one. Jimmy claimed it cost him a thousand pounds when everything was totalled. I don't doubt that things are different now, compared to early tours, particularly in France. The strength of the euro against the pound has made credit card touring financially out of reach for a lot of tourists. The fifty-franc (five pounds) 'chambre d'hote' or youth hostel is a thing of the past. France is now one of the most expensive places to tour in the world. The tent question was raised as an option and was dismissed without any serious thought. The tent had only one attraction and that was of cost. The negatives were compellingly massive; the extra weight and bulk of the tent and its necessary equipment that needed to be dragged over the mountains could kill the spirit of the tours completely. The Penguin tours have been built on the ethos of lightweight touring – long distances with minimum baggage. A travel light, travel far type tour would be a fond distant memory. Then there was the convenience of knowing that on arriving at a destination, the day's work was done, and we could relax. Contrast that with the nightmare scenario of arriving knackered and drained and having to erect a tent in the rain. On the other hand, the reality is that we cannot afford tours as we had known them. The price difference between a fifty-euro hotel and a five-euro campsite makes a strong case for giving the humble tent a trial. Jimmy was sold on the idea of camping. He borrowed a bivvy bag (a cross between a sleeping bag and a very small tent) from a friend and the tour was on. I left the arrangements to Jimmy; the only stipulation was that I could only afford a week off work.

A flight was booked to Bordeaux for 11 July, a Sunday. The plan was to ride back to Calais via Chinon and be back a week later. A night in Chinon with JC guaranteed a night not under canvas. I packed my cardboard bike box with my bike and panniers. There was no chance – no matter how hard I tried – of staying within the eighteen-kilogram limit stipulated by the budget airline. My tent and sleeping bag, packed with my heavy steel touring bike with panniers filled with my essential gear, took my load to twenty kilograms. We got around this obstacle by filling a suitcase with our excess and paying to take a suitcase between us. The old suitcase was sacrificed at the airport. The budget airlines are now penalising passengers carrying equipment such as ours. More reason to keep baggage to the minimum. I was looking at this tour 'with-the-tent' as a fact-finding mission. What was becoming obvious was that using anything other than super-lightweight camping equipment was a problem with budget airlines.

## Bordeaux (Merignac) to Jonzac (120 km)

Bordeaux airport is at Merignac, a few miles to the west of Bordeaux centre. Our route was to take us east, making a traverse of Bordeaux unavoidable. We had the bikes assembled and rolling by 11.00 a.m. Large towns and cities are a pain on a bike. Not for the first time, we found ourselves happily cycling down a road we weren't supposed to be on. A bloke at a filling station told us it would be advisable to find another route, but how? All routes detoured around housing and industrial estates and then, returned us to the fast-flowing semi-motorway again. Eventually we hit the country roads and enjoyed some hot weather. After sixty miles, we stopped at Montendre for some refreshment. It was hot and fatigue had set upon us. There was a compelling argument to stop here. The locals were preparing food stalls for a music festival that was taking place that evening, but we decided to push on another twenty kilometres to Jonzac and a campsite just outside the town. Our campsite turned out to be the best on our trip. It had everything that a campsite should have and more, a bar, a restaurant, showers and a good place to pitch a tent. They even had the World Cup Final on a large plasma screen and all for seven euros a piece.

The evening's entertainment started when we retired to our tents for the night. A fierce thunderstorm raged during the night. Lightning lit the sky as the rain lashed our tents. I peered out of my tiny, leaky, one-man tent to see Jimmy in his bivvy, which was no more than a wet soggy sleeping bag. I couldn't help bursting into laughter at this bizarre situation. I pulled all my gear into the middle of the tent to stop contact with the single-skin canvas. At this very early stage of the tour, I realised the tent was inadequate for my needs. Jimmy insisted his bivvy was fine. I don't know whether he believed it, I had my doubts.

## Jonzac to La Mothe St. Heray (117 km)

From Jonzac we rode through Arciac, Segonac, and stopping at Jarnac for coffee and Chef-Boutonne for lunch. In keeping with the low-budget theme, we used a supermarket to replace the calories we had burned. We found a bit of parkland with a picnic table and ate our lunch in the midday sun. Wet clothing spread over the rear bike rack had now dried out.

Our second campsite was a basic municipal site on the edge of a town called La Mothe St. Heray. The site's facilities comprised of a big field, toilets, washbasins and showers. A girl in a lock-up hut charged us three and half euros each. We pitched our tent, showered and walked the mile into the small town. After a beer or two, we dined at the French equivalent of a fast food outlet – Sur Le Pouce.

My learned friend Jimmy told me it translated to 'food on the thumb.' We sat outside to eat at some tables across the road. It felt a lot more up market than a British equivalent. Our sleep that night was a lot less eventful than the previous one.

## La Mothe St. Heray to Chinon (103 km)

This was the day we cycled to John's place in Chinon for a night's sleep indoors. We headed out on the D938 through St Maixent Le Cole and then D524 and came across the delightful village of Vasles, where we had lunch. We met John in Thenezay and he rode the thirty miles with us to Chinon.

Chinon is a picturesque town situated on the Vienne River. We stopped on the bridge that spanned the river to take photos before going into town. John's place was a small ground floor flat. It had a pretty back garden where we ate and sank a few beers.

The good night's sleep Jimmy and I were looking forward too, turned out to be a big disappointment. John's flat had a single bed, so Jimmy and I slept on a hard-concrete floor.

## Chinon to Tuffe (124 km)

We set off in the rain and it didn't stop all day. What made it worse was I managed to sustain a knee injury. Usually, running is to blame when my knee feels like my bones are grinding together. On this occasion, however, I can only blame a poor choice of gearing on a climb. I felt the knee click as I pushed hard to haul myself over the brow of a hill.

The weather conditions made even the prettiest of places, La Grande Luce and Volnay, take on a drab appearance. The campsite at Tuff was based around a large lake that was made for water sports. We walked into the small town and we were drawn by this brightly decorated – if not wacky café called O Patti Nat. Outside were bright pastel umbrellas, and inside was an equally wacky owner called Natalie. We ate her speciality 'Patti Nat', which was basically based on potatoes with her fillings, hence the name.

## Tuffe to Marcilly Sur Eure (140 km)

The weather was fine as we rode through la Forte Bernard, Belle me, Mortgage au Perches and Lonny. We dined at La Forte Vidame. Coming into this town, a large castle cum chateau comes into view. It is a very impressive-looking piece of architecture on the scale of Chatsworth House in Derbyshire. After lunch, we rode through Brezolles and Nonancourt to our eventual campsite for the night at Marcilly Sur Eure.

We booked in, paid our five euros, pitched tents and then discovered we couldn't get any food. We were in the middle of nowhere with only lager to sustain us after our hard days ride. Drinking four cans of lager on an empty stomach after a ninety-mile ride is not to be recommended. We had very little choice. We had no appetite for riding miles into the unknown in search of a restaurant that may not exist. Followed by a ride back to the campsite in the dark on strange roads. As I expected, the alcohol on an empty stomach went straight to our legs. We retired to bed with our bellies empty, with the intention of finding somewhere to eat a very hearty breakfast – as soon as possible.

## Marcilly Sur Eure to Forges Les Eaux (105 km)

After an early start and a few miles, we stopped for breakfast at Pacy Sur Eure. The locals in a small café were already hitting the alcohol. The café owner asked us what we wanted. On our request for food, he summoned the already inebriated barfly to the Boulangerie in return for having his wine glass recharged. He returned with croissants and pastries. We ate and left still hungry – the French don't do big breakfasts.

We headed off through Vernon, took the small roads to Tourney and stopped at Richeville for lunch. We passed through a town called Lyons la Foret. It was a place that deserved a longer stay. It was a touristy place that had quite a lot of charm. Most of the buildings in the town were 17th-century architecture. There was little evidence of mundane modern-day influence, apart from motor vehicles, to prevent you from thinking you had stepped back in time.

We rode on another twenty-mile to a campsite at Forges Les Eaux. We checked this time that the town was big enough to house a few pubs and restaurants. We walked through the campsite and emerged into a good-sized town where we re-fuelled. On returning to our tents, we were invited for a late-night drink by three middle-aged women out for a week-end in a caravan. They took the piss, but it didn't matter to us. We only picked up the occasional words as a lot of their French conversation was in slang. They were having fun at our expense. It didn't really matter as they were providing the beer and we weren't going to complain.

## Forges Les Eaux to Colembert (148 km)

We set off, hoping to get within fifty or sixty miles of Calais. As it transpires, we went a lot further than planned. We just couldn't find anywhere to camp. We rode through Gaillefontaine, Aumale, and Moyenneville. We tried to bypass Abbeville without much success. All roads led there so we had our lunch in the town centre.

We headed towards Crecy-en-Ponthieu, and Campagne-les-hesdin. We started looking for somewhere to camp. We passed through the towns of Hucqueliers and Desvres without seeing anything. We stopped at a Chambre D'hote sign only to be told by the Patron that they were full. He gave us directions for a campsite, but by then it was starting to go dark. After a few detours down dead ends, we picked up the sign for the campsite.

Up to that point, the campsites have been good value for money. The lack of a restaurant on some of the sites would not have been a problem if we had arrived with our own food and means to cook it, or perhaps eaten before we arrived. A lot of our problems I could accept were due to bad planning or lack of planning on our part. The campsite at Colembert was hard to find and when we had we wished we had treated ourselves to a hotel, regardless of cost. The site was owned by the local farmer who had turned a field with a considerable slope into a nice little earner. We paid our money to allow us to pitch our tent - which wasn't any cheaper than others we had encountered. We discovered that the price didn't include wash and shower facilities. We needed to purchase tokens that allowed access to an allocated metered amount of water in which to clean our sweaty bodies and clothing. Was this a deterrent to prevent us from emptying their stock of precious water, or just a way of squeezing more money out of tourists? To make matters worse, some of the guests played loud music late at night.

In the morning we were pleasantly surprised to find fellow campers more hospitable than the campsite owners. A pair of Dutch cyclists shared their breakfast with us. It was only cake and bananas, but it was very welcome. It was a husband and wife cycling around France on a recumbent tandem. They were more self-sufficient, carrying enough equipment to allow them to carry and cook their own food, but only doing half the distance we were doing. Time for them wasn't an issue, their pace was more leisurely. It was a step that I believe I needed to take in the future. Their tandem was a strange-looking machine. It allowed the front passenger to adopt a recumbent position while the stoker adopted a normal cycling posture.

## Colembert to Calais (40 km)

The final stage of our journey was a mere twenty-five miles at the most. We went through Guines, avoiding main roads with the help of some local cyclists on their club run. Our long day in the saddle yesterday ensured a mid-day ferry.

## Dover to Home

We managed to get the only puncture of the tour when Jimmy punctured on the way to the railway station in Dover. The long train journey home gave us plenty of time to reflect on our first tour with a tent. This was a fact-finding mission. We achieved what we set out to achieve – a journey across France on a shoestring. It was certainly a lot cheaper than previous tours and on the whole enjoyable and therefore a success.

My conclusions from the 2010 tour and fact-finding mission are this: given the choice, I would prefer to carry on to the end of my days with a credit card in my back pocket and the tent covered in cobwebs rotting in my garage. The ten tours I enjoyed from the start of the millennium were priceless; from the first adventure in 2000 to France with Kevin, to the last with Steve to Germany in 2009. The next decade will be different. Half-way through it, I will become a pensioner with all the handicaps that brings. My body might not, sorry, will not, be capable of a hundred miles per day. Also, I found out that going solo isn't as much fun as sharing the experience. What pensioner will be game for an annual cycling tour across Europe – camping or otherwise – not many, I guess? After my 2010 tour I sold my tent on and recouped my outlay. If camping is the future it has got to be better than what I had experienced. Cheap single – skinned tents are a waste of money. If camping is to be the future, I am going for the best money can buy.

In August, the rest of my life took a turn for the better as my daughter and family returned from Australia. I hoped it was for good this time. It just goes to show how things can change so quickly in life.

# Tour 12 – Zadar to Milan

The majority of my free time during 2010 was spent renovating the house I had bought as an investment. In hindsight, it wasn't the best decision I had made in life. What I thought was a six months project took more than twice that amount of time. At the start of the New Year, I had done the majority of the hard work and was looking forward to renting it out and getting my life back. The bad weather of Christmas 2010 put my finish date back further. That Christmas, I ordered the new kitchen and bathroom – a year later, there was still work to be done. I was into March before I completed my project and was ready to rent the house out. Adrian, a work colleague, and quite conveniently, an electrician rented the house from me. He had done me some much-needed electrical work and he was now looking for a house. The deal was done and he moved in.

In 2011 I had also had a rush of blood employment-wise yet again. I had been at Lechler for three years and hadn't had a pay rise. Another promise of jam tomorrow was more than I could stand. When two of my six work colleagues put their notice in for what they believed to be better, I couldn't resist joining them. As usual with things that are decided in haste, this ended up being a mistake. Although not many, there were a few positives to come out of the move, but unfortunately not for me. The ones left behind got a decent pay rise to retain their services. Apart from an increase in salary, there was nothing else going for my new job at MTL. I was working considerably more hours and when they moved premises to Rotherham, I started on the lookout for new pastures. Despite my best efforts, I was stuck there for the time being.

I didn't have much of an idea for a tour, but Steve Worthy had, so I let him get on with the organising. In hindsight a mistake. To his credit, it was done very quickly. It was that swift I didn't have time to get things OK'd with Jane. It was an ambitious trip that would eat into quite a bit of annual leave. For me the trip was a first of its kind - flying out and back with a bike. The logistics of protecting my beloved touring bike with a plastic bag was a little daunting. Steve had already used the plastic bag method and emailed me pictures to prove it. If my bike returned unscathed it would open up a lot of touring opportunities by being able to fly back from a destination instead of using a ferry port for the return journey. Steve arranged this tour over one week-end rather than two – and eating into more of my annual leave than anticipated. Being a retiree, he had considered cheap flights rather than days off work. The plan was to get a flight to Zadar on Monday 6th July and fly back from Bergamo on Wednesday 15th July, the following week.

Up till then, I hadn't experienced much opposition to my cycling holidays from my wife, Jane. This time, it was different. The cycling holiday was due to swallow up the majority of my annual leave. In the past my cycling tour had been an extra. I had always had plenty of holidays due to contracting. Changing into full-time permanent employment left a lot less holiday entitlement than normal, not enough to have a big family holiday and a tour as well.

During my racing days, the amount of time I devoted to training did, on occasion, cause friction between us. I would get carried away with enthusiasm and enter bike races here, there and everywhere. Cycling was an addiction, a compulsive habit, a craving that needed satisfying. Jane would intervene and give me a few home truths about what a selfish bastard I was being. I would then curb my addiction and make promises that I wouldn't keep. Soon after the heat had gone out of the situation, I would start to ramp it up again.

When my racing days came to an end and the children took holidays on their own, my annual bike tour was accepted as long it didn't comprise our other holidays. This year, the bike holiday was jeopardising my annual holiday with Jane. Looking through impartial eyes, it was hard to argue I wasn't being selfish. For a period, I put the holiday on hold and planned not to go unless the heat went out of the situation. I was the bad guy with not much of a leg to stand on. I told Steve and he couldn't see the problem. Being a retiree without any holiday constraints I would imagine he would find it hard to see a problem. In the end I had paid my money, there would have been little point not going, I would have lost that if I backed out now. The atmosphere at home wasn't good for several weeks leading up to the tour and a few weeks after I returned.

I would need to buy another tent to replace the one I used and sold after the tour last year. I did my research and opted for a Force Ten two-man tent. It was 1.3 kg and offered just enough space at a reasonable price. Unlike the other, it was double-skinned and greatly improved my chances of remaining dry.

Steve hired a car and picked me up at 5.30 a.m. on Monday morning. The early flight from Stansted ruled out the usual train journey. The Ford Focus was just long enough to accommodate our bike boxes. We refuelled the car and left it with the hire company at the airport. A method we hadn't used before, but it worked a treat.

## Zadar to Pag (40 km)

We assembled our bikes at Zadar airport and set off early afternoon towards Pag. The island of Pag runs parallel to the main land and is a welcome escape from the busy mainland coast road. The surface is very barren comparable with the lunar appearance experienced at the top of Mount Ventoux. Our first night was at Simuni campsite on the island itself. We camped near the beach in an ideal spot. Unfortunately, the lack of fertile soil meant that it was impossible to secure a tent using normal tent pegs. The rocky surface made for a very hard bed for the night. The campsite was reasonably equipped with restaurants and bars. We settled down at a restaurant bar run by a German, called Sven, and his Spanish wife. Sven couldn't do enough for us – offering food and beer tailored to our taste. The draught beer took seven minutes to produce – why, I just don't know. Being a salesman, he managed to turn this negative feature into a positive. We managed to cope with this problem by ordering the beer well in advance.

# Pag to Selce (100 km)

We set off after a breakfast of sausage and scrambled eggs at Sven's place. We followed the island road to the ferry port at Novalja. The steep climbs and the heat made the going hard. Once on the mainland, we followed the coastal road north. Our journey was interrupted by some heavy rain and we only managed to get as far as the campsite at Selce. We pitched our tents on grass and took a short walk into town, where there were several places to eat and drink. Selce itself was touristy but a pleasant place – a good holiday base. The rain came down heavily all night and our walk back to the campsite involved dodging heavy downpours.

## Selce to Kozina (Slovenia) (100 km)

We followed the coast road to Rijeka where it became very busy. We left the coast and climbed into the mountainous countryside through Matulji, Rupa and the Slovenian border at Starod. I exchanged my remaining kuna for euros at the border and probably got robbed, but never mind.

Slovenia had a good feel to it. The road surface was good, the traffic was very light and the scenery was stunning in places – built for cycling. The lack of tourists however proved a drawback – no campsites. There were campsites but we never found them and had to settle for B&B. In a town called Kozina we found Hostel Kozina.

The hostel was a series of self-contained accommodation within a large old house. The price was a pleasant surprise – twenty euros each including breakfast was good value for money. It gave us an opportunity to wash and dry some kit, knowing it wasn't going to get wet again overnight. We were invited to help ourselves to the fruit growing in the garden. There was a pair of ladders leaning against a cherry tree and we duly obliged. The evening meal consisted of Pizza and Lasko (Slovian beer).

## Kozina to Lavariano (Italy) (90 km)

After breakfast, we got a history lesson from a resident who was a tour guide for the local caves in the area. He was proud of being Slovian and what had been achieved in his country. Apparently, Slovenia created a sizeable amount of the wealth of the old Yugoslavia considering its population of only two million people. He had a dislike for Croatians, and criticised them for exploiting tourists. He was correct – we had paid premium prices in Croatia, and it was about to get a lot worse when we crossed into Italy.

We headed towards Divaca Gorenje and then on the 204 towards Nova Gorica. That afternoon, we crossed the border into Italy. The roads got busier at Lucinico, heading on the 56 towards Udine. We turned off outside before Udine at Percot to escape the traffic. We eventually found a B&B at a town called Lavariano. As we searched for a B&B in Italy, our Slovenian tour guide's words were ringing true. Our B&B cost had doubled be it more lavish – but we were not looking for frills. To be fair, the accommodation was excellent. A collection of converted farm buildings – we were in what used to be the cow shed. In the evening pizza and beer, again the prices had doubled.

## Lavariano to Revine Lago (82 km)

We had breakfast in the dining room in the main building of the original house. The breakfast was a feast. I was nearly starting to think this was value-for-money.

We rode the flattish roads between the coast and the mountains passing through Morteglio, Talmassons, Flambo, Cordovano, Badmara, Cinto Caom, Pramagiori, and Congliano. We stopped at Tourist Information enquiring about a campsite. The nearest one was at Revine Largo in the mountainous area that had been on our right shoulder all day. We rode past Tarzo until we came across our campsite at Revine Lago. As the name suggests it was sited at the side of a lake. The place itself was a bit of an anti-climax compared to our last two nights of luxury. We ventured just outside the campsite to eat pasta dishes.

## Revine Lago to Semonzo (57 km)

The day started with heavy rain. We didn't get very far before we had to shelter in a café, we sat there soaked to the skin until midday. The locals were indulging in a couple of glasses of wine and then driving off in their cars – we just drank coffee. We stumbled towards Cison Di Valmareno and then Bassano Del Grappa sheltering occasionally when the rain became too heavy to ride. We managed less than fifty miles – probably one of the shortest-ever stages. A couple of miles north of Bassano Del Grappa we found the campsite at Semonzo. The small but well-equipped campsite was the best so far. We rode to the town and filled the panniers with food and wine and dined outside in true campsite fashion.

## Semonzo to Torbole (Lake Garda) (120 km)

It was Sunday, the roads were full of bikers on club-runs and some just on their own. We stopped for a D.I.Y. breakfast of cheese and ham and joined in with club-runs through Thiene, Schio and Roverto. We got onto a twenty-kilometre cycle track that took us into Lake Garda. The busy Tobole was not short of campsites. The campsite itself was overcrowded, with hardly enough washing and toilet facilities to go around, which meant queueing was inevitable.

At this time of year, Lake Garda is heaving with tourists and most of the restaurants and bars were packed. We sat in a restaurant waiting for our meals. I was hungry, tired and starting to get more and more pissed off. I was becoming desperate – ninety miles in the saddle and the beer was getting to me. After an hour only a starter had turned up. I repeatedly asked the waiter for our meal. I was more than pissed off; I losing it – the mist was starting to rise. When my head started to spin, I went outside for fresh air and kept walking. I had left Steve in the toilet – what was I thinking? I was joined by Steve and the waiter up the road. I returned to the restaurant to pay. I left not before telling him how bad his service was. He returned the insults by berating tourists – the very people he relied upon to survive. In retrospect, I was out of order, but chronic fatigue, alcohol and an empty stomach don't provide you with a lot of patience.

## Tobole to Lago D'Iseo (125 km)

We travelled by road to Riva Del Garda and then the hard work began. We had to take a mountain –bike track to avoid using the road which we were not allowed on. Riding fully-laden road bikes up a steep track wasn't easy. The track climbed up to Biacesa Di Ledros and then Lago Di Ledro. We had lunch at a supermarket take away at Storo.

We travelled onto Darzo, Lago D'Idro, NozzaCasto, Brozzo and Gardone Val Trompia. We turned right off the main road, climbing to Polveno – then onto Covelo and Lago D'Iseo. The campsite (Camping Sassabanek) on Lago D'Iseo was by far the best campsite and setting of not just this but any tour - it had it all. Besides good washing, toilet and dining facilities it had tennis courts, swimming pools and an area with tables and chairs to relax by a private lake. In the evening we dined at the restaurant on the campsite – which was all reasonably priced.

## Rest Day

We took the decision to spend another night on the campsite rather than try and get accommodation near the airport. We were only thirty miles from Bergamo and an early start the next day would see us make Bergamo airport easily (barring problems) by midday.

We decided to take advantage of the campsite swimming pool. Steve had brought two pairs of Speedos – a pair for each of us. For lunch, we cycled to the supermarket and filled our panniers with food and dined lakeside.

## Lago D'Iseo to Bergamo (48 km)

I was up early – about seven, a little nervous about making the airport. Unlike the ferry we can't arrive late and get the next one. We had breakfast at the campsite and we were off after nine. We followed the lake round and then headed for Bergamo signs. Our biggest obstacle was avoiding the motorway; it seemed all the roads to the airport were pulling us there. We got to Seriate and asked for directions at a news kiosk. An Italian motorbike rider took pity on us and guided us to the airport. At the airport we changed clothing and prepared for the journey home. We wheeled our bikes into our plastic bags, and sealed them with sellotape. I strapped both panniers together and we booked in without drama.

At East Midlands Airport, Jane arranged to pick me up in the car and Steve got a lift with his wife, and we made our separate ways home. Jane hadn't forgiven me fully for the holiday, but she was driving me home, rather than leaving me to make my own way back. I suppose that had to be considered progress.

# Tour 13 – Biarritz to Dinard

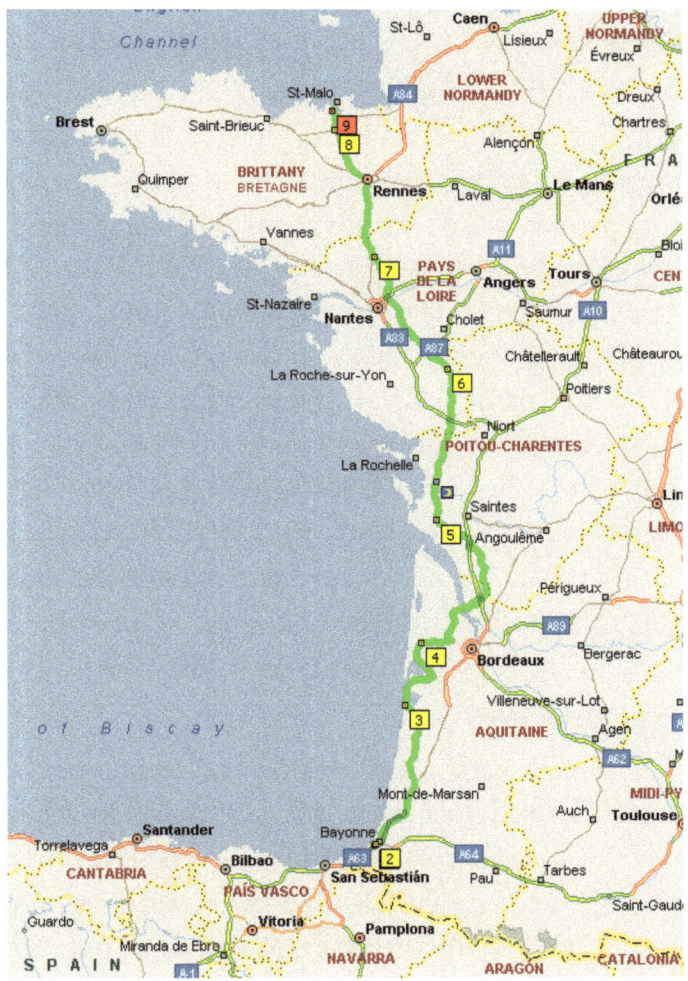

In 2012, the tour took a different format. Climbing some of the highest mountains in Europe and riding for two hundred kilometres a day was no longer possible or desirable. I found myself not going out on the bike if the weather wasn't good when, in the past, weather wasn't an issue. Also, the people, the likely suspects, had moved on. Kevin was no longer with us. Maurice and Steve had retired and could do what they wanted when they wanted. This tour was the third year with the tent. As expected, there wasn't very much interest when I looked for companions to join me on a cycling tour under canvas. Steve, last year's touring partner, wasn't totally happy with camping and I wasn't surprised when he had other plans for this year. That left Jimmy; who is usually allowed a touring pass on alternate years. Luckily, this year Jim was in. We decided on a flat tour, nothing too strenuous. I had read about the Atlantic coast cycle route (called the EV1) that stretches from Biarritz to Baule down the west coast of France. Most of the route is on wooded cycle paths that don't wander too far from the sea. We booked an EasyJet flight on Sunday 8th July, from East Midlands airport to Biarritz. We planned to fly back from Dinard on the north coast of France a week later.

My work situation was looking and feeling better in 2012 – once I moved on from MTL in October 2011. Since joining MTL in Jan 2011 I was never happy with the situation. Forty-three and a half hours per week - what was I thinking of? The strict regime and lack of flexible hours only added to a miserable working environment. On the plus side the work was quite interesting – I was designing jigs and tooling and had a fair amount of autonomy. The owner was something else – a different breed. He was a sixty-something Jewish workaholic who was at work from crack of dawn until supper-time and thought everybody was the same. It was also a very dour, miserable place. The owner had his favourites and the favoured tried all the political tricks to keep things that way. I kept my head down during the day. At dinner-time I chewed the fat with the receptionist. The rest of the workforce had their head glued to a computer screen for thirty minutes. I wasn't on my own in thinking this was an unfriendly environment. People who had worked elsewhere noticed the strange culture that existed and shared my opinion.

I enrolled with several agencies and attended several interviews in my quest to escape. It took me nine months to finally get away – thank you Michael Page. I joined Siemens as a Design Engineer in October 2011 and sincerely hoped job number thirty-six would be my last. The conditions were brilliant: flexible hours, the thirty-seven-hour week, showers and changing facilities and the money was alright as well. Siemens was situated on the Sheffield Airport site, quite close to where Jane and Nicola work, should I ever need a lift. As for the people, they were great – a good bunch of lads who enjoyed a bit of banter and didn't take themselves too seriously. Order book permitting, I saw myself staying there until retirement in 2018.

## Biarritz to Anglet (15 km)

The tour as always, didn't go strictly to plan – they never do. The Sunday we arrived, I had planned to do about thirty to forty miles from Biarritz. Instead we did a mere eight miles to the youth hostel at Anglet. I didn't plan to get away from the airport late and had forgotten to account for the hour you lose changing time zones. It was a busy hostel, but they managed to fit us in. At twenty-one euros, it was pretty good value. At least we ate well and had a good night's sleep.

## Anglet to Briscarrosse (136 km)

From Anglet, we had to head inland up the estuary, cross the bridge and head for Tarnos and then Capbreton, and Hossegar. We stopped for lunch in a small town called Leon. After dinner we rode through Vielle St Girons,

Mimizan and then Briscarosse. We made the mistake of booking the first campsite we came to when we were knackered. The price for two small tents was forty euros – almost as much as a youth hostel. He reduced it to thirty-five when we argued how small the tents were. The site itself had brilliant facilities (swimming pools, etc.) but unfortunately, nothing we would take full advantage of. We used one of their restaurants and chatted and exchanged adventures with an Irishman and his Spanish girlfriend. The Irishman had settled in Madrid, where he had met his girlfriend; they were also on a cycling holiday in France.

## Briscarosse to Le Porge (75 km)

We spent the day on cycle paths as we headed to Briscarosse Plage and then travelled parallel with the sea on our left shoulder. This was a more leisurely ride and a much- reduced speed. We had lunch at Arcachon, where the roads started to get busy around the basin until Audenge. From Audenge to Le Porge, we were back on cycle paths. We had a bit earlier finish as we found this municipal campsite only a kilometre from the beach. It was a two-star site that was a mere eight euros – ideal for our needs. A walk to the beach and we had a choice of restaurants.

## Le Porge to Le Gua / Cadeul (181 km)

The day began with more cycle paths and we stopped at Lacanau for lunch. We enjoyed our last bit of sea, sun and cycle-paths riding through Hourtin, Grayan et Hopital and Soulac Sur Mer. We pushed on to Verdon Sur Mer to catch the 16.30 p.m. ferry to Royan. At Royan, we lost our way a bit – the roads became busy around seaside resorts. We endured fast traffic-laden roads past Le Gua on the road to Cadeul. We were about twenty kilometres south of Rochefort. Eventually, we found a campsite on the road that was very good. We had a lakeside pitch, which was guaranteed mosquito-free. It turned out to be true. The campsite was a bit of an institution. As we arrived, an aerobics class was in full flow. We dined there and the meals were very good. Later on in the evening they had a rock band on that was also excellent. They sang English rock ballads and cavorted around the stage and I really was impressed. We talked to an English guy and his wife who had been coming back to this site for many years because he enjoyed it so much.

## Le Gua to Pouzauges (160 km)

At this point, we were down on schedule. We had covered the mileage, but the cycle-paths had been misleading. We needed a couple of hundred-mile days to get us back on track. Today was to be one of them. We headed in a straight line towards our destination rather than following coastal tracks. We hammered on through Saint Agnant, Tonnay Charante, and stopped at Aigrefeulle D'Aunis for lunch. We travelled past Fontenay Le Comte and made our last stop at Pissotte. Our hundred miles took us to Pouzauges and a mile or so after was a lake and a campsite. The campsite was a bit of a disappointment – probably more to Jimmy than it was to me, in its facilities. The owner was English and had a hard luck tale, which was easy to sympathise with. He had moved to France when his daughter was ill with a complaint that he thought would benefit from the better climate. She had died the year before year and this left him and his wife to battle on regardless with their campsite venture. He cooked us a microwave meal which was cheap enough but was probably the worst that I have experienced - not just on this holiday but any holiday. Jimmy found it hard to hide his displeasure, but I didn't have the heart or the strength to leave it and walk the mile up the valley into the town. We later chewed the fat with another traveller who knew better and had dined in the town and had come back to have a few beers. Obviously bottled beer is something that he couldn't spoil. He told us a few tales of his travels as the rain poured down. In the morning he decided to stay another day as the rain was so heavy. For Jimmy and I, that wasn't an option as we needed to get to the airport on time.

## Pouzauges to Nozay (130 km)

We headed out of Pouzauges towards Les Herbiers in a north westerly direction. The rain was still torrential and made riding conditions difficult. We lost time when Jimmy and I lost each other going through a town. I stopped to check the map whilst Jimmy pottered on before pulling in at a shop. I went past him, thinking he was in front when in fact he was behind. It only added up to more frustration as the rain continued to pour. When we eventually regrouped, we stopped at Clisson for lunch and sheltered from the rain, knowing that the day would not after all be high mileage. We headed in the direction of Nantes but not wanting to go there. We crossed the Loire at Les Bout des Pont, about ten kilometres east of Nantes, where we crossed into Thouare Sur Loire. We travelled north to Nozay to clock up eighty miles – which wasn't too bad considering the circumstances. At Nozay, we found the luxury of a chamber d'hôte far too tempting to resist. For twenty-five euros, we had a chance to dry our gear and a dry bed for the night.

## Nozay to Dinan (118 km)

As we headed out of Nozay on the last big mileage day of our tour, we had travelled ten miles before we realised, we were going in the wrong direction. Brittany isn't blessed with brilliant road signs. On the main roads, there is no problem and car drivers have the benefit of good wide empty roads. The minor roads are poorly signed – if at all. We looked for places that didn't exist and there were signs for places we couldn't find on the map. We needed Marsac and the Gemene Penfao without hitting the Route Nationale or the motorway. We eventually got on track through Pipriac (where the road was closed due to Bastille day), Pleian Legrand, Paimpont and St Maugmn; then Becherel and Dinan. The youth hostel at Dinan was a nightmare to find, and when we had, we wished we hadn't bothered. There were few facilities beyond a bed in very nice surroundings. The people who ran the place were away on holiday. Some of the inmates sorted us out with a bed and we left the money with them. Dinan, however, wasn't short of good restaurants. A five-minute walk and we were into the heart of this popular tourist town. We ate probably the best meal of the holiday – a contrast to the night before.

## Dinan to Dinard Airport (25 km)

From Dinan to Dinard is only about fifteen miles. The last thing you want is a long ride to the airport on the day of your flight. The airport, we discovered, is not in Dinard but in a small place called Pleurtuit. It pays to give yourself loads of time on the day of the flight and find the airport first then explore the surrounding area after if you don't want to spend your time there. These small airports don't provide much in the way of facilities so we left our arrival there as late as possible. Everything went to plan packing the bike away in the plastic bags. It was a new experience for Jimmy and like the first time I presented a bike in a plastic bag, he was a little apprehensive.

The ride home from East Midlands airport wasn't an enjoyable one. Unlike small French airports, there weren't any minor roads. There was a cycle-track but it didn't seem to travel in the direction we wanted. We headed for Derby as opposed to Nottingham and ended up on the busy A50 – what a nightmare. Just before Derby, a motorcyclist suggested quite strongly that we shouldn't be on this busy road and asked why we weren't using the cycle-ways. We asked directions and cycled in that direction and finally got off the road. It felt like a long time before we finally got through Derby and to some more familiar roads.

When I parted company with Jimmy at Dronfield, we had covered six hundred and forty miles in the week. Not a bad effort for two almost pensioners.

# Tour 14 – Limoge to Carcassonne

In 2013, I turned sixty. I wanted to do something special and planned to take my son, Matthew, if he wanted to come. Matthew borrowed one of my bikes and started doing some cycling in 2012 with the intention of getting himself fit enough to tour. At first, he struggled but got stronger with every ride. During the winter months he took to running to improve his core fitness. He started running home and before long, I found it difficult to keep up as he matured into a very good runner.

At Christmas, Matthew announced his engagement to Amy, his girlfriend and early in 2013 told me I would be a granddad in August. He had made known his intentions to go with me on a bike tour, but now the timing was critical. It would have to be no later than June. The race was on to try and get a bike and equipment ready. I had no idea where or how far to go. The tour would be like all the others no doubt – booked at the last minute and without much attention to detail. If the bikes are ready, we would pick a place at random and just go with the flow – that's just how I like it.

As with most plans, things go wrong. I came off my bike at the end of March and broke three ribs and dislocated my shoulder. I was off the bike a couple of months while the ribs healed. The pain and discomfort of broken ribs has to be endured to be believed. The ribs eventually got better, but the shoulder didn't. If I was to get on my bike for a tour it would be July at the earliest. It would definitely be too late for Matthew. He wouldn't want to be somewhere else when his first child was born. I blamed myself for the accident, but perhaps it wasn't to be.

I received an operation date in October for my shoulder. I was in a bit of discomfort, but nothing was stopping me from riding a bike, be it far from my best. I had a holiday in Corfu to recover with Jane in April. It was a leisurely holiday with a lot of sunbathing and reading.

That is all I could manage. I was on Tramadol strong painkillers, which left me with very little energy. I had another holiday in Spain in May with Matthew and Amy. By then, I was feeling more like myself. I was managing a run in the morning as I regained my strength. I had thoughts of a cycle tour in July, but it would have to be far more leisurely than anything I have done in the past. I didn't have the fitness I had in previous years due to missing time off the bike. Also, I had very little strength in my shoulder, which meant I might have to modify my riding style and avoid pulling heavily on the handlebars.

This cycling tour was something new – a holiday rather than a war of attrition or an endurance test. I worked everything out in kilometres rather than miles. A tour based on a maximum of a hundred kilometres a day rather than the hundred miles per day of previous tours. Also, I planned a circular route rather than an out and home journey by the shortest route. This way we were under no pressure to maintain a schedule as we could cut short or lengthen the route as we felt fit. I provisionally planned a route from Limoge in central France to Narbonne Plage on the south coast and then on to Carcassonne in the south west, where we would fly back from. If I wasn't up to the task, I would take a more direct route straight to Carcassonne. Jimmy was coming with me and I was a bit fearful that he might find the route a little tame for his liking.

# Limoge to St Yrieix la Perche (50 km)

We arrived in Limoge on the mid-day flight from East Midlands Airport and we were welcomed by boiling hot weather. By the time we had set the bikes up and were ready to roll it was 4.00 p.m. – we lost an hour due to British summer time.

Getting out of Limoge airport and finding our way was simple compared to busier airports like Bordeaux, for example. We turned out of the airport and the road we wanted was in front of us, a very straightforward ride to the first stop. The short 50 km ride had Jimmy struggling to maintain a reasonable pace – which he put down to the travelling and the intense heat.

The campsite at St Yrieix La Perche was just before we got to the village at a big lake. There was water-sport activity going off around the lake, which looked inviting to two weary cyclists. We pitched the tents. Jimmy hadn't improved his tent erecting skills from last year. It still took him ages and after what seemed like hours, we dined at the restaurant on site. The food was OK but not as good as the restaurant staff thought it was. They were frying a few strawberries in a pan of alcohol and charging ten and a half euros. We decided it was a delicacy we could manage without.

## St Yrieix to Martel (88 km)

The very hot weather continued to be a feature of this tour, making our progress slow. We rode through Beyssenac, Juliac, Objat, Varetz, and Cressensac. We got lost a bit between Objat and Varetz as we tried to avoid the major roads. Finally, we stopped for a coffee and enquired about campsites. The small site at Martel was recommended and it was very good. It was a hundred yards from the town and was cheap. The meal in Martel wasn't particularly cheap though as it was designed for tourists. We had a drink with a fellow traveller who was recently divorced and was celebrating by riding around France for several weeks. The guy was from Bath (a plumber ironically) and he had been divorced from a millionaire's daughter and was walking away (riding away in his case) with a considerable sum of money.

## Martel to Limogne en Quercy (52km)

We took a slight detour and rode to the spectacular Rocamadour. I'd been before, but Jimmy hadn't. We had a bit of climbing to do on minor roads to get on track. We ran out of water and had to ask a local if he could fill up our bottles. Losing fluid was becoming a big problem. Once we hit a major road, we stopped at a trucker's café for drinks. We headed through Livernon, Brengues, and stopped at Carjac for what was probably the best meal of the tour. It was only a French version of a Spanish omelette, but it was excellent. We picked up a booklet on campsites in the area and then went off in pursuit of one.

The campsite we found was cheap and had free access to an adjoining swimming pool. I took advantage of the pool to cool off. The town was a ten-minute walk away. The only restaurant which was open served cordon bleu food that was more visually pleasing than filling – pretty useless for this hungry cyclist at least. Later on, we found an open-air theatre that was staging a version (I think) of the Hunchback of Notre Dame. We did find a bar later which served more suitable meals, but it was too late. We had already been fleeced.

## Limogne En Quercy to Realmont (100 km)

We used minor roads to Vidaillac D24, then Puylagarde on the D97. After this, we took the D33 to Parisot and Cornusson. We picked up the D600 through Corde Sur Siel and then Albi. We had lunch at Albi amongst the many cafés on the cobbled streets near the massive cathedral. We had stayed there twelve years ago on route to Serignan. As I remember from the previous tour, the youth hostel is probably the worst youth hostel I had experienced – it seemed a shame in such a beautiful city. We picked up some accommodation brochures from the Office de Tourisme and headed off to Realmont via Oulan Pouzol and Combers.

The campsite was two kilometres from the town of Realmont. It meant using the bikes for a ride into town for a meal and a drink. The meal was up there with the Spanish omelette at Carjac. We kept alcohol consumption to a minimum and bought a bottle of wine from the supermarket. Wine somehow doesn't taste the same out of plastic drinking bottles. During the night we experienced the only rain of the whole holiday.

## Realmont to St Pons de Thomieres (75 km)

We followed minor roads through Finotes, Venes, and Roquecourbe to Castres. Castres proved a difficult town to get through. It was a series of cycle lanes and dual-carriageways. We headed for Mazamet where we luckily stumbled across a bike trail that we followed for 35km. The trail was a real bonus because the main road was steep and laden with big lorries. The trail was an old railway line that climbed gradually rather than steeply like the road – which came into view regularly.

The campsite was a privately run one that was expensive for what it was. It had the benefit of a restaurant and a swimming pool on the site. The restaurant was adequate, and the food wasn't up to much. We were too tired to venture off the site and find anything better.

# St Pons de Thomieres to Narbonne Plage (70 km)

The first part of the morning we were climbing gradually on the D907 through Condades and to Ste Colombe. We descended through the small towns of Agues–Vives and Marcorignan until we arrived at the very large city of Narbonne. I thought Narbonne Plage would only be a few kilometres away. In reality we still had a few more hills to climb before our destination. By the time we got there, we had run out of water and Jimmy was suffering for it. We found the municipal campsite about a few hundred metres from the beach and shops. The short day in the saddle meant we had dinner on the coast, followed by a swim in the sea. In the evening, we had moules et frites – my favourite coastal meal.

## Narbonne Plage to Carcassonne (120 km)

We found a route to Narbonne that didn't involve the climbing we had encountered on our arrival. We headed down the coast to Gruissan (D332) and then Ricardelle. It was a case of avoiding the major roads to Carcassonne. We went through Nevian D607 and stopped for breakfast. We then followed the D6113 all the way through Lezignan Corbiere until we arrived at La Cite – the old town part of Carcassonne. We had a tour round the old town and located the whereabouts of the campsite, which was only a few hundred metres away. The campsite was well equipped, with a swimming pool and more. We set up camp, had a swim and then headed to La Cite for the evening.

## Carcassonne to Dronfield

We had packed everything and we were ready to roll by 7.00 a.m. From our map, we could we had a 15km ride to the airport, which was on the outskirts of town. We gave ourselves plenty of time to allow for things to go wrong and we reached the airport within forty-five minutes. We were the first there. Only Ryanair flew from Carcassonne and there were two flights, both departed around 10.00 a.m. – our flight and one to Holland. By the time the bikes were packed, the tiny airport was full.

We took a different route back from East Midlands airport and it turned out to be a more pleasant journey than last year. We turned right out of the airport and headed for Castle Donnington. After that, we rode to Derby through Shardlow. From Derby, we used the more scenic A61 through Belper, Ambergate and Matlock. Baslow Hill was climbed at a sedate six miles per hour as the energy levels dropped. We afforded ourselves a couple of well-earned pints of beer in the Rutland at Holmesfield before getting back home.

Matthew's son Elliot was born two days after I returned from touring. In the end, he could have come with us, but he would have been unwise to take that gamble.

I had a shoulder operation in October, which appeared to be a success. I was then faced with a three-month layoff from the bike. This will not be a big problem as December, and January are not the best months for riding a bike.

I had six weeks off work to recover from the operation. As for future touring adventures, who knows? I have found plans nearly always go wrong, so I don't waste too much time doing it. Most importantly, never put off doing anything you want to do until a later date, or it will never happen.

# Tour 15 – Milan to Dronfield

In 2014 I probably did one of my hardest tours ever. It only goes to show that you don't always get wiser as you get older. It would have been a daunting task for a cyclist half my age and definitely not one for a sixty-one-year-old recovering from injury.

I was keen to regain my fitness as early as possible after surgery. As soon as I got the green light from the physio, I was running and cycling again, even if it was not as fast as I would have liked. By March, I was getting back to where I wanted to be fitness wise and I was well up for a cycling tour. My companion from last year, Jimmy had made plans for a cycling holiday in Majorca so I couldn't count on his company. Luckily, I still kept in touch with Steve Worthy from the Fire Brigade.

On a night out in Sheffield with two of my ex-fire brigade mates, Steve Worthy and Adrian Robinson, a plan was hatched to ride from Milan back home an estimated nine hundred miles. I didn't know at the time, but this was probably my last tour of this magnitude. It is far too easy to commit to something when the beer is flowing freely. When I look back on this tour it is not one that I have fond memories of. The overriding memory is of being cold, wet and suffering severe exhaustion. Also, these conditions contributed to tetchiness, probably on a level not experienced on a tour before. The result being I made very few notes of the journey and took very few photos, thus the brevity of what I can recall. My energy was focussed on surviving what was a very hard tour. For once, and to my regret, I took too little clothing. It may have been an overcompensation from other years when I had taken more than needed.

## Bergamo to Lecco (40 km)

I travelled with Adrian down to East Midlands with a relative who had a large SUV type capable of carrying our large bike boxes and ourselves. We met Steve at the airport and we boarded our flight for Milan. The flight was in the afternoon and it didn't give us much time for cycling any reasonable distance.

The first leg was to get somewhere to camp for the night. The drive down to the airport, the Ryanair flight and the bike assembly took its toll on our energy levels. The weather was cold and wet, which was uncharacteristic for this time of year. We camped at the side of Lake Como and the rain continued all night.

# Lecco to Splugen (104 km)

In the morning, we were met by heavy rain as we headed up towards Bellagio. At Bellagio, we lost a couple of hours as the ferry we required to Verena didn't materialise. This was very frustrating as we had only cycled 40 km and it was almost mid-day. Eventually, we crossed the river and headed for the Splugen Pass. Nothing could have prepared us for the severity of this climb. The climb twisted in switchback turns, which seemed to go on forever.

On the lower stretchers of the climb, Aide and I took photos and an impatient Steve kept going. We must have easily lost five or ten minutes just stopping to admire the views. We made an effort to catch our companion and in doing so, we started to suffer – Aide in particular. We stopped for food as the dreaded bonk took hold. The closer we got to the summit the colder it became and harder the gradient. We asked a local how far to the top and he told us twenty kilometres – our morale sank. We were in trouble, but our only instinct was to keep going regardless. The road came back on itself many times and the speed dropped as we tried to maintain momentum.

About six kilometres from the summit, a familiar bike was leaning up against a wall outside a hotel that was set back from the road – luckily, I spotted it. Inside the hotel Steve was already into the beer and had warned the owner of our imminent arrival. We ate and drank, even better, as we reflected on what was probably the hardest days on a

248

bike we had experienced in a long time. I was still shivering from exhaustion and found it hard to keep warm. The next day, we still had another six kilometres of hard climbing to reach the summit.

## Splugen to Rapperswil (135 km)

We looked out at the mist-covered mountains and headed out with trepidation. The scenery was spectacular all the way to the summit. We reached the Summit of the Splugen Pass and couldn't believe how cold it was for July. Ice was on the river that flowed down the mountain. Alarm bells rang. I had insufficient clothing for this tour. In the attempt to keep the weight down I had made bad decisions on what to bring along. I was mad at myself for not researching the route and being unprepared for what we encountered.

We descended the other side of the mountain into Splugen itself. We continued on flat terrain through Chur, Sargans and onto the youth Hostel at Rapperswil. The rain continued to be a feature of this tour and the low temperature made for miserable riding conditions. The most memorable part of the day was getting a police escort to the youth hostel when we asked a policeman for directions. Fortunately, the policeman was a cyclist himself and felt sorry for three lost, rain-sodden cyclists.

## Rapperswil YH to Schulsee YH (73 km)

We left the youth hostel and followed the road parallel to Lake Zurich all the way into the city itself. I remember not being impressed by Zurich. It was a lot of busy streets and trams. Steve almost became a casualty, skidding on the tramlines made greasy by the rain. We headed north towards Waldshut on the Swiss-German border. The weather continued to be wet and cold. A night under canvas was not an option; it had to be somewhere warm and dry. We had been cycling in the cold and wet all day.

This was becoming a tour to forget. We headed for Hausern and then Schulsee Youth Hostel.

The dormitory on offer had only two beds with the provision for one person to sleep on the floor. We had no choice but to take it. Steve threw his gear on one of the two beds and announced his intention as to his sleeping arrangements. Normally, this wouldn't have been a problem, but in the frame of mind I was in, it was. I wasn't bothered about sleeping on the floor – I was opposed to the idea that Steve assumed he wasn't. My back was up and I let him know it. I was open to tossing a coin or whatever.

The situation caused a lot of bad feelings. Adrian, to his credit, remained impartial. It resulted in Steve sleeping on the floor, which made me feel awkward. I think this situation wouldn't have arisen under normal circumstances. For an hour or so, a strained silence created an uncomfortable atmosphere.

Schulsee was a tourist place with another lake-side position. We had a mile bike ride into town for an evening of beer and pizza. After a few beers the arguments about the sleeping arrangements had been put to bed.

## Schulsee to Ville (138 km)

We had just the night in Germany. We went through Frieberg and Reigal as we headed out of Germany into France. The weather improved and we considered camping for only the second night of our journey. Camping Le Giessen near a place called Ville was a typical French campsite, outdoor barbeques and plenty of beer and wine. This would be our last day in the flat; the next day, it would become a bit lumpy. By this time, I had bought a jumper at a supermarket to combat the cold weather. It was perhaps a little late as the very cold weather conditions were behind us.

## Ville to St Avold (127 km)

This was a tough day in the saddle. The climbs were not mountainous, like the Pyrenees, but they were hard going. The col du Dunon was a hard climb without panniers, with panniers it was exhausting. The day comprised of hard climbs, forests and minor roads. The campsite was a mile outside St Avold on a hillside. The campsite had no eating facilities, so we walked back into town to eat. The World Cup was on in a bar, but I was too exhausted to stay awake, much to the amusement of my companions. I spent the night in the bar asleep, unable to function. My body was telling me I had done too much, but unfortunately there were many more miles in front of us.

## St Avold to Marville (119 km)

The scenery on this stage was typically small French villages and rolling countryside. We got lost occasionally, which was not unusual. The rolling hills were taking their toll on Steve as he started to suffer, dropping off the pace on the climbs. The weather, at last, was starting to pick up after riding mostly through rain for the majority of the tour. At Marville, we opted for a two-star hotel. It was only a small place and we didn't have the strength to ride further in search of a campsite. The hotel had a restaurant and a television to watch the World Cup again. It wasn't long before I was asleep – pint in hand. The last few days, we had clocked up big mileage, making up for a slow start due to the bad weather. We were now nearly a full day ahead of schedule and would be going back a day early unless we hit problems.

## Marville to Chimay (125 km)

As we headed into Belgium, we still maintained a good pace. We flitted from France into Belgium and back again. We were now spending time on a cycleway characteristic of this area. I didn't realise until we arrived in Chimay what the town was famous for. Chimay Brewery is located in Scourmont Abbey, a Trappist monastery in southern Hainaut, Belgium. It is only one of the eleven breweries worldwide that produce Trappist beers. We set up camp on a site just outside the main centre and walked into the main part of the town. We sampled very strong premium beers and paid premium prices. Chimay Red, Blue and Gold labels are all different strengths and tastes, but all very good beer. They were probably the best I tasted – even upstaging Leffe which up to now had been my favourite beer. Unfortunately, the price limits how much you can drink of the stuff. On holiday it is ok to make an exception, but not on a regular basis.

## Chimay to Ronse (103 km)

Travelling from Chimay to Ronse, we took a northwesterly route, flitting from Belgium to France and back again. To add to the confusion, towns have two names one in Flemish and one in French.

We broke our journey, stopping at the half way point at Mons or Bergen, depending on what side of the fence you sit. In the centre of Mons, there is a large square where people sit, and chat – usually outside in cafes drinking beer or coffee. Mons has been branded as the cultural capital of the world so, as you would suspect, nothing is cheap. My companions opted to queue at a nearby McDonalds to save money on a coffee – something I felt was more than a little pathetic but for some reason, I went along with peer pressure. Afterwards, I couldn't resist calling Steve a tight bastard – which didn't go down well.

We carried on to Ronse which was approximately a hundred kilometre from the ferry port of Zeebrugge. This is what we felt was a comfortable distance to ride on the last day to allow a little time in Brugge en route. The youth hostel at Ronse was called 'De Fiertel' and was situated about five kilometres from the centre of Ronse in a secluded wooded area to the north of the town. The hostel was a large modern building with plenty of glass and great views of the surrounding area. The guy who ran it, Frank, had a well-stocked fridge full of beer but couldn't provide food. We set off back into town on the bikes to search for food to take back. We found what I thought was a Moroccan supermarket that sold everything we needed to produce a good meal. We made a massive amount of salad accompanied by meats and cheese. We even had some weird-looking deserts that were washed down with reasonably priced beer provided by Frank's fridge.

## Ronse to Zeebrugge (100 km)

The roads north of Ronse tend to head to Ghent, which we wanted to avoid. We used the minor roads travelling towards Brugge, where we arrived just after mid-day. Brugge is a nice place to visit apart from having to put up with the massive amount of tourists which I suppose we are classed as too. We stayed on the outskirts this time as we had exhausted the centre on previous visits and ate lunch.

Steve had a route planned that would avoid the main route from Brugge to Zeebrugge. I was a little sceptical as usually these detours more than double the travelling time as a rule. On this occasion, the journey along cycle-ways and paths turned out to be a worthwhile diversion. The busy dual carriageway was replaced by canals and beautiful scenery. Once in Zeebrugge the journey to the actual ferry port wasn't so good. The route we chose wasn't at all bike-friendly and it seemed to take ages to arrive at the port.

Finally, at the check-in we were dealt a harsh lesson. What we expected to pay as a small administration charge for changing our day of sailing turned out to be a very large proportion of our fare. I think it was another eighty euros between us. This eroded any benefit we had gained from our early booking.

# Hull to Dronfield (130 km)

As opposed to the rest of our tour, we rode home in very hot weather. The journey from the ferry port to the Humber Bridge is the worst part of the journey. At Scunthorpe, we parted company with Steve. Adrian and I headed for Rotherham and then onto Dronfield. The Rotherham detour for me added a bit of mileage but I was glad of the company on a very hard journey home. I have done this journey a few times now and each time, the memory erases just how hard it is with a fully laden bike.

Looking back, the tour was too hard. The total mileage was about 880 miles. I was probably the strongest in the saddle in the daytime. I certainly suffered most once I had stopped pedalling and was overcome by exhaustion. I had used every ounce of strength and energy during the day and didn't have the tiniest bit of strength for anything other than sleep. It was a trick honed from my racing days, any energy not used up during a race was a waste. To arrive at the finish line totally and utterly spent was what I aspired to. I think it affected the others in different ways. Steve became a bit prickly. He responded badly to a bit of banter when, on other occasions, it wouldn't have affected him. We did have a few differences of opinion where he took exception to comments. Adrian was probably the least affected, but then he was only fifty years old. He would recover quicker and adapt better to the pressure we exerted on our fragile bodies.

Lessons were learnt the hard way. It may be unwise to take too much clothing, but it is stupid and dangerous to take too little. I had become paranoid about taking too much equipment. The bad weather totally caught me out, so instead of enjoying the tour I was made miserable by the wet and cold. Looking back, it was hard to comprehend what I was thinking.

# Tour 16 – Belgium

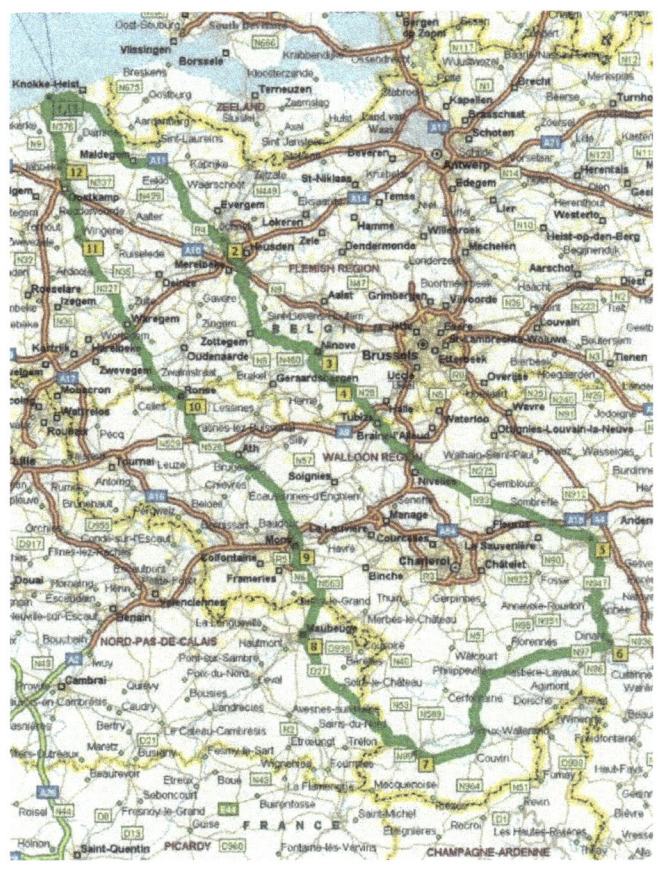

In late 2014, I took an enforced break from cycling. It was mid-December on a dark, quiet road. A driver cut a corner and obviously hadn't seen me despite my bright clothing and lights. My beloved Kevin Winter, with the now famed Penguin logo, was in a bad way. I had used it for commuting for the last few years. It lay on the garage floor, waiting for the insurance company to assess. For the dark winter months, I commuted to work like all the other workers in their cars. My son Matthew had moved to Dronfield and I got a lift so far and walked the extra four miles to compensate for the exercise I was missing.

When spring arrived, I started riding the bike again. My enthusiasm returned and I was again looking forward to taking some sort of holiday on the bike, but perhaps nothing like my past exploits. My son bought a fold-up bike and started commuting to work. It wasn't long before he was riding strong and we discussed touring in Scotland for a few days. I was short of a bike after the crash, so a trip to the bike shop was required to braze on some pannier bosses onto an old mountain bike and after a well overdue re-spray, we were ready to roll. Matthew was using my second-hand tourer which I had bought off eBay. It was the bike I had used for the Milan trip the previous year. It was an old-fashioned tourer with loads of clearance for big tyres and subsequently weighed in a lot heavier than the Kevin Winter. We had a tight window as Amy – Matthew's partner, was expecting their second child and was due in late August. The end of July was the latest we could go. The tour nearly didn't happen. Reputations die hard and convincing people that things are going to change is difficult. My son was having second thoughts - he had heard stories from the past of hard days in the saddle and when my touring partner Jimmy was mentioned, Matthew backed off. I had a little persuading to do. I assured him that the hard-core tours were over – for the time being. I explained to Jimmy that the Scotland trip was a father and son affair and arranged to go with him later in the year, if that was something he wanted to do.

I chose Scotland for its wide-open spaces and lack of traffic. Unfortunately, Scotland has a reputation for poor weather and it didn't disappoint. The weather had been the main reason my tours had been abroad and this will continue to be the case. However, for a few days of trial for a novice like Matthew, it would be fine. If anything should happen and we needed to get home quickly, we wouldn't have to catch a plane. We drove up to Inverness and parked the car at the Youth hostel there. We rode from Inverness across to the west coast. It was a hard sixty miles as the wind and rain were in our faces whole the way. I had pre-booked three youth hostels, Inverness, Torridon and Gairloch. I wasn't taking any chances of not finding anywhere to stay. I didn't entertain the idea of taking a tent. This was to be a holiday, not an endurance test. I couldn't contemplate putting my son through what I had done – I was hoping maybe, if things went well, we would be going again together. The first day to Torridon was by far the hardest. On the second day riding up to Gairloch was easy and the youth hostel was a small and very friendly place. Riding back to Inverness was eighty miles, but with a tailwind and Matthew managed the distance with ease. It was a very easy tour without drama and hopefully it will happen again – somewhere where the weather is better.

As for the tour with Jimmy – it did materialise. The plan – if you can call it that, was to see as much of Belgium as we could in the week we had.

## Dronfield to Hull (130 km)

We rode the eighty miles from Sheffield to Hull and caught the ferry to Zeebrugge. I rode to Jimmy's house and an old racing buddy of ours Stuart Wales was riding part way with us. We gave ourselves the full day to ride the eighty miles to Hull ferry port. We parted company with Stuart at Blyth after about thirty miles. We crossed the Humber bridge and found a quiet road up to the ferry port. We arrived early in the afternoon in plenty of time for an 18.30 departure.

## Zeebrugge to Oetingen (115 km)

From the Ferry port, we headed towards Ghent – passing through wasn't easy, as it never is with all cities. We headed south easterly on a route which would avoid Brussels at all costs. We went through Aalst and Ninove, stopping to find a B&B at Oetingen. The accommodation was excellent, although a little more expensive than we were looking to spend. However, after covering 115 kilometres, we were running out of options.

## Oetingen to Dinant (106 km)

We headed to Namur. Namur is a very grandiose place with splendid architecture and more importantly, the start of the Meuse de Velo. Riding alongside the river down to Dinnat is probably the highlight of the tour – it really is very picturesque. Dinnat is quite a place with its La Citadelle and the famous saxophone bridge. The bridge is lined on both sides with massive saxophones in honour of the man who invented the instrument. We camped on the riverside at a campsite about a mile out of Dinant. During the night I could hear the trains that clattered by. I hadn't realised how close we were to the train line.

## Dinant to Maubeuge (105 km)

We were now on the most eastern part of our tour and we started to head back via a different route. After talking with a local, we were told about the Ravels, which were old railway lines that had been converted to cycle tracks. We managed to use some of the tracks on our return journey. We passed through Chimay, one of my favourite stops in past tours. Chimay is famous for its very strong beer, but unfortunately, there was no overnight stop to sample some of its brews. We travelled back through southern Belgium to our campsite stop was actually just over the border in France. We cycled into Maubeuge centre to eat some Turkish food and cycled back to our tents, a bit pissed.

## Maubeuge to Wingene (122 km)

From Maubeuge, we headed north west and passed through Mons or Bergen – depending on which country you are from. I had been through these places on my tour back from Milan with Aidrian and Steve in 2014. It was new to Jimmy, so we spent time in Mons, which is an impressive place. We headed for Ronse and the youth hostel I had stayed at on the Milan trip. This time, we had to push on and find somewhere nearer Brugge. A bad decision in hindsight, as accommodation was thin on the ground.

As the light was fading, we asked an elderly-women on an electric bike coming back from her shopping trip if there was anywhere nearby where we could get a bed for the night. She turned out to be our saviour. She took us through the back lanes as we pedalled hard to hold her wheel. The B&B place she had in mind was deserted. Undaunted, she led her back to her house, a very modern, large place on a well- to-do estate. She initially offered to put us up for the night but we could tell by his body language her husband wasn't keen on the idea. We weren't happy causing her that sort of inconvenience after what she had done to help us. After consulting the Belgium equivalent of the Yellow Pages, she located a B&B, but not before Jimmy and I had enjoyed some fish and chips at the local shop/restaurant. She then took us to the B&B, with Jimmy and I tucked on the back wheel of her electric bike. Luckily, it was only a couple of miles away. We thanked her and took a few photos of this very generous and wonderful human. She had put herself out for us, and without her, we may have been sleeping in a gutter. I put Wingene as our destination, and it was somewhere around there, but our exact location was much more vague!

## Wingene to Brugge (25 km)

The B&B was excellent and the women gave us local maps of the area so we could find our way back to Brugge quite easily. We only had 20 km to do, so we arrived at Brugge by mid-day with plenty of time to explore. I had been to Brugge a few times before but still found new things to fill the time.

## Brugge to Zeebrugge (18 km)

It's about 18 km to the ferry port. We booked on-board waiting with the bikes and motorbikes to embark. The overnight ferry docked at about 8.00 a.m. the next morning. I would usually ride the eighty miles back to Dronfield. This time, however, was different; the Blades were playing at home and I fancied getting back for the game. Jimmy and I shot off to the railway station and took the train back to Sheffield, thus enabling me to get back home in plenty of time for kick-off.

The total for the tour was logged at 383 miles, but with a few detours and the ravels (old railway lines) we used, which I couldn't measure on the map, the total was probably nearer 400 miles.

# Tour 17 - Bergerac to Dinard

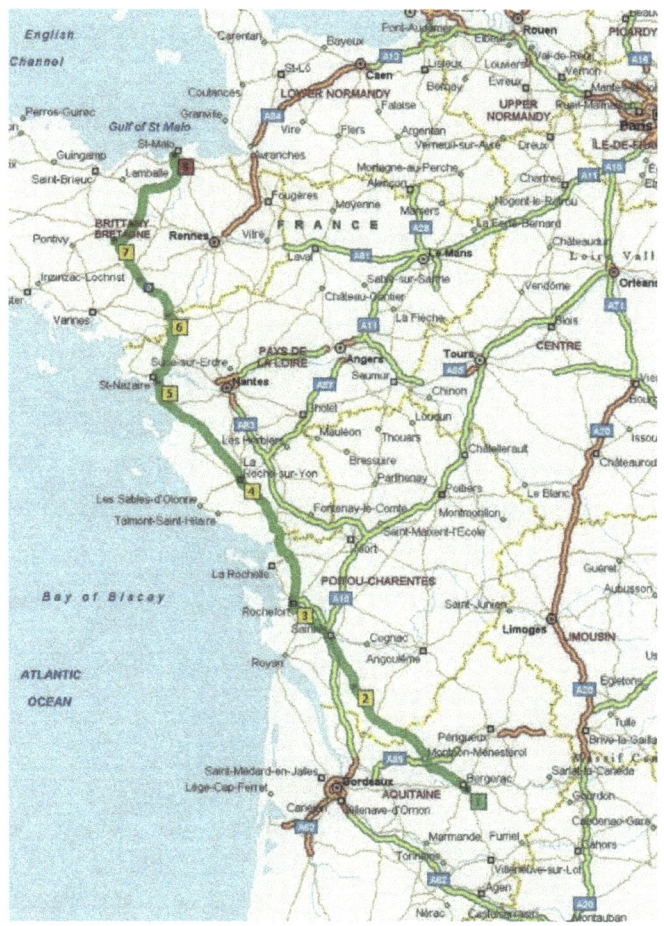

Since at least as far back as 2012, I had been suffering with a bunion, which was getting worse. Surgery was required, but it was never the right time, even though wearing cycling shoes was very painful. Now, however, I decided the time had come to get it sorted. I had the surgery in March and stayed off work for ten weeks with a large air boot on my foot. and was able to do nothing but hobble about and lost my fitness. I did manage to get to work occasionally when my wife or daughter would drive.

When I was given the green light to start light exercise, I didn't waste time getting on a bike. I bought a pair of Shimano sandals with cycling cleats, that allowed me to cycle pain-free until my foot was healed, much to the amusement of my cycling buddies. The return to some sort of fitness was a long and painful process and it was August that year before I was back to a level that would allow me to tour.

In the middle of September, I was on a plane with my son for a tour in France. The old Kevin Winter tourer was up and running, with a new pair of forks and wheels and became Matthew's tourer, after The Insurance company paid out. He borrowed a tent from his future father-in-law. It was a Vango Banshee (an excellent tent) acquired from free cycle. Matthew bought a sleeping bag and we were ready to roll. We flew to Bergerac from East Midlands airport. The tour was to be from Bergerac to St. Malo, returning via Pleurtuit airport, a modest four hundred miles. The tour covered a lot of familiar ground from previous tours, but I didn't want any dramas that might put Matthew off cycle-touring for life. So, some of the places and I had already visited through my touring exploits got revisited.

## Bordeaux to Jonzac (118km)

The first day was an eighty-mile bike ride to the campsite at Jonzac. Jimmy and I had stayed there in 2010 on the Bordeaux to Calais tour. I knew it was a good site so we pressed on despite it being a long ride the first day. Besides recovering from injury, an added difficulty for me was following a vegan diet. Matthew was vegan and I decided to make things simple, and join him. It meant substituting dairy produce with guacamole and hummus. We rode the short distance into the pretty town, where we found plenty of places to eat that accommodated our diet.

## Jonzac to Rochefort (76 km)

The next day we headed west the next day towards the coast for about sixty-mile arriving in Rochefort, a touristy place with adequate campsites. We wen to the supermarkets to pick up our daily fix of hummus and tomatoes. So far, we had still managed to keep to the vegan diet.

## Rochefort to La Roche Sur Yon (104km)

The route up the coast proved to be problematic. Negotiating our way around La Rochelle on a bike was a nightmare and we got lost or found ourselves heading in the wrong direction several times. La Roche-sur-yon we found, to our cost, was to be avoided. Large lorries and heavy traffic were not what we came here for. We did, however, find a campsite in a small village on the outskirts.

## La Roche Sur Yon to St Brevins (93 km)

The coastal road up to Saint Brevins went through Pornic, a nice seaside place. Soon the Saint Nazaire bridge came into view on the way up to Saint Brevins les Pins. I had stayed at a youth hostel there on my first tour back in 2000. The hostel, sadly, had closed so we settled for a campsite instead.

## St. Brevins to Redon (57 km)

From Saint Brevins, we went over the Saint Nazaire bridge and headed north to Redon. Again, I was cycling on the familiar ground of my first tour with Kevin sixteen years ago. I remembered the old guy who gave us shelter from the rain all those years ago, just outside St. Nazaire. When we arrived at Redon, we suffered a bit of a blow as we were informed at the Offices de Tourisme that the youth hostel was closed from the end of August. With the help of the assistant at the tourist office, we were able to find a farm that offered a unique camping option. A wooden hut on stilts that had a sprung floor and a table underneath to eat off. When we reached the farm on the outskirts of Redon, we found it was remote, with no restaurants nearby. We had no option but to accept the farmer's offer of eggs, cheese and bread. This went against Matthew's vegan values, but we had no choice. Being a vegan in France was difficult.

# Redon to Plumieux (57 km)

The road to Plumieux took us through La Gacilly, where there was a photographic exhibition. The houses were decorated with murals and we stopped to admire the artwork. The journey up through Ploermel and the Lac au Duc was where I had spent holidays with my family as well as my cycling buddies. My original plan was to head for La Trinity Porhoet a couple of miles south of Plumieux. I intended to call in on John Cantrell in Plumieux but not put John and Linda in the awkward position of offering us a bed for the night. I had stayed in La Trinity Porhoet with Jane, her sister Sally and her husband Keith when we came over in 2003 for my fiftieth birthday. The people who owned the bed and breakfast had moved on and no alternatives were available.

We pushed onto Plumieux and knocked on John's door with a bit of trepidation. A gobsmacked Linda opened the door to us and we had a drink and catch-up until John arrived from his daily bike ride. Despite my insistence that we found digs elsewhere he insisted that we stayed with him. We accepted their hospitality and took them out for a meal of pizza, at Killian's bar in the village. Before this, we had a trip to La Cheze to see Mathilda and Bernard. They owned the L'Auberge de Lie, a pub where we had spent many a happy hour. Matthew and I were a bit saddened to see the state the owners and the pub had sunk to. John did warn us that things had changed and Mathilda was drinking heavily and smoking at the bar. The clientele had mostly disappeared and only a few hardy regulars were there drinking. We didn't see Bernard at all, and there was no evidence of people dining in the back as we had many years ago. We had a photograph with Mathilda and retreated back to Killians in Plumieux. I thought that would probably be the last time we would visit La Cheze. Things just weren't good. Matthew described it as like finding out that Santa Claus didn't exist. He had great memories of visiting La Cheze in his teens and that the reality of what we saw now was such a sharp contrast and disappointment.

## Plumieux to Dinard (88 km)

John rode half way to Dinard with us. He took us on the quiet roads that he knew like the back of his hand. Matt competed with John on the climbs much to my amusement. Matt was going really well and was more than a match for

John despite Matt having to haul heavy panniers over the climbs.

We arrived early enough at Dinard to be able to spend time sightseeing and drinking coffee at the many restaurants before booking into the youth hostel. I had used the Youth hostel many times. It was situated a couple of kilometres from the main night life and restaurant areas. Bike lights came in handy pedalling back to the hostel after an evening meal on the waterfront.

## Dinard to Pleurtuit (10 km)

The distance to the airport seemed a lot further than the 10 kilometres it said on the map. I always struggled to find this small, out-of-the-way airport. We then had to prepare our bikes for the flight home. It involved turning the handlebars through 90 degrees, dropping the saddle and removing the pedals. The bike was then squeezed into the plastic bag purchased for the purpose. The bag was then filled with our luggage and sealed with tape. Give me the ferry every time as it removed the necessity for this ritual.

# Tour 18 - Brittany

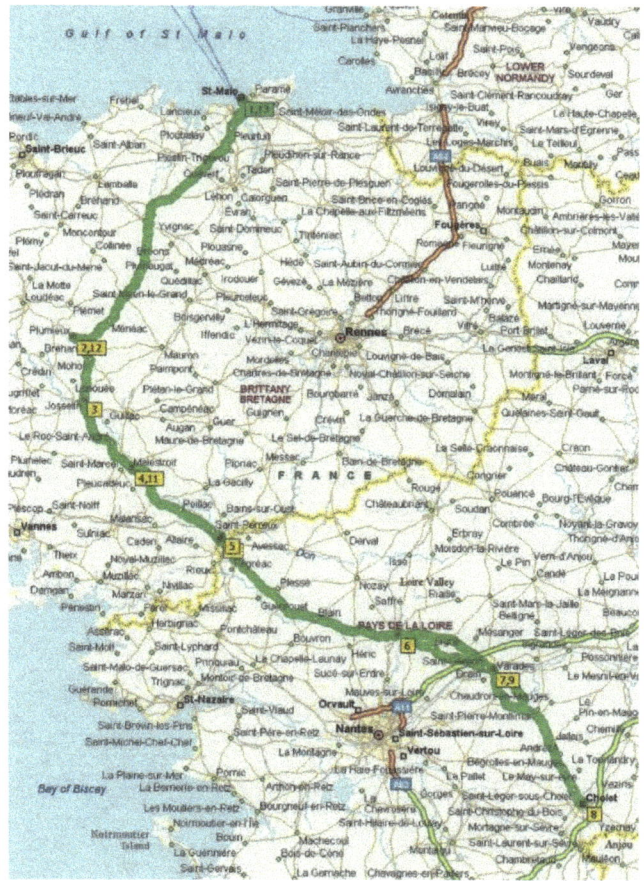

In 2017, I didn't manage to get away on tour. After the first operation in 2016 for a bunion, I followed it up with an operation to correct my hammer toes. If I was feeling sorry for myself, I had to spare a thought for my touring partner Jimmy, who was diagnosed in December 2015 with throat cancer and spent 2016 undergoing treatment. Jimmy didn't go back to work until December 2016 and wasn't fit for any sort of cycling in 2017. We marked time and looked forward to a 2018 tour. I was retiring from work that year and for the first time in my life, holidays would not be a problem.

In July, Jimmy and I decided to tour France and catch a few stages of the Tour de France. Due to our lack of fitness, the tour would be tame by past touring standards. We intended to Meet John in Saint-Malo and cycle down to Cholet for the team time trial and take it from there. We booked a ferry from Portsmouth to Saint-Malo and a return ferry a week later.

I picked Jimmy up at midday in the old Rover and set off on the 220-mile journey to Portsmouth. I bought a second-hand Thule roof rack, from a friend at work just before I retired with this trip in mind. We arrived at the Holiday Inn at 6.00 p.m. and parked up, ready to cycle the 10-miles to the ferry. It was advertised as being 3-miles from the port, but it took us the best part of an hour, so I suspect it wasn't.

## Saint-Malo to Plumieux (100 km)

We waited at Saint-Malo for John. When he didn't show on time we set off and proceeded to get lost and ended up on a major road where we weren't supposed to be. We eventually found John, who had turned up late. He was a bit pissed off that we had not waited and decided to set off -not a good start.

Heading out of the ferry port, we had dinner at Dinan. We took canal paths to avoid the roads. At Caulnes, we stopped for more food as Jimmy was feeling knackered. With a few detours and a wrong turning, I think we probably covered an extra 10 km by the time we arrived at Plumieux. We had beer and pizza at Killian's bar. It was the time of the World Cup and we watched France beat Uruguay and Belgium beat Brazil.

## Plumieux to Nort sur Erdre (150 km)

We rode on the roads to Josselyn, famous for its grand chateau. I had been there many times. This is where we got on the Brest to Nantes canal path to Redon which was a good road surface. In hindsight we should have used the youth hostel at Redon and watched the football. Instead, we continued along the canal path to Guenrouet. By this time Jimmy was suffering from fatigue. We used the road from Blain to Nort Sur Erdre. There was beer and pizza at the campsite for two very knackered cyclists. Whilst John had booked a hotel and he was enjoying a slightly better evening meal.

# Nort sur Erdre to Ancenis (30 km)

We had a very short ride to Ancenis. I struggled to understand John's thinking and how he had split the journey. It was all about hotel availability, but this tactic had totally knackered Jimmy, and he needed a couple of easy days to recover. Ancenis is a lovely place. The Le Loire runs through the town. The campsite had a swimming pool and a special place earmarked for cyclists. We booked two nights at Camping de l'le Mouchet. It was an ideal base for riding to watch the team time Trial in Cholet. The day was red hot and a couple of hours watching the race was just as exhausting as riding. I got a few good photos as the teams thundered through Cholet. We rode to Beaupreau for food at midday and returned to Ancenis for a Tapas.

## Ancenis to Redon (100 km)

We retraced our route and arrived at Redon at 4.00 p.m. Jimmy and I booked the youth hostel for a night of relative comfort. We watched the tour come through at 4.30 p.m. After this we went into Redon for a meal and watched France win the football 1-0. The town went mad.

## Redon to Plumieux (100 km)

The following morning, we had a bit of a sleep in and we set off at 10.00 a.m., which was a late start by our standards. We met John at Maletrout on the canal route. We followed the canal route past Josselyn to les Forges, then took the road to Plumieux.

It was Wednesday and Killian's was closed, so Linda cooked tea. She also did some washing for us which was much appreciated as the hot weather meant we had used our full kit of clothes. We watched England get beaten by Croatia. We hadn't expected anything better. We booked youth hostels in advance for the next couple of days at Dinan and St. Malo.

## Plumieux to Dinan (90 km)

John rode with Jimmy and I as far as Merdrignac – about half the distance. We found a supermarket and ate our dinner on tables outside.

We arrived at the youth hostel which was a bit of a dump and seemed to get worse. It's a pity because Dinan is a beautiful place. We enjoyed some Moules frites at a restaurant by the river Rance.

## Dinan to St. Malo (30 km)

We found a cycleway that avoided using the main road. We went to the Tourist Information and eventually found the youth hostel, which was a fair distance outside the town. We rode into town but found all the restaurants far too expensive. Having spent eight and a half euros on a beer, we retreated to the suburbs. We found a reasonably priced Italian restaurant and returned to the youth hostel for a few beers.

## Ferry and Home

Usually, when we got on the ferry and arrived in Portsmouth, the adventure was over. However, on this occasion, I had made the error of losing the paperwork relating to where the car was parked. After the ferry docked, we set off from Portsmouth in the direction we

283

thought we had parked the car. After a couple of hours of aimlessly following our instincts, we decided to try a different approach. We were now in a seaside part of Portsmouth with people geared up for a good time. Our enquiry for directions to the Holiday Inn was met with blank looks. There was more than one Holiday Inn – in fact it could have been one of four. We tried a few eventually finding the one with a Rover 25 in the car park. We retrieved the postcode and with the help of Jimmy's phone, we eventually found our way back to the car. What should have been a thirty-minute journey turned out to be a three-hour stressful ordeal. A note to myself: ensure I have directions back to the car because after a week or so away on holiday, you just can't rely on memory. We loaded the bikes on the car and headed home without further drama and arrived home in the early hours of the next morning.

# Tour 19 – Land's End to John O Grouts

I had been retired a year when the desire to do this iconic ride couldn't be put off any longer. Apart from a couple of small tours in the UK the majority of my touring had been abroad. The main reason for this was my touring had been a holiday rather than ticking a box. The Land's End to John o' Groats (Lejog) had always been on my list to do eventually – but always next year. I could hardly call myself a proper tourist until I had added this tour to my CV. It's not that I was daunted by the distance or the weather; it was a case of not having a strong appetite for touring in a country which is so car-orientated and basically, in a lot of cases, anti-bike. When I had completed it, I would then be in a position of knowing, rather than assuming that the UK has less to offer than our European neighbours when it comes to cycle-touring.

Trying to find anyone with an appetite or desire to do Lejog among my cycling buddies was proving difficult, if not impossible. The weather, traffic congestion and time off work being the main reasons. The only firm interest from likely candidates was from Phil Mason – a guy I went running with on Tuesdays with the Sheffield Striders. The only reservation I had with Phil managing to complete the tour was not his fitness but his bike. This was an old Dawes, which wasn't in the best of health, to say the least. In fact, when Phil showed me the Dawes, he was planning on using for Lejog, a voice inside me was saying, 'He's got to be joking,' – but sadly he wasn't.

After a couple of meetings to discuss some details like route, accommodation and time scale, we were ready to roll. We decided on youth hostels and B&B rather than camping. We opted for Ride by GPS rather than maps and to do minor roads and paths rather than the most direct main roads. We set ourselves ten days to do the near thousand-mile trip. We booked a train to Penzance 15th May, the cheapest option being the 1.50 p.m. train (£57

286

with a rail card) that travelled direct and took seven hours. We booked a night in Penzance Youth Hostel (which was only 3.5 miles from the station) where we enjoyed a few beers to prepare for an early start.

## Day 1 – Penzance to Launceston via Land's End (99.6 miles Elevation 8556 ft of climbing)

We had to cycle the 10-mile to Lands to start our trip and to take photos for our records. We had a tailwind down to Lands' End. Which meant we set off into a head wind. This remained with us for most of the tour. We stopped for fish and chips (Phil just had chips) at Perranporth, putting my vegan diet firmly in the bin.

We found riding the Sustran paths was hindering our progress. We met two guys who were taking a month doing LeJog on this terrain. It would have taken us a lot more than ten days to follow this type of route. So, at Bodmin, after an Aldi stop for food, we decided to brave the busy A30 for the last twenty miles. In hindsight, it was a mistake, as we were riding in the nearside gutter to avoid the heavy traffic. Phil's narrow 23mm tyres punctured three times on the debris-strewn carriageway. The tyre walls were blown out and we limped into the White Heart at Launceston after doing temporary repairs. We found a Chinese restaurant (Red Lantern) and had a few beers and a decent meal. We knew that the next day, radical changes were needed to Phil's bike if we were to make it to John o' Groats.

## Day 2 –Launceston to Bridgewater (96.5 miles Elevation 5787 ft of climbing)

We located a bike shop, called Launceston Cycles that opened at 9.00 a.m, in order to buy a couple of decent tyres for Phil's bike. An Ideal tyre would be 28mm but they didn't fit in the frame, so we had to settle for 25mm. It was 11.00 a.m. before we were on our way after some other minor repairs. The bike shop man was concerned about the wear on Phil's front bike wheel and we made the decision to get to Dronfield, where I would loan Phil a wheel.

After ten miles, Phil had his fourth and thankfully, his last puncture. By the time we got to Oakhampton, I had broken two spokes in the back wheel. It was my turn to need a bike shop. When we found one in Oakhampton, there was a 'back in 30 minutes' sign on the door and it was more like an hour before the young lad turned up. We used this time to refuel with pastries at a bakery. I purchased four spokes, two for spares. I fitted the two spokes myself to save time, and we were on our way.

At Tiverton, we followed Cycle Route 3 down canal paths which, on occasions, were like a ploughed field. Just when I thought things couldn't get worse, I came off my bike on a sandy surface, narrowly avoiding ending up in the canal. A dog walker dragged me out of the nettles and I only suffered minor bruising. As darkness fell, Phil lost my phone, which was mounted on his handlebars for navigation, because the battery was flat on his phone and he couldn't charge it. We now had no phone or means of navigation. We turned around in pursuit of the phone, retracing our route back down the path. Luckily, a woman walking her dog handed it back to us. We were thankful. After leaving the canal path we encountered a road diversion to add to our woes. Not to be too over dramatic, but this was probably one of the least favourite days I have experienced on a bike. We arrived at The Admiral Blake Guest House, our digs, at 11.30 p.m.! By the time we had showered, everywhere was shut except a Domino pizza house – not a first choice. After eating our food and walking back to our digs, we finally got to bed at 1.30 a.m. Things could only get better.

## Day 3 – Bridgewater to Evesham (109.5 miles Elevation 2776 ft of climbing)

Thankfully, the cycle ride, this day went smoothly and without drama. It was mostly on cycle paths through Bristol and Gloucester, which was quite picturesque. Crossing the Avonmouth Bridge was particularly impressive. We stopped at an Asian store for lunch and Phil bought a charging cable to get his phone working. We made a decision to use the A38, which we were advised was ok for cycling by another cyclist. At Cheltenham we used the A46 to Evesham. We booked into the Northwick Arms at 8.00 p.m. Phil's wife had done the research and this was the cheapest we could get at £101 between us. It proved to be the most expensive of the tour, mainly because of its location in the Cotswolds and the fact that it was Saturday night.

The only disaster we had was that Phil knocked his meal on the floor at the hotel; when he tried to reorder another one, it was already after 9.00 p.m. and they had stopped serving food! I did give him some of my chips.

## Day 4 - Evesham – Dronfield (112.5 miles Elevation 6253 ft of climbing)

This was the highest mileage of the trip, with Phil clocking 118 miles to his house after picking up a front wheel from my home at Dronfield. We set off just before 7.00 a.m. It was a good day, there was no wind and the roads were good for cycling as we headed through Alcester and set a course for Meridan – the centre of England. We stopped at Morrisons in Atherstone and narrowly avoided ejection by an overzealous employee for eating a Morrisons sandwich in their canteen – hooligans!

I was now into familiar terrain as I used to cycle back from Coventry when I contracted at Peugeot many years ago. Derby was familiar too with cycle paths through the busy city and then onto the A61 to Chesterfield, and then Dronfield. My daughter rode out to meet us as we made Dronfield for 6.00 p.m.

## Day 5 - Dronfield to Northallerton (96 miles Elevation 1778 ft of climbing)

I met Phil at 7.00 a.m. at Midland Station to avoid rush hour traffic as we headed through Meadowhall, Rotherham and Doncaster using cycle paths where possible. Riding through Rotherham, we narrowly avoided being wiped out by a car driver who halted inches to the side of us. A brief reminder, if we needed it, that we were very vulnerable as cyclists on these busy roads. We stopped for dinner at a sandwich shop near York. We made good progress except where we lost time on some bizarre cycle paths that were only fit for experienced mountain bikers.

We used the A19, which was a little unsafe for bikes and we arrived at Northallerton at 4.15 p.m. We stayed at the Golden Lion which was good value and had a friendly atmosphere. The breakfast next morning was the best so far and set us up for the day.

## Day 6 - Northallerton to Wooler (105 miles Elevation 5276 ft of climbing)

From Northallerton we rode through Yarm, (which looked like a nice place), Durham, Chester-Le-Street, and then Newcastle. We stopped at a sandwich shop near Newcastle for lunch.

We were using the Google bike route by now and abandoned the ride GPS. For some reason, we found ourselves on a stretch of the A1 near the Angel of the North and it was a nightmare. Although Google directed us there, it wasn't for cyclists. We came off into Newcastle Centre and tried to pick our way through which proved to be an unpleasant experience. Crossing the Tyne Bridge was a high point and we stopped to take photographs of this impressive structure. We had lost hours by the time we hit Morpeth on the way out. The last thirty-mile ride to Wooler was a joy on Northumberland country roads with beautiful scenery.

The youth Hostel at Wooler was almost empty. There was a cyclist there from Edinburgh who gave us some useful information on how to navigate through Edinburgh, which proved invaluable. We ate at the Milan Italian restaurant and sank a few beers at the local pub.

## Day 7 - Wooler to Kinross (93 miles Elevation 5958 ft of climbing)

We opted for the full breakfast and didn't get away until 9.30 a.m. After a few miles, we crossed the river Tay and we were in Scotland. Thirty miles down the Edinburgh road we turned off at Dalkeith as the old guy suggested. We had fish and chips at Morrisons at 55 mile, which was just the job. We picked up the cycle paths through Edinburgh, heading for the Firth of Forth Bridge stopping for photographs as we reached this monumental landmark.

North of Edinburgh, the scenery became rural and we rode along undulating forestry roads into Kinross and onto the Green Hotel. We arrived too late to eat at the hotel, so we brought back a Chinese takeaway to eat there.

## Day 8 - Kinross to Aviemore (105 miles Elevation 5797 ft of climbing)

We declined the optional £12 breakfast and had a 7.00 a.m. start. We stopped at Dunkeld, a tourist town, after thirty miles for a poor, disappointing, posh meal. It was something you might expect at Betty's Tea Rooms and totally unsuitable for two hungry cyclists. We refuelled at a convenience store in the same village.

We spent most of the day on a cycle path that ran parallel to the A19. It was a tough day on a poorly surfaced road into a headwind, cycling predominately uphill. It was the only time Phil began to suffer as we ground out the miles. We came across a few cyclists coming in the opposite direction and we exchanged experiences of our trip, which gave us a break. We refuelled at a café and Phil regained his energy and was back to normal.

In the last ten miles or so of this leg, we enjoyed long descents into Aviemore. The youth hostel at Aviemore had great facilities and was positioned well for restaurants. We opted for La Taverna, an Italian buffet where you could return as many times as you wanted, which was just what we needed.

## Day 9 - Aviemore to Portgower (103 miles Elevation 5249 ft of climbing)

We rode on cycle paths parallel to the A9 into Inverness for breakfast at Morrisons. How I loved these breakfasts! Phil broke a shoe cleat. He had worn it out to the point where it no longer clipped into his pedal. We had a detour to Cycles of Inverness, who replaced them. I purchased a decent pair of gel gloves (£37), my Aldi ones left my hands blistered. It was not the only part of my body that was falling apart. While Phil's bike was letting him down on the early part of the journey his investment in a pair of what he called 'game-changing' £200 shorts were proving they were worth every penny. My investment of £30 for a pair of cheap shorts was proving painful!

We rode the last thirty miles on the A9 as the traffic thinned out. The weather and scenery were bleak as we rode into a headwind towards Portgower and our isolated digs for the night (Jutta's B&B). The view from our accommodation was nothing but fields and sheep. The owner of the B&B was an eccentric German who had filled his house with antiques. Our only chance of food was at Helmsdale two miles away downhill. That meant a two-mile slog uphill to our digs with our fish and chips and a few cans of beer to wash it down. We had no choice, so we took it.

## Day 10 – Portgower to John o' Groats (54.5 miles Elevation 3192 ft of climbing)

On the final day we only had 55 miles to reach our final destination. We then had to ride back to Wick, which was another 15 miles, to catch the 4.00 p.m. train. We couldn't afford any problems as there was only one train available and we had to be on it.

We arose at the crack of dawn and ate the breakfast the owner had kindly left out for us. By 6.10 a.m. we were on the road to allow plenty of time for the necessary ceremonial celebrations at John o' Groats. There were two massive climbs from Helmsdale to Wick that went on for what seemed like miles on an undulating coastline, which involved using the 'granny ring' (26). We met two young guys on the way who were doing the route in thirteen days. They were in good spirits and had opted for camping so they were carrying more equipment and moving at a leisurely pace.

At Wick, approximately forty miles into our journey, we stopped for a second breakfast at a Morrisons supermarket. The road from Wick to John o' Groats was fairly flat and we arrived at John o' Groats at midday. We posed for pictures in Tam-O-Shanter hats, given to us by a lady waiting for her husband, who was also doing Lejog. We had a coffee to savour the moment and celebrate our achievement and then headed back to Wick. We had cycled 974 miles in ten days (994 miles in total) unsupported and had navigated our way through confusing, congested cities along the way. By any standards, it was a decent achievement.

We had dinner at the Bridge Café in Wick whilst killing time waiting for the 4.00 p.m. train to Inverness. In the evening, we booked into Inverness Youth Hostel for the night and headed for Jimmy Chung's Buffet there, we ate several plates of Chinese food, which was only heading for the bin, at a reduced rate of £10. We had a few beers at Wetherspoons, but we were too exhausted to get drunk.

At 9.00 a.m. the next day, we picked up a hire car from Kennings and loaded up the bikes, called for the mandatory Morrisons breakfast, and headed down the A 19. It was something approaching a five-hundred-mile journey. Our preference would have been the train, but the £200 plus train fare each made it a very expensive option. The car rental plus petrol came to £90 each, which equated to a considerable saving over the train. It was nearly 7.00 p.m. by the time Phil dropped me off at the Hyde Park pub in Dronfield, where a few family members gave me a hero's welcome. I did manage to drink a few pints that evening.

# Tour 20 – Bike Packing in Scotland

At the beginning of 2020 everything in my world was looking good. I had entered the Manchester Marathon and was upping my game running-wise. My friend Graham at the running club was putting in some long runs with me mid-week and Matthew was joining me on runs up to twenty miles at the weekend. The Marathon was on May 4th and I was following a programme aimed at hitting the distance before the event.

On the touring front, I was planning on doing the French equivalent of the Lands' End to John o' Groats. I had purchased an excellent book called France en Velo by John Walsh and Hannah Reynolds which provided the route details of the journey from St. Malo to Nice. My friend, and French resident JC showed interest and we just needed to firm up a date for the tour to happen. Ah well. That was my plan for the year that never was.

History will show that Covid 19 happened and everything I had planned got cancelled. I had just done my long twenty-mile run one weekend when my daughter informed me that the marathon was cancelled. I opted not to re-enter at a later date as I guessed we were in this crisis for several months. All my holidays, including the bike tour, were off. The only outlook to adopt was to be philosophical about it – such is life. Many people lost their lives and others their loved ones. Losing holidays was annoying but not life-changing.

The year 2021 was not much better, and life was no nearer returning to any sort of normality. The opportunity for getting away on tour – particularly abroad looked very unlikely. It wasn't until early 2022 that an opportunity arose and it was from a very unlikely source. The usual suspects that I'd toured with were otherwise engaged or disinterested in touring in the UK. Travelling abroad in 2022 was not an option as European countries had imposed sanctions on us Brits.

Eric (not his real name), from the cycling group I rode with regularly, was talking about doing The Great North

Trail. I had two great reservations about embarking on this adventure. Firstly, I must confess to not being a mountain-biker. I purchased a Bianchi mountain bike on retiring but never graduated above novice. I descended on the brakes when others would just relax. I spent a lot of time picking myself off the deck when I had applied the brakes when I shouldn't have. On loose gravel, non-technical stuff, I was okay and climbing hills was not the problem – bombing down technical descents was. My second reservation was the group I was going with. Eric, although I thought I knew him, was prone to, shall we say, lose his cool occasionally. He was a bit of a marmite character amongst his peers and divided opinion. I liked the guy and I was prepared to take the gamble. Perhaps I am a poor judge of character. Or perhaps I was that keen, no desperate, to tour that I was a little naïve. I had no idea of their ability or temperament of the other three members of the group. Also, if their ability on the technical off-road stuff was a lot better than mine, would I be slowing them down? Also, would that be fair to them? I had a lot of reservations about the trip, but if I didn't go what other option was available? I could stay at home and wonder what if? With hindsight I should have stayed at home because the tour was a total disaster.

I went to a meeting at Eric's house, where I met three of his friends. Sometime later, I was to discover that they were mountain bike instructors – but didn't know this at the time. If I had known this, I may have bowed out gracefully. I didn't, and never one to shy away from a challenge, once committed, I was in. A group was set up on Signal where information and banter were shared. A date of 11 June 9.00 at John o' Groats was provisionally given for the start date for four of us. Another person was starting from Durness and was meeting us on route at the end of the first day.

Gravel bikes are the vogue for these sorts of adventures with their wide tyres and bike-packing carrying ability. I would have to use the mountain bike, and I needed to buy bike-packing equipment as my panniers wouldn't be suitable. Eric opted for a mountain bike and the other three opted for gravel bikes. Strangely, Eric opted for a single-speed mountain bike, which raised an eyebrow or two. It seemed a strange choice of stead. But then again, Eric wasn't your regular sort of guy. I couldn't believe that someone could be that brave or some would say stupid.

I spent time researching equipment as this was a brand-new format in touring for me. I bought budget gear, which I thought would do the job. I purchased a Big Papa seat from Alpkit and a front bag from Planet X cycles. I bought a small bag for the top tube off E bay by Rock Brothers for my camera and glasses and small items like cutlery. Where a gravel bike scores is that it has a large triangle under the top tube, whereas a mountain bike hasn't. A large bag can fit in that triangle. I opted to take a small rucksack for items I wouldn't be able to fit in the bags I had. This was mostly food, which I would need for the first three days when we were away from civilisation.

This was my first off-road escapade and I made some big mistakes. I opted to cut down on items that I should have taken but space was at a premium and difficult decisions, wrong ones, it turned out, were made. These decisions came back to bite me and hard lessons were learned. I took spares I would normally take on a road tour; spare tubes, tyre levers, pump, lube and spokes. What I should have taken and didn't was spare brake pads and a spare rear mechanism hanger. Most importantly, I should have taken a Garmin loaded with the route and the knowledge of how to use it. Instead, I was totally reliant on others – which was a very big mistake. If I should get separated from the group, it would be disastrous. A few dry runs were organised at weekends to check equipment and socialise as a group. I didn't attend as these dates clashed with other social events that I already planned. Perhaps I should have gone but I had never had a dry run before on a tour. I could have learned something, who knows?

It was up to each individual to organise their own means to arrive at the appointed time and place. Bill and Ben (not their real names) travelled up by car to Edinburgh and caught the train from there to Thurso. Gary (not his real name) flew from Manchester to Inverness and then by train and ferry to arrive at Dunness. I researched the train option and through the TrainPal app managed to book a journey for £46 albeit using my senior rail card and four changes. I booked my bike on each train journey to ensure that my bike could travel, as this can be a problem if not. I told Eric of my plan and he did likewise, as the journey going the standard route through Doncaster was showing a price of £238! To summarise; we travelled Sheffield to Manchester, Manchester to Edinburgh, Edinburgh to Perth, Perth to Inverness, and finally Inverness to Thurso. We arrived at Thurso about 6.30 p.m. and then we had a twenty-mile ride to John o' Groats, arriving there about 8.00 p.m. Obviously, this plan was relying on the trains running to time, which we know they rarely do.

## Friday 10 June – Rail Journey to Thurso

Jane gave me a lift to Sheffield to catch the 5.07 a.m. Manchester train, as I had a flat tyre on the bike. Luckily, it was not a puncture. I had not tightened the valve properly after fitting puncture-proof (slime) inner tubes. I met Eric at the station and the journey to Manchester went without drama and we arrived on time. Unfortunately, this is where it went badly wrong – the 6.26 a.m. Edinburgh train was cancelled.

Eric was ready to throw the towel in at this stage and to be honest, things didn't look good. We decided to push on, after a little coercion, and see where fortune would take us, but the journey now looked complicated. We were advised by a rail staff to take the Blackpool train and get off at Preston and catch an Edinburgh train from there, which we did! We arrived at Preston and went for the Edinburgh train. When we tried to board the train, we were stopped by a rail staff operative because we hadn't got a reservation for our bikes. By this time, Eric and I were getting a little tetchy, Eric more so than me, which is Eric's trademark from his experience with motorists who upset him. After a few frank exchanges of views with the jobs-worth rail operative, we went to the ticket office and booked our bikes on the 8.03 a.m. to Glasgow and were advised to get off at Carlisle – which we did. We got bike reservations on the 11.03 Edinburgh train.

At Edinburgh, we went to the ticket office and recounted our woeful day to the staff at Scot Rail and asked how they were going to get the two of us to Thurso. After conversations between the various rail organisations, a plan was formalised and at last, the rail companies were being helpful. We were put on the Inverness train and were told a taxi would be waiting for us at Inverness to take us to Thurso. Sure enough, they were as good as their word. I received a text from a guy called Scott, who was waiting with a VW transporter to take us to Thurso. We finally arrived at Thurso at 8.30 p.m., having put the world to rights with Scott, who had strong opinions on all subjects we raised with him, from the War in Ukraine to Scotland's independence. We tried to get him to take us to John o' Groats instead of Thurso, but to no avail. We accepted the situation of a late-night ride to our evening destination of John o' Groats.

We donned our cycling gear and set about the twentyish miles to the Sea View hotel at John o' Groats where Bill and Ben had already arrived and were enjoying a few drinks, no doubt. We passed a few campsites on the route and I suggested to Eric that we could use one of them. Eric was keen to meet up with his two mates so onward we went. We had a tailwind and Eric's legs were twiddling away on his single-speed. I was wondering whether he was regretting his choice of bike already. It was 10.00 p.m. by the time we arrived at the Sea View Hotel. I was physically and mentally drained and fancied a final night of comparative luxury in a hotel as well as a few pints of ale. As much as I tried, I couldn't persuade Eric to do the same and off he rode to put his tent up for the night somewhere in the wild. Little did I know that, that would be the last that the group and I would see of Eric on this trip.

## Saturday 11 June – John o' Groats to Altnaharra 70 miles

We had arranged for a 9.00 a.m. start and the three of us, Bill and Ben (immaculately turned out in matching Rapha kit) and myself, headed for the famous John o' Groats signpost to have the obligatory photo shoot. We waited, but no sign of Eric at this point (or any other point). What the fuck was he playing at? All the months of planning and preparation and the guy dips out before we start!! At first, I was worried that something had happened to him. I was to find out later that such eccentricity was not out of character. We set off to a lighthouse a couple of miles up the coast, which was (I didn't know) the official starting point for this escapade. After more photos, we set off in earnest along single-track roads into a very strong headwind. Progress was very slow. We were averaging less than ten miles per hour as we had several breaks to recover our strength and press on. We took turns at the front to preserve our strength in what was becoming, and we all agreed, one of the hardest days encountered on a bike.

We received messages from Gary, who had ridden down from Durnes and was meeting us on route, somewhere near Altnaharra. He was camped in some trees, sheltering from the wind and rain. Gary flagged us down as we approached the seventy-mile mark by which all of us were exhausted. There was a campsite a couple of miles up the road on Loch Naver but this was only available to caravans and motorhomes. Gary had seen Eric earlier on the road. He met Gary and told him he had ridden off on that first night until 2.00 a.m. while the rest we were fast asleep in The Sea View Hotel. He had camped for a few hours, then got up early and set off and was now several hours in front of us. The reason for this, we may never know. Apparently, this behaviour was not uncommon for Eric. If only I had known this beforehand, I would never have signed up for the tour. We camped, we ate, and we slept in preparation for another hard day in the saddle.

## Sunday 12 June – Altnaharra to Oykel Bridge 55 miles

We rode a couple of miles up the road and stopped at the campsite and bought water and food from the camp shop. We had water filters but the guy at the shop said we should boil water otherwise, we would have health problems. He proved to be correct. The water filters had been used frequently on this trip and so far, I hadn't experienced problems.

The strong winds and rain continued to blow in our faces as we now encountered rough off-road surfaces. Our destination was the Oykel Bridge Hotel, where we hoped to get something to eat. There was nothing in this part of the world and it was our only hope of some decent food. On arrival, we didn't experience any hospitality and food was for residents only. They didn't have any vacancies, so we left with our bellies still empty. The Rapha twins thought that the hotel had a chronic shortage of staff and blamed Brexit. They were very sure of their theory and I offered nothing in response.

Our destination for the day was a bothy that was about another ten miles away. This is basically a wooden or corrugated hut in the middle of nowhere that provides shelter from the wind and rain. There were wooden benches that were off the floor, but no heating. There were a few rules as to its use. A shovel to bury any human waste as there was no toilet. At this point, there were two items I should have brought and didn't; one was a stove and the second was an inflatable mattress. I had a piece of foam that was ok on grass but not on a wooden bench. I was desperate for a hot drink and luckily, Gary offered me one, which I gratefully accepted. There was a river about thirty metres from the bothy, I stripped off and had a full body wash, which was freezing but was necessary if I wasn't to suffer from saddle boils. Gary was already suffering from chafing and I returned the favour from the hot drink by giving him some antiseptic cream – something that should have been on his list and wasn't.

## Monday 13 June – Oykel Bridge to Contin 45 miles

This was the least mileage we did on the tour. The main reason was the stop at a pub to get a decent meal and recharge our electrical gadgets. The wind, rain, and terrain still provided a challenge, but the fish and chips at dinner certainly lifted the spirits of our group.

We also had an added bonus of Bed and Breakfast accommodation at the Achility Guest House in Contin. We bought food and wine at a shop in Contin as the guest house didn't do meals and there were few in the way of pubs in Contin. We showered, washed our gear and dined at the guest house with the food we had bought. The next morning, we had breakfast at the guest house before departure.

Tuesday 14 June - Contin to Fort Augustus 51miles

On this day, we cycled on the most boring, barren terrain I have ever come across. The bleak weather only added to the gloomy landscape. In under two hours, the desolate landscape was broken by a large dam – the Orrin reservoir but I couldn't be too sure. By this stage, one of our crew was having toilet stops which didn't bode well. After what seemed like several hours, we descended off this stark landscape onto a narrow road with passing places. After a few miles we found a café to have dinner. We had curried lentil soup and a sandwich, which was excellent.

After some tarmac riding through woodlands, we turned off onto some technical, narrow tracks, which for me especially, involved walking with the bike. It was extremely tiring. After a few miles of this we encountered a river which we had to wade across. It wasn't a paddle it was a full-scale wade which covered most of the bike. I would have preferred not to have submerged the bike in water for the obvious problems water poses with bearings, etc. There was no option as the bike was used, and needed, to provide stability as we waded across.

The final section was a long technical descent on a narrow, muddy track where I came off the bike and landed badly on my shoulder. A slight touching of the brakes was enough to take the wheels from under me. I was the least competent on the technical sections and this was the third time I had managed to hit the deck in only a few days. It was a fact I accepted. I was the eldest and the least experienced off-road. I had strength going up the hills and could hold my own in that department.

The final section brought us to Fort Augustus and the hostel there. As we put our bikes away, we noticed the dropping of the wind had provided an opportunity for the midges to attack for the first time on this trip. We showered and changed, then headed out to try and find somewhere to eat. Fort Augustus was a small but busy place and we had to wait for over an hour for a table to become free at the pub restaurant. After we had eaten and had a couple of beers one of our team told us, due to illness, it was the end of the trip for him. He would take a flat route and catch a train home.

# Wednesday 15 June – Fort Augustus to Corrour 45 miles

The team was now down to three. I wasn't feeling in the best of shape. It was a combination of fatigue, a stomach upset and backache. The rucksack was a big mistake on my part. It was causing back pain as it was heavy and awkward. I had avoided getting a frame bag that fitted in the triangular space where the bottles fit. In hindsight, it would have been better if I had carried a small hydration pack on my back. It was too late now I would have to live with my mistakes.

We filled our bags with food and drink as we were heading into the wilds. The hostel to which we were heading would have cooking facilities, so we needed pasta, cheese, and sauce – enough ingredients for an evening meal. I bought bananas and dried fruit to eat on route.

Shortly after leaving Fort Augustus, we took an overgrown single track. After a few miles we started climbing the Corrieyairack Pass. This climb had been talked about as being a beast and it certainly was that and more. The gradient and the length of it, on its own would have been classed as very hard. Add to this the fact that we were riding on shingle and loose boulders that skidded under every pedal stroke the climb became an awesome challenge. Some parts were so steep that walking was the only option. My arms ached from pushing my laden bike over the rough terrain. To make things worse, we were passed by motor-assisted mountain bikers. One of our group, the youngest by some way, did manage to ride most of the climb. We did have stops to rest and compose ourselves as fatigue crept in.

I hadn't found the descents so far much fun and this descent was no different as I relied far too heavily on the brakes. Streams ran across the road accompanied by stone slabs probably 30-50 cm high. Some I jumped and some I slowed right down as I was unsure whether they could be jumped without the risk of somersaulting over the handlebars. At the bottom we needed a break as the descent took a lot out of us as well as the ascent. I realised at this point the brake pads on the rear wheel were nearly worn out. Spare disc pads are things I should have packed but hadn't. The irony of this is, if I was a better mountain-biker I wouldn't have used the brakes as much as I did and therefore, they wouldn't have worn out.

The terrain to Corrour was undulating but not testing. Gary, at this point, was suffering with a knee problem that was eventually to end his tour. I was suffering a little just from the accumulation of fatigue in my body. I accepted as much on any such adventure. This wasn't a walk in the park, it was taxing mentally as well as physically. Steering the bike over boulders and keeping the bike upright added another dimension to test the system. This type of riding also puts a strain on the arms and the upper body. A fifty-mile ride under these conditions is devoid of any rest or freewheeling to allow you any recovery. However, my biggest problem was the painful bunion on my left foot.

Whenever we stopped for a break, my shoe was off to relieve the pain. It was becoming a talking point and a notable characteristic of mine. The bunion and hammer toes in my left had gradually become worse this year. I had been given a steroid injection just before setting off on tour, which reduced the swelling. I had purchased extra wide shoes that helped, but the ten hours a day was enough to inflame the hardiest of feet. It was back in 2016 and 2017 that I had the operations on my right foot to correct the bane of my life. At that time, my left wasn't that bad, an annoyance but nothing like the pain I was enduring at present. I made a mental note to myself that this problem would need to be resolved as soon as possible upon my return.

By the time we reached the remote hostel at Corrour, I was exhausted. The hostel was very remote and not accessible by road. An elderly woman ran the hostel on her own. She was originally from Sheffield, so we had a good chat about the city we both knew so well. After a shower, we enjoyed a cooked meal of pasta with tea to wash it down. Over the meal, we confirmed what we already knew, that the tour was over. I needed brake pads if I was to continue. It was unlikely I would see a bike shop to get the parts I required. I have been exhausted before and battled on – it's par for the course. To ride with just one brake on unknown terrain is not wise. I was annoyed with myself and if the others had been continuing, I would have taken the risk, perhaps.

Gary and I walked a few hundred yards up a hill from the hostel to get a phone signal enabling us to book a train from Corrour station to Glasgow. From there, I would be able to get a train to Edinburgh and onwards to Sheffield. At Glasgow, Gary was travelling a different route to Manchester. The remaining Rapha was riding to Glasgow on his own, where his vehicle was parked.

The next morning, I packed and rode to the station. Luckily, there weren't any issues with the trains and everything went smoothly. I rode the seven miles back home to Dronfield in bright sunshine – the only good weather I had seen all trip. I had mixed emotions, the relief of being home and also disappointment. The trip had been a nightmare for several reasons. The weather was foul and the terrain wasn't easy and I was woefully under-prepared for the trip in terms of equipment and spares. I was too blasé in my approach and this time, I was found wanting. A Garmin, a stove, a sleeping mat, and spare parts such as brake pads were essential items that were missing. Also, my touring companions needed to choose more carefully. I didn't expect my touring buddy to set off on his own on day one. It has never happened before and it was something I never expected or could have anticipated. As for the foot, I had been there before. The bunion alone wouldn't have stopped me from finishing the tour had it not been for other factors. There was very little enjoyment or many memorable moments in this tour at all. There were too many negatives to make this an adventure worth pursuing any further than we did.

The first thing I did on returning was to pursue some relief from the bunion that had blighted my trip. I went to Scarsdale Hospital in Chesterfield, where they administered further Cortisone injections to give me some temporary relief. This was followed up by adding my name to a waiting list for surgery, sometime in the future. The mountain bike received a full service. The Bianchi took a hell of a battering during that week and needed several new parts. The big papa carrier was put on eBay to recoup some of my investment in something I was less than impressed with. It was a positive attempt to purge any idea in my head that I would ever mix mountain bike riding and touring again. A famous Chesterfield saying of, 'I'll stick to what I know duck,' sprang to mind and felt quite appropriate to the situation.

# Tour 21 – Bergerac to Dieppe

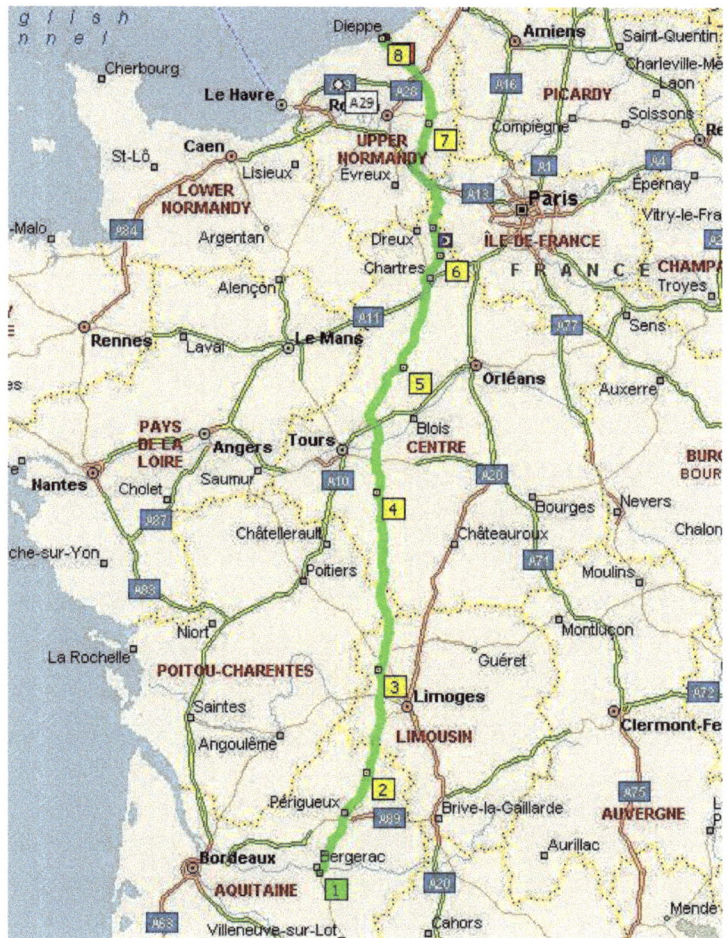

It was early January 2023 before I had the surgery on my left foot. I opted to have all the corrective surgery done in one session as opposed to three separate operations, which I had on the right foot. Two months of inactivity was the consequence, I had my meals brought to me whilst I lay with my foot elevated. I flitted between watching Netflix, reading Haruki Murakami books and pencil drawing. It wasn't long before my thoughts turned to musing on a possible tour.

It had been five years since I had toured overseas on my bike. This wasn't a conscious choice. Covid was to blame for the last two, or perhaps three years. It was 2018 when Jimmy and I met JC for a tour in France that included watching a couple of stages of the Tour de France.

Since 2018, JC had moved from his home, of more than twenty-five years, in Plumieux Brittany, to a modern and more luxurious property in Blond in the Haute-Vienne department of France. Also, this year I had reached the age landmark of seventy. Not that this should be a barrier to preventing me from doing things I enjoy. But perhaps I should be aware that my capabilities won't be that of a younger self. Seventy miles a day would now be a more realistic target and perhaps less if the terrain was particularly hilly.

Jimmy, my occasional touring partner over the years, was due to retire in early August and was eager to tour in France again. I say occasionally but in reality, we had been on ten tours together and two base holidays, making him my main cycling companion. I wasn't inclined to go abroad, for August can be very hot in France, but leaving it later in the year would interfere with other plans. I was starting an art class in September and the football season would be in full swing. The Blades were in the Premier

League, probably just for one season, so I needed to enjoy it while I could. So, France in August it was to be. My initial thought was to take the Golf (car) down to Portsmouth and take the ferry to St. Malo. However, the cost for a return ferry crossing was coming up at £209. Added to this, the parking and cost of fuel made this option expensive. I dislike flying, finding the experience stressful. As much as flying went against the grain, I explored the option. Good old Ryanair was offering flights from East Midlands to Bergerac for £14 plus £60 extra to ship the bike. I could get a ferry one way from Dieppe to Newhaven for £42, and a train journey from Newhaven to Sheffield for £27 with my senior railcard. Keith the Taxi was £80 between the two of us for a one-way trip to East Midlands. I calculated a saving of about £70. It would also be a more interesting tour travelling South to North. I had used St. Malo several times before and Bergerac to Dieppe would provide new roads to explore.

I contacted JC and Jimmy to agree on the dates and booked the flights for Wednesday, 16th August, and a return ferry the following Friday, 25th August. The tour dates were based on a hundred kilometres per day and two nights at JC's. This was a more relaxed schedule than previous tours for a number of reasons. Mostly, it was going to be very hot and Jimmy's ability to cope in the past under these conditions wasn't great. Ideally, I would have preferred to be back a day early as I was told at the ticket office, when I picked up my tickets, that a national rail strike was planned the day after. Nevertheless, we went ahead with the plan, the trip was booked and there was no turning back. I picked a couple of bike boxes from J.E.James Cycles – the staff there are only too happy to off-load large boxes as it makes less for them to dispose of.

This trip was going to be a first in that it was going to be paperless. I purchased a Garmin 1030 a couple of months before and was still finding my way. I intended on plotting the route on Strava and leading the route from onto my Garmin. I got some instruction from Barry, a mate of mine and by trial and error, I was ready to roll. Jimmy purchased the same Garmin and was busying himself plotting the route on Komoot. Between us, I was confident we wouldn't get lost. I intended to take an A4 map of the area of France that didn't carry any great detail just as a rough guide.

A week before we were due to fly, Jimmy injured himself while riding his bike. He embarked on a training regime aimed at getting himself fit enough for the tour and overdid it. He hoped that a week's rest would cure the problem but it wasn't to be. On Monday night, Jimmy phoned, almost in tears, to inform me he wasn't going to make the trip. I half expected this, and it didn't come as a massive shock. I phoned a few likely candidates in the cycling fold, but at this short notice, I would have been amazed if anyone would be available. I was still going, and would miss the companionship, but in a bizarre way, I was glad that I only had myself to worry about. Obviously, Jane was concerned that I was going it alone from the safety aspect. The lack of companionship for me wasn't a big deal.

## Bergerac to Thiviers (Nantheuil) (88 km)

The day started very early – about 3.00 a.m. Keith, the taxi was picking me up at 4.00 a.m. to get me to East Midlands in plenty of time for my 7.00 a.m. flight. Jane packed me sandwiches and I had my breakfast at the airport. The flight went ahead on time without any drama. I made conversation with the lady sitting next to me. She was going to visit her sister who lived in France. She showed me photographs of her sister's house, which looked very grand and impressive by any standards. I told her about my upcoming adventure. My thoughts were that I needed to make an effort to talk; otherwise, I would go mad over the coming weeks. If people didn't want to get involved in conversation, I would accept it and wouldn't engage with them. Generally, people travelling alone welcome interaction with others given the opportunity.

Bergerac is a tiny airport and I was soon through and assembled my bike when it arrived off the plane. The airport was empty well before I'd dumped the cardboard packaging and was pedalling towards the entrance. Once out of Bergerac, I headed towards Perigeux and then hoped to at least get as far as Thiviers and look for somewhere to camp. Just after midday, I was looking for somewhere to eat. I had only been riding for an hour and a half, but it felt like a long time since I had eaten. At my first restaurant stop, I struggled to find food that didn't contain meat. The plat de jour was duck, but I asked the waiter to replace the duck with cheese. He was a little bemused but eventually dished up a large salad with eggs. I played with the Garmin only to realise I hadn't set it going. I thought it started recording automatically as soon as I followed the route, it didn't. A bit of a hiccup, but soon rectified. I started recording from the restaurant leaving me to estimate the mileage up to that point.

On arriving at Thiviers, I asked some motorcyclists if there was a campsite nearby. One of this group took pity on me and asked a local shop owner for information. She came out with directions, but I could only remember the first few directions. The campsite was towards a small town called Nantheuil. After a few kilometres, I asked again and eventually arrived there. The tent was erected. I showered and then enjoyed pizza and a few pints of draught Leffe. The pizza and leffe became a recurring theme on this trip. The pizza I tired of, the leffe I didn't.

## Thivirers to Blond via Oridour sur Glane (93 km)

I rode up a rough track out of the campsite, which took me back to the centre of Thiviers. The Garmin seemed to get its knickers in a twist in town centres and sent me down alleys I wasn't sure I should be taking. I was using my instincts rather than any science and headed in the wrong direction before asking some cyclists, who put me right. I wanted to head towards Chalus. One of the cyclists, who spoke excellent English couldn't help giving me a history lesson. Apparently, Richard the Lionheart was mortally wounded in 1199 and died at Chalus. He was replaced by King of France Phillipe Auguste. I arrived at Chalus and asked for directions from a waiter at one of the restaurants in the town square. You can't always trust the Garmin in towns but you can always rely on waiters speaking English. The waiter directed me to take a right at the King Richard statue. The Garmin let me down again. I followed it down the Rue de Napoleon, of which there are a few, as it ran parallel to the main road. This came to a dead end. Rather than go back a few miles, I clambered over a ditch and some scrubland until I reached the main road – not an easy task with a full-laden tourer. My socks had been decorated with a type of sticky bud that was very hard to remove. My next navigational error was at St. Victunien. A local put me right, I crossed the La Vienne river and rode to Oradour Sur Glane.

I rode up through the village and I could see the museum on my left hand side. I sat on a wall and had some food before I locked up my bike and entered the modern museum building. There was an old black homeless guy who had a bike laden with what looked like his worldly goods. I passed him one of my bananas, which he accepted with a nod before I moved off. Photographs lined the wall of the museum of the 643 victims slaughtered on June 10th 1944, during WWII. There was no entry fee to the village.

I wandered around the old village that had been left as a shrine to those slaughtered. It was quite a sad experience wandering around and taking photographs along with the other tourists.

I phoned JC after the visit for instructions. I was only twenty kilometres away and his place wasn't hard to find. There was only one road into and out of the place – you could blink going through and miss it. On arrival, I couldn't help being impressed by John and Linda's new home, it was in stark comparison to the fugal abode at Plumieux. It was very spacious, well-equipped and nicely decorated without being elaborate. It was single storey, through plan with three large bedrooms, with one bedroom being used as an office. A large garage on the side housed six bikes, one of which used to be mine, that is now sat on a trainer. The back garden wasn't massive back but he had a small orchard to the garage side of the house. In the UK a house like this, in a reasonable area, would command a million pounds. In Blond, it wouldn't cost half of that.

On past visits I had taken John and Linda out for a meal at their local restaurant. On the day I arrived, Linda had already cooked a meal. We sat outside to eat and drink beer under an umbrella to shield ourselves from the strong sun. For the next day's meal, John suggested buying food from the supermarket in Bellac rather than using the only restaurant in Blond, which John wasn't that impressed with. So that's what we did; we drove to Bellac and shopped in the morning at the supermarket and paid a visit to the bike shop, where I stocked up on energy bars and tablets to put in my bottles. Adding a little flavour to the warm water, I would be drinking made it somehow more palatable. Later in the day, we watched the tour of the Limouson bike race that was passing through the village. The evening was a repeat of the previous evening. I made sure I had plenty to eat and drink as the following day would be a long one.

# Blond to Loches (153 km)

With two good night's sleep and no gear to pack away, I was away early – about 9.00 a.m. It was another hot day as I passed through Bellac heading for Le Blanc. At the seventy-mile mark, I was looking to call it a day as the heat was getting the better of me. At Chatillon Sur Indre, there was a campsite. Initially, it looked ideal. On further examination, it proved not to be. It was an unmanned site and according to a Canadian cyclist, who was camping there, gaining entry to the washroom was proving problematic. There was no-one to contact who could help, so I took the decision to press on. The next big town, Loche Sur Indois, didn't have a campsite. My Google search for a campsite took me to Loche, which was to the west of my direction of travel and wasn't getting me nearer my final destination.

By the time I reached Loches, I had done a hundred and fifty – three kilometres, (ninety-five miles). My Garmin was giving me data in miles and the road signs in kilometres. I knew I was doing too many, miles or kilometres, in a day. In the relentless heat and this pace was not sustainable. Loche was a reasonable size town and the campsite took some finding. It was a tourist destination and, as a result, was charging a premium price to camp. The price of twenty-nine euros was the most I had paid to pitch my tent. To be fair, it was well equipped with a swimming pool and eating and drinking facilities. I took a swim in the pool before indulging in the usual pizza and leffe.

## Loche to Moree (112km)

I decided on a breakfast before setting off. I picked a few croissants in a Loches pastry shop (the café didn't offer anything apart from coffee) and sat drinking a very strong coffee at the Italian café whilst I watched the locals buying that at the market that was in full swing. I then set off on my bike; after an hour or so, I stopped at a large chateau around dinner time to eat at the restaurant that was part of the tourist attraction. The restaurant was for the visiting clientele to Chateau de Montpoupon, and not for passing cyclists. The women did take pity on me and filled my bottles with water and ice which was most welcome on this very hot day. I stopped at a shop and bought a family tub of ice cream. I sat outside the shop at a table and devoured the tub in no time. My mouth and throat were so dry with the heat that it seemed the only solution on probably the hottest day so far.

Later in the day, I crossed La Loire and arrived at Blois. Trying to navigate through Blois using the Garmin turned into a nightmare. It was a big place and the Garmin was sending me down blind alleys. It felt like an hour before I finally headed out towards Oucques-la-Nouvelle. Seventy miles took me to Moree, which was probably my favourite campsite of the tour. It was a large municipal site with a large lake to swim in, the bonus being it was only seven euros to camp. I went for a swim in the lake to cool off and then enjoyed the usual leffe and pizza.

## Moree to Maintenon (114 km)

This was a bad day for the reason I rode most of the day on an empty stomach. It was a combination of bad luck and poor timing. I hit small villages that had shops at the wrong time of day and they were shut. I consciously avoided big towns like Chateaudun and Chartres to avoid the bad experience I had in Blois the previous day and paid the price for this decision. I survived on a couple of energy bars I had and water that I was given by residents on route. I meandered through the countryside, calling at villages in the hope of finding food without any luck. I found a campsite near Maintenon and arrived there hungry, hoping for at least the usual beer and pizza. To my surprise, it was the only campsite without a restaurant or any access to food or drink. I hadn't the energy or inclination to travel further to find another campsite. The owner of the site, a nice Portuguese lady, said she was going shopping at a supermarket several miles away and offered me a lift there to buy some food. We arranged to meet in an hour – giving me time to pitch a tent and shower. I stocked up with food at the supermarket for the evening and enough food to last the next day. On the way to the supermarket and back, we shared how we arrived where we were, at this campsite in the middle of nowhere. She told me of her ambition to quit the campsite and return to her native Portugal. It was nice having somebody to share a few tales with.

I sat at a table to eat my meal of bread, tomatoes, salmon and cheese. For dessert, I had yoghurt and bananas washed down with a few beers. I noticed some young boys camping nearby who had an extension and were able to charge their devices. There was a charging point, but it was in the toilet several hundred metres from where I pitched my tent. I didn't fancy leaving anything overnight in the washroom to charge. I made a mental note that this extension was something that I definitely needed if I was to keep my devices topped up and would get one at the next opportunity.

## Maintenon to Lyon la foret (122 km)

I left Maintenon with enough food in my panniers to last me all day. I passed through a lot of picturesque places en route to Lyon la Foret. Nogent le Roi was a particularly pretty place, very much like York with its old wooden buildings. At just over halfway, I crossed the river la Seine at Vernon. The day was a lot cooler and having plenty of food meant it passed without any drama. Before I arrived at Lyons la Foret, I travelled through a lot of forestation. The town itself was very pretty. I wandered round taking photos and it felt familiar – had I been here before? The campsite was on the outskirts of the town and had all the facilities I could have wished for. I picked up an extension for thirty euros that allowed me to charge up my devices. A bit late in the day, but an investment worth making. I pitched my tent and dined on pizza and beer again.

## Lyon la Foret to Pauville Sur Mer. (100 km)

I was only a hundred kilometres from Dieppe and had two days to get there. I was heading for a coastal resort that was about ten kilometres from Dieppe where I planned to spend two nights. I had built in an extra day as a contingency – luckily it wasn't required. If my companion Jimmy had made the journey with me, I'm sure we would have used it.

The route to Dieppe was well-signposted and was mostly on purpose-built cycling paths. I stopped for dinner at a café that was on this track and was used by many tourists and locals. On arrival in Dieppe, I used Google to locate the campsite. The coastal seaside town in which the campsite was situated was a short climb out of Dieppe. I pitched my tent at the side of a lake where a few of the site occupants were fishing, then I went for a meal at the restaurant on site. It started to rain very heavily for the first time on this tour.

The next day, I rode into Dieppe to locate the ferry port in preparation for tomorrow's departure. It was a midday sailing and I needed to be there in good time. On returning to Pauville Sur Mer I decided on a swim in the sea. The water was warm and ideal for a cool-off. Afterwards, I found a good restaurant and treated myself to a decent meal comprising of salmon and vegetables. It made a change from the pizza I had endured all holiday. The evening meal was a return to the usual, but I did have company. A German couple, who had a motorhome parked near my tent, started a conversation and we chatted into the evening. Afterwards, I joined them for a drink. We sat outside their motorhome under an awning as the rain came down heavily. We shared life stories until it was time for me to crawl into my tent.

## Pauville Sur Mer to Dieppe (9 km)

The next morning, I was up early to grab a drink and some croissants at the restaurant before departing for Dieppe. I arrived at the ferry port two hours before sailing. The gate didn't open for another half hour. A handful of cyclists joined me in the queue for the ferry and dozens of motor cyclists. A very loud, brash American guy, from New York as it happens, punctured while in the queue. Neither he or his petite Swiss wife had a clue how to change a tyre, so I intervened and did it for him. He was very grateful and offered to buy me a coffee on the ferry – which he did, to be fair.

We docked at Newhaven at 3.00 p.m., and I was at the train station at 3.45 p.m. I had anticipated not getting off the ferry and through the controls until after 4.00 p.m. I had booked on the 5.00 p.m. train to Brighton but boarded the

4.00 p.m. Luckily nobody checked the times on the ticket. I also boarded the earlier train to London St Pancras and there wasn't a problem. I found London St Pancras a nightmare to navigate and find my platform. I needed the extra time to find my platform and negotiate the lifts with my bike. I chained my bike up and hunted for food and the toilets. I needed to go down the elevator and didn't fancy negotiating it with a fully-laden bike. Why they don't have toilets on all levels in a station of that size is beyond me.

When the train arrived, there was a mass dash through the gates to board. The staff at St. Pancras weren't at all forgiving. A guy tried to get on the train without a booking for his bike and was quickly removed. Luckily, all the trains ran on time despite the imminent train strike planned for the next day. The train pulled into Sheffield at 9.45 p.m. Jane came to Sheffield to pick me up and spared me the ride home in the dark. I crave to get away on these trips, but I love returning home to the comforts of a warm, comfortable bed. We take a lot for granted in life and these trips, if nothing else, make me appreciate what I have.

# Tour 22 – St. Malo to Nice – France En Velo

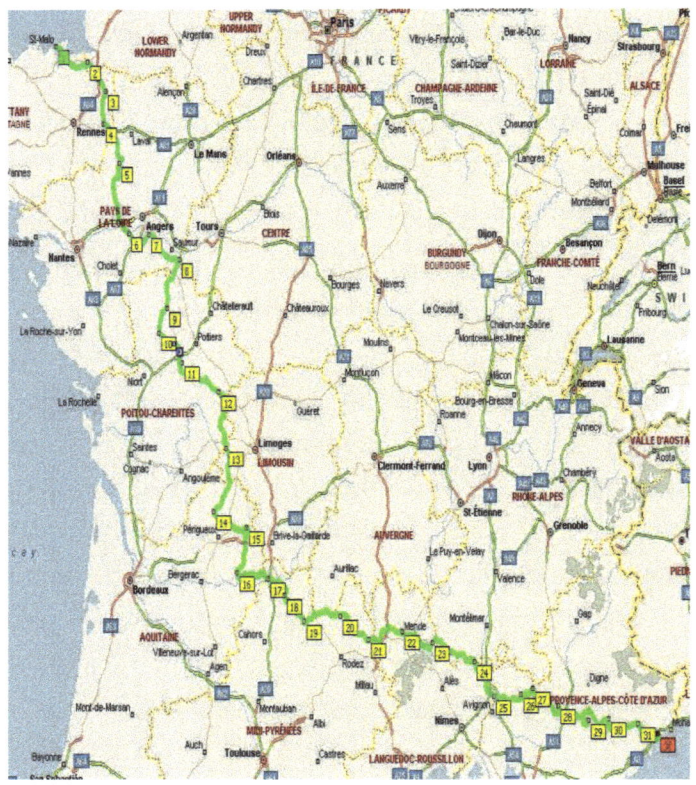

I made a decision at the time that this was going to be my last long-distance tour. When I told Jane, she didn't believe it. I don't know whether I believed it myself. I was going to take more than two weeks away from my family duties of babysitting and dog walking. I did feel a little guilty leaving Jane to do all the domestic stuff I usually do, but I needed to get this tour done, which had been tormenting me for some time now.

In reading this book it is apparent that the country of choice for me and the one featured most prominently on my tours has been France. France is so entrenched in the culture of cycling, everyone knows about 'The Tour de France' but not everyone knows that The Vuelta (Tour of Spain) or The Giro (tour of Italy) exist. Having completed the Land's End to John o' Groats in my own country, I looked to complete something similar in my country of choice, France.

I came across an excellent book about five years ago called France en Velo by John Walsh and Hannah Reynolds. It describes in detail the ultimate cycle journey from the Channel to the Mediterranean. A thousand-mile journey from St. Malo to Nice. This wonderful book was thumbed through many times as I contemplated doing it one day. Covid 19 came and went, which gave me the excuse to shelve the idea. Eventually, I decided that 2024 was the year. I was seventy-one. So, it was now or never. The book breaks the route down into three options. The Challenge: A ten-day itinerary; The Classic: A two-week itinerary and The Explorer: A three-week itinerary. Twenty years ago, it would have been the ten-day challenge without a doubt, at my age, carrying my equipment on an unsupported tour, I decided upon the two-week option. Of course, I could have paid £3,000 and had a company carry my bags and stay in a hotel each evening, but where's the adventure in that?

My biggest issue was to find someone to join me on this epic ride. Jimmy pulled out of the tour last year with a knee injury. He was diagnosed with cancer later in the year and had spent twelve weeks in hospital. Hopefully, he would make a full recovery, but this tour was out of the question. Steve Worthy was diagnosed with prostate cancer and was also undergoing treatment. My running mate, Phil Mason, was a likely candidate to step up to the task. He was training for a marathon and after that, he was free. Phil had completed Land's End John o' Groats with me five years before and thankfully had purchased a new bike. After a round trip of two hundred miles to see a mate in Saltburn, he announced quite nonchalantly that he was up to the challenge.

I plotted the route on Strava, dividing it up into fourteen stages, one for each day. Now with Garmin technology, gone are the days of ordering all the relevant maps required from the bookshop, and then marking the route in coloured pencil. Phil booked the trains to Portsmouth, the ferry to St. Malo and the flights home from Nice. I also had to acquire/borrow a tent and a sleeping bag. Obtaining a plastic bag for the return trip was proving difficult. Cycling UK, my previous source, had decided that plastic bags were no longer eco-friendly. I finally located a bike shop on the internet that had some old stock. We were going the second week in June and we only had a couple of weeks to get organised. Luckily the plastic bag arrived in time. The ferry sailed from Portsmouth at 8.15 p.m. on Monday, 17<sup>th</sup>

June. The train to St. Pancras was booked for 11.00 a.m. from Sheffield.

I set off from Dronfield on my bike, giving myself an hour to cycle the seven miles to Sheffield just in case of a bike issue. I sat having a coffee at the station and reflected that it was twenty-four years since I did the very same thing, waiting for Kevin on my very first tour. I was a lot younger and fitter then. Although I'm older, the buzz of excitement doesn't go away. The anticipation and fear of what awaited me before each tour kept me alive and coming back for more.

The journey to Portsmouth involved a change of station and a cycle ride. We had to get from St Pancras to Waterloo Station which was a couple of miles ride through the centre of London. We arrived at Portsmouth and found a pub to eat, drink and watch Slovakia surprisingly beat Belguim 1-0. There were a half-dozen Slovaks enjoying the moment. Later we boarded the ferry and watched a poor comedy-come magical act whilst having a few more beers. We decided on an early night. We had paid an extra £50 each to have an over-night cabin to enable us to have a good night's sleep. We had fourteen nights in a tent ahead of us, so it made sense to enjoy the luxury.

## Day 1 - St. Malo to Vitre (96 km)

We headed out from the ferry in light rain. We weren't alone, several other cyclists were tackling some part of the journey we were doing, notably a father and son partnership. They were on lightweight titanium bikes and were doing the ten-day option and had booked all their accommodation in advance. We proceeded to the seafront at St.Malo and asked a passer-by to take a photograph of us to mark the start of our tour. The weather was disappointing; it was overcast and I felt light rain.

The early part of the stage hugged the northern coastline. We travelled on cycle-paths that headed towards Mont St Michel. We stopped at a café for some breakfast as we hadn't had anything on the ferry. So, after an hour's riding, we were ready to eat. The riding was easy and we made good time before we stopped for dinner at Fougeres. The first stage was only seventy-two miles on flattish terrain, so we were on target for a 5.00 p.m. finish. This was quite unusual. In our last touring exploit together, Land's End to John o' Groats, we were arriving a lot later but the mileage was greater.

We rolled into Vitre and noticed it had bags of character. I was desperate to get the camera out but getting to a campsite and drying out was the priority. The Tourist information directed us to the campsite, which was about two miles outside the town. Once we set up camp and showered, we asked at the campsite office for directions to the nearest restaurant. We fancied walking and we weren't looking for a ride home in the dark. After a twenty-minute walk, we arrived at what appeared to be a micro-brewery. To be fair, the beer was great and the manager gave us a tour of the workings of the brewery. Unfortunately, in the food department, it was lacking. I shelved my vegetarian diet for the night and tucked into some spicy sausage while Phil stuck to his principles and just had cheese. The pub was shutting quite early but the bar staff offered to drop us in town where we hoped to eat. We found ourselves unlucky once more, no food. We walked back to the campsite in the dark after consuming another two pints of beer. I put this down as an epic fail on our part. We need to eat a substantial amount of food when undertaking a massive calorie-burning activity such as this. In future, we needed to ensure we ate, even if it meant stopping somewhere before we camped.

## Day 2 - Vitre to Brissac – Quince (141 km)

This stage was more than twenty miles longer than the first stage, and it was probably the wettest I had ever experienced on a bike. If we could have afforded to have an easy day, this would have been it. We rode through it. Phil donned his waterproof hiking trousers and I rode bare-legged. It was not only wet it was cold. Wet clothing makes it even worse. I had both undervests, both cycling tops and a waterproof jacket, five layers in all.

We stopped after an hour at a café for breakfast and it took a lot of resilience to climb on the bike afterwards. In a café we stopped at—and there were a few—we left a trail of water and wet seats. I can't imagine we were popular when they discovered the wet seating.

We were heading into the Loire region and in any other conditions, I would have been stopping for photographs and admiring the view. Today, we were on a mission to get to our destination as quickly as possible and dry out. Occasionally, when the heavens opened and became unsafe to carry on, we'd take shelter under trees or in a cafe or boulangerie. I stopped to take a photo as the road flooded in a town, and we were reduced to riding on the pavement as the road became impassable.

A couple of miles before our destination, Phil dropped off on a climb. I waited at the top of a climb, and he showed up a few minutes later. He was struggling with the dreaded bonk. I handed him an energy gel and he recovered sufficiently to make it to the campsite destination. He decided to have an alcohol-free evening. He thought the previous night's alcohol intake was to blame for his drop-off in performance.

The campsite at Brissac-Quince (camping Etang) had a restaurant so we didn't have to venture off-site for something to eat and drink. Phil stuck to his word and didn't have any alcohol. The food on campsites is usually limited to pizza, salads and chips. On this occasion, we were grateful. In comparison to the previous night, it was a feast. I had one big regret that day, my Sony camera never recovered from the drowning it received. I should have packed it away in my waterproof panniers and not taken it out. Instead, it was in a seat pack that got waterlogged.

# Day 3 - Brissac-Quince to Airvault (111 km)

As we headed off to our next destination, there were signs the weather was at last changing for the better. We stopped at an l'epicerie in St Remy la Varenne. It was a popular stop with cyclists and we shared our tales of adventure with some Australians. They were on a cycling holiday, which was a lot easier and more structured than ours. The shop sold sandwiches and fruit, which kept us going for a while. We rode for a long period parallel to the Loire River. We stopped at a purple Citreon near Saumur for lunch before taking a more southerly direction and leaving the Loire.

Heading towards Loudun is where we had not one, but two crashes. I analysed it over and over again how this could possibly happen. For the past fifty years since I'd been riding a bike, I was quite comfortable riding in a tightly packed group, either in a road race or just a club run. With this comes an awareness of people around you and a responsibility to ride smoothly and without any sudden braking or change of direction. You take a lot for granted when riding and avoid individuals who you think are a danger to the group's safety. Phil, by his own admission, wasn't comfortable riding in a group and tended to avoid them. So, I should have perhaps been aware of this when Phil pulled quickly because of a wrong turning and I hit the deck. The first crash wasn't that bad; I sustained a bruised thigh and grazed elbow and Phil was unscathed. I didn't learn from this crash, several miles later, Phil was startled by a gunshot and we both hit the deck. This time, I seriously damaged my hand and ribs. Phil was also hurt but not as badly, just cuts and bruises. Another concern was that both our front wheels were damaged and would need attention if we were to finish our adventure in Nice.

We needed to cut short this stage and evaluate our options, that was for certain. We had planned getting to Parthenay which would have been an eighty-two-mile stage. Instead we needed to get to a campsite to patch up our wounds and sort the bike wheels out. We found a place about twelve miles short of Parthenay called Airvault. The campsite was called Camping de Courte Vallee. It was owned and run by an English couple who had moved to France from Hampshire. When we arrived, the guests, all Brits, were in a bar area watching the television as the England game was about to start. When Jayne, the owner, saw my hand, she produced a massive first aid kit and bandaged up my hand. The iodine and alcohol she administered were painful. I did consume a good amount of alcohol orally that night to combat the pain. She advised me to go to a hospital tomorrow for medical attention. I nodded in agreement, but I had no intention of doing so. We spent the rest of the evening drinking English beer, eating fish and chips and watched England bore the pants off us.

The other good news was that we didn't have to put up a tent. Jayne said we could sleep in the games room as it wasn't in use. I was relieved as I had consumed five pints of beer and I would have struggled putting up a tent with my injuries. By next morning, we had formulated a plan to get the bikes repaired and push on.

## Day 4 - Airvault to L'isle – Jourdan (129 km)

My first task was to put a spoke in Phil's broken wheel. The wheel was better but not great. My wheel had not broken any spokes but wasn't running true. Phil had located a bike repairer in Parthenay en route. It wasn't a bike shop as such. The guy was working out of his garage. He trued our wheels the best he could and charged us ten euros each. The wheels were still not running true, but they were good enough to continue.

I visited a pharmacy and stocked up with plasters and paracetamol. I asked the pharmacist to have a look at my hand and she waved me away, saying I needed to go to the hospital. They painstakingly gave me directions to the hospital. I considered going but we just couldn't afford to lose any more time. I also had a damaged rib. However, I knew there was no magic cure, having broken three ribs once in a bike crash many years ago. I knew the ribs would be a problem later on when the long climbs started the next day. Up to now, the roads had been flattish and the few hills had been short, at less than a mile.

The campsite at L'isle – Jourdain was up a hill outside the town. It was a municipal site and was the unmanned type where you have to purchase a card, which is then used to gain entry to the shower block. Luckily, Phil had more patience with these situations than me. Last year I cycled an extra twenty-miles to avoid the faff of using these places. It may be an age thing, but I like dealing with people, even if they can be unhelpful at times. I avoid using self-service checkouts at supermarkets as I usually make a mistake and have to send for assistance anyway. A pointless waste of time.

We erected the tents, showered and Phil located a restaurant that was open within a short cycle ride. We had picked a bad night to find a restaurant open after 8.00 p.m. France was playing a football game and that was a reason for the nation to shut down. We did find one restaurant open owned by a Polish woman who stayed open to serve us. We were the only two in the restaurant. The food and beer were excellent and we cycled back with our bellies full, ready for the next stage.

That stage was the last of the flat stages. The first four stages had two miles of climbing over two or three climbs. From stage five onwards, things were to become a lot harder.

## Day 5 - L'Isle – Jourdain to Brantome (136 km)

The Garmin has revolutionised touring. Not only did we not need maps but it told us the number of climbs, the severity of the gradients and where on the stage we would encounter them.

This stage had eleven climbs with a total of nearly ten miles of climbing and the steepest of the climb has an average of 7% for nearly half a mile. This indicates we have a tough day ahead of us.

The weather was improving and although there were plenty of hills, this stage didn't produce any problems. We followed the La Vienne river southward and it came into view several times. I had hurt the ribs on my right-hand side, so I avoided pushing myself on the hills so my breathing didn't become heavy. I used paracetamol occasionally throughout the day. If I lost any ground to Phil, I made up the deficit on the long descents. Descending was not Phil's strong point. It wasn't mine particularly, but Phil made me look good.

We adopted a strategy of buying a lot of food at a supermarket in case there wasn't anything available at the campsite. This turned out to be a good idea as it was a long day in the saddle and the campsite took some finding. Phil used Google to locate campsites, but on this occasion, we weren't getting anywhere. We travelled up and down this road looking for the elusive campsite. Eventually, in desperation, I asked a local and that proved to be successful.

The campsite was full of motor-homes and had few spaces for camping. We finally found a spot that had electricity to charge the gadgets and phones. At the bottom of the campsite was a river with deck chairs and a manmade beach where we ate our supermarket food of bread, cheese and tomato, followed by a couple of bottles of beer.

# Day 6 - Brantome to Les Eyzies – de – Tayac (113 km)

A shorter day in the saddle and the Garmin told us there were less than seven miles of climbing spread over seven climbs. It was the first day of really hot weather. We were following the La Vezere river and the scenery had become more impressive and less agricultural.

We stopped for dinner near Montignac. For the first time on this trip, we searched for a table in the shade. We both had a seafood salad, which was massive. A couple of women on the next table had the same and then ordered Steak afterwards. We found this amusing as we would burn off the calories while the overweight women sipped their wine and would probably go for an afternoon nap.

As we rode into Les Eyzies we had a bit of shock in store. The campsite Le Pech Charmant was up a very steep gravel road that was perhaps a mile long. The severity had us clambering for our lowest gear. We just hoped the effort was worth it. Once we reached the site, it was probably the best we had encountered so far. The owners were friendly and they cooked homemade pizzas of the highest quality, on-site. This was a massive relief as there wasn't a chance of cycling back into town and returning up that hill afterwards. The site was fully equipped with facilities to wash and dry our clothing. Our cycle clothing received a long-overdue wash.

# Day 7 - Les Eyzies – de – Tayac to Gramat (85 km)

This day was a short day in comparison with the others. It was very hilly in places and very hot. There were seven miles of climbing and seven major climbs. There were three climbs in the first ten miles. After that, we had about twenty miles of cycle paths that took us around Salart. The cycle paths were busy with leisure cyclists. There were bike hire stations – a very well-subscribed tourist area. Along the way were places to stop for drinks and snacks. One of the places used to be a railway station and had the remains of a platform in front of it. Obviously, an old disused railway line had been transformed into a leisure facility for the locals and tourists to explore by bike.

After coming off the cycle path, we had two major climbs as we approached Rocamadour. Although I had been to Rocamadour several times, I couldn't resist stopping for photos. We then pushed on to Gramat, our destination for the day. The campsite was a couple of miles south of Gramat on an old farm and was a strange one. The grass was long and the site was occupied mostly by young people, probably in their late teens. I was informed by Phil that it was an eco-friendly type with mud hut buildings that could have come from an African village. I was unimpressed but equally intrigued. I wondered how the farmer had the nerve to take twenty euros from us for camping there. However, it was the only option in town so we put up with it.

We set up our tents and rode back into Gramat to eat. I had a beer at a bar in the town square while Phil located a pancake house. The food was good and had all the carbs we needed, but a bit niche and pricy for pancakes. We rode back to the campsite to find some sort of spiritual meeting of the young residents. They were sat in a circle conversing in French of which we had little understanding.

## Day 8 - Gramat to Entraygues – sur – Truyere (105km)

We went from what I thought was our worst camping experience to probably my favourite place. The weather now was hot. We had four climbs and less than seven miles of climbing.

Entrague was on the river La Truyere. A more picturesque town you are unlikely to find. The mileage was moderate and it was a day of taking photographs of the beautiful landscape.

The municipal campsite was at the far end of Entragues and its location couldn't have been better. It didn't have a restaurant but that didn't matter. A five-minute walk across a bridge and we were in the middle of a choice of bars and restaurants. The French football match was on the television. As soon as the match had finished, the French had no interest as to what followed. We had bought some beers on arrival at the campsite and put them in the fridge for later. The campsite did have a television room on site. Phil and I watched the England match on our own.

# Day 9 - Entraygues – sur – Truyere to Mende (122 km)

This stage wasn't the longest stage at seventy-six miles but it was by far the hardest. It involved a total of five climbs and fourteen miles of climbing. The severity of the climbs was something we hadn't previously encountered. One climb in particular had me in bits. It was nearly three miles long and had a gradient of 7% and was 14% in places. A young, fit man on a stripped-down racer would be struggling to stay upright, so two old men carrying camping equipment had a massive challenge. In several places, my bike was hardly inching forward. I could have probably done with a lower gear than the 26 x 28 I had available.

The day started with a very gradual incline out of Entraygues following the La Lot River. It was a day for photographs as we passed through Estaing, another picturesque town. The Lot region of France is a particularly beautiful part of the world with one blot on the landscape, which is the Mileau Bridge. Even so, I had to take a photograph of the structure and struggled to get it all in the frame because I didn't have a wide enough lens.

After a hundred kilometres, we arrived at the dreaded Col de Goudard. The sign at the top indicated an altitude of 1022m. This wasn't a massive climb by comparison with others I'd encountered. But for the severity of the gradient, I thought it stood alone. As it finished at the small village that gave the climb its name, I was very happy to see the top. I was unable to pull up hard on the handlebars due to my hand injury and was avoiding trying to get out of breath to avoid rib pain. This all added to my lack of forward motion. With very little time to recover, we encountered the last climb of the day. This climb wasn't as severe, but it was on a busy road that did present a different challenge, with traffic threatening to hit us if we veered off-course.

The descent into Mende was steep, and on a traffic congested road. Mende is a large busy town in comparison to previous destinations. We located the campsite, perhaps a mile outside the town, just off a busy dual carriageway. We arrived a half hour before the campsite shut as there were some negative comments about the site refusing entry after 7.00 p.m. I was totally drained of energy. My reserves were spent and I struggled to find the strength to erect my tent. We pitched at the side of a river a short walk to the shower block.

There wasn't a restaurant on the campsite but neither of us had the appetite or energy to ride back through the traffic into town. Instead we decided on a McDonalds that was a two-minute walk from the campsite. I hadn't been in a fast food establishment since my children were young, probably thirty years ago. I hated everything about such establishments from the processed food down to the ordering system. I let Phil familiarise himself with the touchscreen ordering system while I concentrated on staying awake. I had a fish burger with chips washed down with two large lattes. To be fair, the lattes were quite nice, however the fish burgers hadn't won me over. The potions were meagre, and the taste wasn't great.

## Day 10 – Mende to Pont D'Arc (117 km)

This stage wasn't a stroll in the park, because every day was tough, but in comparison to the previous day, it felt easy. It had half the climbing and was a few miles shorter in distance. We needed an easy recovery day. The next day was the longest of the tour.

Two of the three climbs came within the first ten miles. The Col des Tribes was the highest at an altitude of 1132m. We stopped at Villefort, where we had dinner. We had one more climb of the day, the Col du Mas de L'Ayre, and then a long descent into Les Vans. I liked the long descents; I was a confident descender and I could have a minute or two rest waiting for Phil to catch up. After that climb, we were halfway through our ride. We were approaching the gorges of the Ardeche, where the scenery was stunning. The hot weather was becoming a problem as the temperature was now in the thirties.

Approaching into Pont D'Arc we stumbled on the campsite. It was the first one we came across. We didn't bother with the usual research for other campsites as this looked well equipped with everything we needed. We could have climbed out of Pont D'Arc and found a campsite en route and saved having a big climb in the morning, but decided not to. Tomorrow was a long day, so the attraction of eating on-site at their restaurant and getting an early night was an appealing factor.

## Day 11 – Pont D'Arc to Sault (162 km)

Shortly after leaving the campsite, we had a four-mile climb that took us up into the gorges of the Ardeche. We left the river of the same name, snaking along the valley below. The river eventually took a southerly path and we headed east towards Chateauneuf-du-Pape, which was roughly the halfway point of this stage. I had been to this place before when I toured with Jimmy and Maurice way back in 2006. I knew there would be ample opportunity to eat in this vibrant town made famous by the wine that bears its name. The place was buzzing with tourists and we paid premium price for salmon, chips and a bit of salad. A pudding and coffee meant we had blown forty euros without feeling that full.

We headed towards Carpentras which was a very busy town and a nightmare to navigate through on a bike. We got caught up in a lot of traffic but couldn't really avoid riding through it, there was no choice. After Carpentras, we had Mount Ventoux on our left-hand side. The mountain was in view for several miles as we skirted around it. We found a small café on route to Villes-sur-Auzon. We filled our water bottles as we were getting through the water at an alarming rate as the temperature soared. At Ville-sur-Auzon, there was a water fountain and we debated whether or not to fill up our water bottles. A sign on the fountain indicated that the water source was uncontrolled. I used my water filter as a precaution.

We estimated we had twenty-five miles to go as we started the ascent up the Gorge de la Nesque. The road rose steadily and the views were spectacular. There were several viewpoints along the way. The temperature was 41 degrees, about 109 Fahrenheit. We had to stop every few miles to rest and drink water. The hot air we gulped in dried out our mouths and throats. The heat was sapping every bit of our strength. The last twenty miles were very tough going as we suffered from a combination of dehydration and fatigue. We had covered over a hundred miles that day.

The campsite was on the far side of Sault and by the time we reached our destination it was 8.00 p.m. The campsite reception was closed, so we planned to camp and pay in the morning.

Luckily for us there was the French equivalent of a burger van parked at the campsite entrance. Several of the campsite residents made use of the facility as obviously there was nothing on-site. The site was very basic with the bare minimum in facilities. The van was serving food until 9.00 p.m., so we ordered cheesy chips with an extra potion of chips and several cold drinks to rehydrate. I had already twice sacrificed my vegetarian principles, but I didn't fancy any meat that this van was offering. We found a bench and ate our meal. We started to lose the light as it was getting late and we still had to erect our tents and take a shower.

We had to pitch our tents quite a distance from the shower block in an attempt to find suitable soft ground. The ground close to the shower block was rocky and hard and wouldn't accept a tent peg. We didn't pack a mallet on our tours for obvious reasons. By this time, darkness had descended on the campsite and there wasn't any lighting or paths to follow or any visible landmarks. When I came out of the shower block my brain was scrambled with fatigue. I was totally disoriented and set off in the wrong direction, away from where my tent was pitched. The site was in darkness and I was lost. Lost on a campsite sounds bizarre, but I was clueless as to which direction to take. I phoned Phil, who had retired to his bed, and asked him to find me. I latched onto his torch beam and found my way back. I felt totally stupid. An unbelievable experience!

360

# Day 12 – Sault to Moustier Saint Marie (111 km)

This was a low mileage day in comparison with the previous day. But with six climbs and nine miles of climbing, it was still a tough day. What made it even tougher was the very strong winds – gale force – at times that made riding a bike dangerous.

We were hoping for an early finish, but events conspired against us. We stopped for dinner at a Thai restaurant in La Brillanne and had a fish dish with plenty of rice. The food was good, the price was cheap but the service was atrocious. Several customers left in frustration as the man and wife team struggled to cope with the number of customers. We had been there over an hour by the time we had eaten our main dish. We waited so long for the dessert to arrive that we decided to forgo it. The owner had a meltdown, so we decided to stay for our long-awaited second course. Shortly after leaving, we encountered our second delay. A railway barrier malfunctioned and the barrier remained down. Police arrived as frustration mounted amongst motorists. I asked the police if we could walk the bikes across the barrier, but we weren't allowed. We waited nearly an hour until an engineer remedied the fault.

The landscape after our delays was dominated by mile after mile of lavender fields. It was a big tourist attraction and cars were everywhere as tourists stopped to take photographs. This only made our journey more difficult as the gale force winds made it very difficult to keep our bikes upright as we dodged in and out of traffic. The landscape was rolling and it made for a very unpleasant twenty miles. Our route took us through Valensole and Puimoisson considered the heart of lavender and sunflower fields of France. We would have enjoyed the journey under normal circumstances. The lavender fields made for a spectacular tourist sight, but the strong gusts spoilt the experience for us.

After leaving the Lavender fields and a bit of climbing we arrived at Saint Jean Camping at Moustier. The campsite was run by a Dutch woman who was friendly and made us welcome. There was Leffe on draught and Pizzas to order. We stayed on site as it had everything we wanted. It was a tougher day than we had envisaged due to the very strong winds. The draught Leffe ensured a good night's sleep.

## Day 13 – Moustier Saint Marie to Castellane (46 km)

I had done two routes for this section. We decided to take the shorter version because it was hot and the England game was on in Castellane and we wanted to have time to spare before the game. There were still nearly nine miles of climbing to be done over three major climbs.

This was a day for taking it easy and sightseeing along the magnificent gorges de Verdon. We even left the bikes and went for a walk from the aptly named Auberge du Point Sublime. There was an information office and then a short walk to take in the view at a viewing point. The shortness of the ride allowed us to just chill and take in the stunning scenery.

We arrived in Castellane at dinner time and ate well at one of the many restaurants in the town. We settled on a campsite that was five minutes walking distance from the centre of Castellane. The campsite owner had a handlebar moustache and wasn't that friendly, but it didn't matter as we wouldn't be drinking or dining there. Castellane was a busy place. It was polling day in France and some places were turned into polling stations for the day. After pitching our tents and showering, we walked the short distance back into town. We got some pre-match food at a boulangerie and found a bar that had football on. We watched England win and progress through to the next stage.

## Day 14 – Castellane to Nice (86 km)

We called at the same boulangerie in Castellane on our way to Nice. We filled our panniers. We had three climbs to encounter, but the majority of riding would be descending. We had a couple of climbs early on. The biggest was the Col de Luens, which reached an altitude of 1054m. The scenery once again was stunning and we tried to do the scenery justice with our photographs.

After thirty miles, we had dinner at Greolieres. The restaurant in the square of this old town was busy with other cyclists. We had smoked salmon with salad, which seemed to be a regular meal for a pair of cyclists trying to avoid meat.

From Greolieres, the road descended for several miles through the Gorge du Loup. We hit a town with plenty of traffic before we hit the Mediterranean-sea front at Cagnessur-Mer. We sat and gazed, enjoying the moment. We cycled on a cycleway that ran parallel to the busy main road until we reached the Nice sign, where we posed for selfies to officially record our journey's end.

We had made the decision earlier that we wouldn't camp the final night. Our flight was at 10.00 a.m. and we had to have our bikes packed for about 8.00 a.m. We needed a place near the airport instead of a campsite several miles away. Phil booked provisionally the Campanille hotel that was within sight of the airport. We dined and had a few beers at the hotel before experiencing some clean linen and a comfortable bed. Something we hadn't had for two weeks.

We left the Campanile hotel before 7.00 a.m. and rode the short distance to terminal two. We packed our bikes in our plastic bags and stood in a long queue, only to be told we were in the wrong queue. The EasyJet desk was in turmoil as they had experienced technical problems. This caused chaos along the line, resulting in our plane being delayed ninety minutes.

At Manchester, we unpacked our bikes, made our way to the railway station and booked our tickets home. We changed trains at Manchester and reached our destination of Dore station, Sheffield. I had the short cycle journey to Dronfield reflecting on another tour completed. I stopped and phoned Jane to tell her prodigal husband would shortly be returning home.

I felt totally knackered on arriving home and had no appetite for the bike for a week. I had punished my body for two weeks solid without rest. On reflection, it wasn't surprising that I was in a state of chronic fatigue. Sleeping in a tent isn't the best way to recover from a gruelling bike ride day after day. Added to this I don't think we consumed the calories we needed. Finally, carrying injuries to my hand from day three only added to the difficulties. I have been here before and after a couple of weeks, I was thinking about the next tour. Such is the life I enjoy, and I will keep on doing so while I am able.

# Epilogue

I rode my last serious bike race in 1997. It was three years later, in 2000, that my love with cycle touring began and it has stayed with me. Every year since that first tour, in 2000, I have been counting down the days to the next one. It started with a plan hatched between Kevin and myself at Bramall Lane. A quarter of a century later the annual cycling adventure has continued each year, halted only temporarily by injury and Covid.

Sadly, over the period of writing this book, the cyclists I have shared precious memories with, Kevin and Doug, have passed away. Kevin, who started this ball rolling, passed away in 2007. There will never be anyone like him again. Doug passed away in 2020. He was a lot older but was a real character – salt of the earth. Since Kevin passed away, Jimmy and Steve have been the main go-to tourist companions. Unfortunately, Jimmy and Steve have been suffering from health problems. I'm still in contact with them both and hope to tour with them again someday. Maurice has moved back up to Newcastle and rides around Northumberland, still enjoying his cycling. Ade, who I'm still in contact with, continues to work for the Fire Service.. As for Denis and Sherby, I haven't seen or heard from them in several years. Luckily, I still see Phil, my present touring companion, at the running club on Tuesdays. He's ten years younger than I am and is my most likely touring companion for any future escapades.

If I have learned anything over my many years of cycle-touring it is firstly, to choose and plan your journey wisely.

It has not always been the case! Know your fitness, and the terrain and always, plan a few easy days to recover. Secondly, take the appropriate bike, well-maintained and suitable equipment that will allow you to complete the tour without drama. And thirdly, and most importantly, choose your touring partner with care. The fitness of your companion is a major factor, but temperament is more important.

I hope this book has given you some insight into a different kind of holiday and the inspiration to plan and undertake a cycle tour of your own.